M000117119

COUNSELING AND MENTAL HEALTH SERVICES ON CAMPUS

A Handbook of Contemporary Practices and Challenges

James Archer, Jr., Stewart Cooper

JOSSEY-BASS
A Wiley Company
www.josseybass.com

Published by

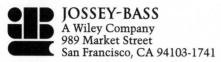

JOSSEY-BASS
A Wiley Company
989 Market Street
San Francisco, CA 94103-1741

www.josseybass.com

Copyright © 1998 by John Wiley & Sons, Inc.

Jossey-Bass is a registered trademark of John Wiley & Sons, Inc.

No part of this publication may be reproduced, stored in a retrieval system, or transmitted in any form or by any means, electronic, mechanical, photocopying, recording, scanning, or otherwise, except as permitted under Sections 107 or 108 of the 1976 United States Copyright Act, without either the prior written permission of the Publisher or authorization through payment of the appropriate per-copy fee to the Copyright Clearance Center, 222 Rosewood Drive, Danvers, MA 01923, (978) 750-8400, fax (978) 750-4744. Requests to the Publisher for permission should be addressed to the Permissions Department, John Wiley & Sons, Inc., 605 Third Avenue, New York, NY 10158-0012, (212) 850-6011, fax (212) 850-6008, e-mail: permreq@wiley.com.

Jossey-Bass books and products are available through most bookstores. To contact Jossey-Bass directly, call (888) 378-2537, fax to (800) 605-2665, or visit our website at www.josseybass.com.

Substantial discounts on bulk quantities of Jossey-Bass books are available to corporations, professional associations, and other organizations. For details and discount information, contact the special sales department at Jossey-Bass.

We at Jossey-Bass strive to use the most environmentally sensitive paper stocks available to us. Our publications are printed on acid-free recycled stock whenever possible, and our paper always meets or exceeds minimum GPO and EPA requirements.

Wiley also publishes its books in a variety of electronic formats. Some content that appears in print may not be available in electronic books.

Library of Congress Cataloging-in-Publication Data

Archer, James.
　　Counseling and mental health services on campus: a handbook of contemporary practices and challenges/James Archer, Jr., and Stewart Cooper.—1st ed.
　　　　p. cm.—(The Jossey-Bass higher and adult education series)
　　Includes bibliographical references (p.) and index.
　　ISBN 0-7879-1026-0 (hardcover: alk. paper)
　　1. Counseling in higher education—United States—Handbooks, manuals, etc.　2. College students—Mental health services—United States—Handbooks, manuals, etc.　I. Cooper, Stewart E. II. Title.　III. Series.
　　LB2343.A726　1998
　　378.1'94—dc21
　　　　　　　　　　　　　　　　　　　　　　　　　　　　　　　　　　　　　98-22390

FIRST EDITION
HB Printing　　　10 9 8 7 6 5 4 3 2

THE JOSSEY-BASS

HIGHER AND ADULT EDUCATION SERIES

Consulting Editor
Student Services

Ursula Delworth
University of Iowa

CONTENTS

**PART TWO: STRATEGIES FOR OUTREACH
AND SYSTEMIC INTERVENTIONS   117**

PART THREE: ADMINISTRATIVE AND PROFESSIONAL ISSUES   191

LIST OF PROGRAM EXAMPLES

PREFACE

The need for effective counseling and mental health services on college and university campuses has never been greater. Rapid economic and social changes continue as an educational backdrop for traditional and returning adult college students. The changing nature of the job market and the economic transitions that are part of the new global economy make career choice and planning for the future difficult for students. Changing family structures (some would say deteriorating family structures) and numerous social problems, such as poverty, violence, racism, and substance and alcohol abuse, have had a profound influence on the formative years of students, and a considerable number of them suffer from resulting psychological and emotional disabilities and deficits. It seems clear that personal and career counseling will continue to be important parts of the college experience and that many of our students will not be able to function as students or effective citizens without it.

In addition to the needs for traditional counseling, demands for campuswide consulting and educational programs to deal with a variety of health and social problems and to create a diverse environment that allows for productive learning and scholarship have increased dramatically. Prevention and education programs on topics such as AIDS, alcohol abuse, sexual violence, eating disorders, racism, homophobia, and gender discrimination are needed on every college and university campus. From an economic standpoint, colleges and universities must respond to these needs in order to ensure that their, and society's, investment in

the higher education of students is not wasted. Whenever students drop out of
school or do not succeed academically because they could not get the help they
required to overcome a problem or negotiate a challenge, the college or university and its funding sources lose valuable resources, not to mention the future
loss to society of an educated taxpayer and citizen.

College counselors and mental health workers have an important role to play
in responding to these needs for counseling, consultation, and education. The purpose of this book is to identify the specific challenges that four-year colleges and
universities confront in these areas and to suggest models, methods, and programs
that will be useful in meeting the challenges. Counseling services in two-year community and technical colleges, which are usually quite different, are not covered.
Also, the focus is primarily on mental health issues, with career and academic
advisement being covered only in the broad context of their impact on student
development. The book includes a survey of much of the current research and
practice in a broad range of counseling, development, and prevention areas that
are particularly germane to college counseling, and it provides suggestions for the
practice, organization, and administration of college counseling. Examples of existing programs as well as of hypothetical programs that merit implementation
are included throughout the book.

College and university counseling and mental health staff and administrators,
as well as university administrators, will find the material useful from both a practical and theoretical standpoint. Counselors will acquire information on the latest
current practices and suggestions for approaches they can use in the future.
Administrators in counseling and mental health centers will find information on
the organization and management of systems and programs, and general university administrators can gain valuable insight into the value, role, and efficient
management of counseling, prevention, and developmental services. Graduate
students and professors will find that this book includes a wide range of information about counseling and college student development.

The Introduction includes a discussion of the general higher education context and how college counseling and mental health services must confront the
changes and transformations in society and in our colleges and universities. A brief
history of college counseling and mental health services is also included as background for the suggestions presented throughout the book.

The provision of counseling within this context of increasing need and limited resources is the focus of Part One. In Chapter One the many counseling needs
of contemporary college students are documented, and the challenges facing college mental health counselors are identified. Chapters Two and Three include a
discussion of the two models of choice for college counseling, brief therapy and
group counseling. Chapter Four examines the possibilities for expanding coun-

seling services through the use of paraprofessionals, faculty and staff, professional volunteers, and part-time staff, and Chapter Five contains suggestions for a number of alternatives and adjuncts to counseling.

In Chapters Six and Seven the counseling needs of several specific groups of students are described, and ways to meet these needs are suggested. These students include those with specific problems such as substance abuse and eating disorders, those with developmental concerns, and specific campus groups such as women, minorities, gays, lesbians, bisexual students, and adult learners.

Part Two urges counselors to take an activist approach to the campus community. Many of the issues and topics covered in Part One are again discussed here but from the perspective of education and prevention rather than counseling. Chapter Eight covers prevention and development theory as it applies to college students. This discussion serves as an introduction to the description of the initiator-catalyst approach to consultation and outreach in Chapter Nine. This approach is a logical extension of previous models and applications. Chapters Ten, Eleven, and Twelve describe and give examples of different kinds of preventive and developmental programs in order to highlight how an initiator-catalyst model might be applied. Chapter Ten covers faculty development and student development programs. Chapter Eleven discusses preventive programs in several important campus public health areas, and Chapter Twelve focuses on the role of college counselors in promoting diversity and improving the campus environment for several different minority groups. Examples of various kinds of outreach and consultation programs and descriptions of hypothetical situations are included throughout. Although some of these programs represent traditional, direct-service approaches (that is, counselors directly providing prevention and development programs), ideas for moving to a facilitative and catalytic role are highlighted.

Part Three examines a number of professional and managerial issues that apply to the administration and leadership of college counseling and mental health services. In Chapter Thirteen the role of program evaluation and research is explored. Chapters Fourteen and Fifteen analyze contemporary ethical, legal, training, and accreditation issues as they apply to college counseling. Chapter Sixteen covers institutional administrative and organizational issues that affect the counseling or mental health center, and Chapter Seventeen focuses on internal issues such as leadership, management, and quality control. A set of general conclusions summarizing the main points of the book is included in Chapter Seventeen.

May 1998
Gainesville, Florida   James Archer, Jr.
Valparaiso, Indiana   Stewart Cooper

THE AUTHORS

James Archer, Jr., is professor of counselor education and psychology at the University of Florida. He was director of the counseling center there for thirteen years, and before that he served for ten years as psychologist and associate director of the University of Delaware counseling center. He holds a B.A. in history from the University of Rochester, an M.A. in counseling from San Francisco State University, and a Ph.D. in counseling psychology from Michigan State University. He has a diplomate in counseling psychology awarded by the American Board of Professional Psychology, and he is a fellow of Division 17 (counseling) of the American Psychological Association.

Archer's main professional interests are college student counseling and prevention. He has written two books, *Anxiety and Stress Management* (2nd edition, 1991) and *Counseling College Students* (1991), and he coauthored a third, *Multicultural Relations on Campus* (1991). He has also written a number of chapters and journal articles on prevention and college student mental health, including a coauthored monograph in *The Counseling Psychologist* on counseling centers in the 1990s. He has served on the editorial boards of the *Journal of College Student Development*, the *Journal for Specialists in Group Work*, and the *Journal of Counseling and Development*.

Archer served as president of the International Association of Counseling Services and was also chairperson of the Association of University and College Counseling Center Directors. He has served on accreditation teams for college counseling centers and has been a consultant for college and university counseling and mental health services.

Stewart Cooper has served as director of counseling services for the past eleven years and is professor of psychology at Valparaiso University. He earned his B.A. in psychology as well as his M.S. in counseling and his Ph.D. in counseling/research methodology at Indiana University, Bloomington. Before joining the staff at Valparaiso University, he was a staff psychologist at the University of Missouri at Rolla. He holds a diplomate in counseling psychology from the American Board of Professional Psychology and is a fellow of Division 13 (consulting) of the American Psychological Association.

Cooper's research has focused on the application of multivariate perspectives and methods to diverse counseling-psychology topics. He has published articles, book chapters, and monographs on prevention, psychometric analysis, substance abuse, dual-career issues, organizational consultation, and sex therapy. Most of this scholarship has been on the college population and college mental health issues. He currently serves as case section editor for *Consulting Psychology Journal*, and he has been a reviewer for *Psychological Reports*.

Cooper just completed a term as a member of the governing board of the Association of University and College Counseling Center Directors and serves as the organization's liaison to Division 17 of the American Psychological Association (APA). He has performed lead and support roles on college counseling center accreditation visits and has conducted numerous regional and national presentations on college mental health topics. He is also a member of the Professional Practice Advisory Committee of Division 17 and was 1998 APA Convention program chair for Division 13 (consulting psychology). His professional activities include clinical work, supervision, outreach and consultation, administration, teaching, and research.

INTRODUCTION

Overview of Current and Emerging Challenges

The challenges facing college and university counseling and mental health services in many ways mirror those confronting society at large. Students, both those of traditional age and returning adults, are products of a society that is confronting unprecedented change. As economic philosopher Peter Drucker puts it, we are in an age of "social transformation" (1994). College students must cope with the economic and social problems of our time, a historical period that will transform us from this age to the next. These rapid changes exacerbate the personal and psychological problems students bring with them.

These changes also bring into focus the need for the development in students of a sound identity and a clear sense of ethics and social responsibility. It is not too dramatic, we believe, to say that the future of our civilization depends on how new generations learn to handle the ethical and social issues facing them. Our technological advances have far surpassed our social, moral, and spiritual ability to deal with rapid change.

Students undergoing this complex and difficult personal and psychological journey are attending higher education institutions that are themselves undergoing significant if not transformative change (Schroeder, 1996). Faculty members and administrators have never agreed on the scope of higher education and in particular on how much the college experience should involve personal and character development; this basic educational issue will certainly continue to be addressed as colleges and universities are forced to clarify their priorities and goals in order to survive during a time of increased costs and decreased revenue. The future of counseling and mental health services and other student services will depend on how the central goals and definitions of higher education evolve. If the belief survives that one cannot educate a person without integrating academic learning with the development of strong character and self-identity and of a philosophy of life oriented toward leadership and service to society, then counseling and student development services and programs will continue to be significant parts of the higher education enterprise. Although the developmental issues related to identity and character are somewhat different for returning adult students than for traditional students, they are no less important. For example, women who are returning to school after raising children or becoming single are often faced with significant identity issues, as well as the stress of returning to a college environment.

Specific data documenting the nature and severity of college students' counseling concerns at colleges and universities across the country were collected by the Research Consortium of Counseling and Psychological Services in Higher Education and summarized by August Baron (1993) of the University of Texas at Austin. These specific concerns are discussed in detail in later chapters. The broad philosophical and practical contributions of college counseling and mental health units to their institutions have been elaborated by the Elements of Excellence Task Group of the Association of University and College Counseling Center Directors (AUCCCD) (1996). The major points of this report are discussed in the remainder of this Introduction and throughout the book.

Survival of college counseling and mental health services will also depend on how well administrators understand the economic benefits to the institution of helping students maintain psychological health and develop personally in ways that will allow them to stay in school and effectively use the educational resources being made available to them. This economic argument has not been adequately considered by many administrators, faculty, and politicians responsible for planning and funding higher education. For a relatively small investment in counseling and other support services, a large increase in effectiveness and efficiency can be realized. One need only talk to a few students, either those of traditional age or returning adults, to understand how much of a college education is wasted because students are not able to focus on the task before them. The reasons are varied and complex, but they usually involve personal or developmental blocks that interfere with academic pursuits.

The economic crunch in public and private higher education may, however, push colleges and universities toward a narrower focus than they now have by forcing decreases in or elimination of courses, departments, and services (Barba, 1995). The challenge for counselors and others interested in a broad definition of education is to get planners and administrators to understand the significant short- and long-term economic benefits of counseling and student development services and programs.

Distance learning and other technological developments will have a profound impact on higher education in the future (Andrews, 1994), and counseling and other student services will clearly be a part of this movement. If the university of the twenty-first century consists of a central core of computers and interactive video equipment connected to various parts of the state, country, and world, how will the character development and other non-information-based aspects of higher education fare? Even with this kind of rapidly advancing technology, it seems unlikely that colleges and universities can abandon concern for the students and their development and learning in a broad sense. The need in our society for effective and productive citizens is too great, and the forces of technology and economics described above create a strong need for finding ways to provide an education that encourages personal and character development.

Student Challenges

The complexity of the world that students who enter higher education face is reflected in variety of ways. Students in college today must cope with the fact that our economy has undergone significant change for college graduates (even in strong economic times), and opportunities may never be as unlimited or stable as they were in the past. Many students must motivate themselves to complete college when they know that many who have graduated are unemployed or underemployed and, in some cases, have returned home to live with their parents. Adult students who have often made great sacrifices to return to college and pursue a dream of a better and more satisfying life may find themselves facing great difficulty in achieving their goal of having a new or enhanced career. Many of our students have grown up in impoverished homes and desperately want to break the cycle of poverty and improve their economic lot, yet this improvement may not be as easy to accomplish as it has been in the past. Others have grown up in comfortable middle- or upper-class surroundings and face the possibility that they will have less material success than their parents.

Students today face an increase in all kinds of violence. Gruesome murders and serial killings have taken place on a number of college campuses. Violence is glorified on television, in movies, and in video games. Children spend thousands of hours watching murders, fights, and other forms of violence on these media. Sexual and family violence is not uncommon in our culture, and many students have personal experiences with sexual, emotional, or physical abuse before they enter a college or university (Stone and Archer, 1990). For those students who have experienced rape, murder, or some form of physical violence, the effects are direct and often take the form of posttraumatic stress reactions. For others, particularly women, the fear of being assaulted or raped is either a daily reality or, if denied, is just beneath the surface.

Today's students have grown up in a world with problems of racism, sexism, heterosexism, and other "isms." The movement toward a truly multicultural society, even in the face of demographic data projecting large percentage increases of several different minority groups, is certainly not smooth or assured. Many minority students (defined here to include any kind of minority) come to our colleges and universities already victims of these forces in our society, and they often continue to experience prejudice and discrimination within higher education institutions. It is still quite uncomfortable for gay and lesbian students to be honest about their sexual orientation with their classmates, and many African Americans and other minorities still find themselves judged with stereotypes (Feagin and Sikes, 1995). Although the Americans with Disabilities Act has greatly increased programs and services for disabled students, life for these students is often punctuated with instances of intolerance and lack of understanding. International students are often rigidly and inaccurately stereotyped. Many of the racial and ethnic minority students must struggle to develop an identity that allows them to keep their own heritage yet become an integral part of the powerful majority culture. The growing number with biracial parents face different and perhaps more challenging identity questions.

All our students have grown up in a culture that seems no longer to have a defined or agreed-on set of values. Their culture is divided about the answers to many fundamental questions and contains zealots on all sides who fight for their particular interests and points of view. Many members of the campus community see efforts by colleges and universities to promote multiculturalism as threatening. It is exceedingly difficult to build a consensus on how to "reconstruct" academia and its disciplines to preserve the best of Western culture while including important and previously ignored aspects of non-Western civilizations (Goebel and Hall, 1995).

Many of our students do not come from stable, healthy families. Many have not had fathers or mothers present in their lives, and a surprising number have not had the love and attention that is necessary for a child to grow up to be a psychologically healthy human being. The family structure of the United States has changed dramatically, and, in fact, the "typical" intact, nuclear family is the exception. Less than 10 percent of current families have both a mother and father living together and a single breadwinner (Glick, Clarkin, and Kessler, 1987). Although the traditional nuclear family is not necessarily the only effective form for raising children, lack of affection and attention from a parent or parents has a decidedly negative effect on children. Divorce and the subsequent emotional upheaval experienced by children can have deleterious effects on their psychological development, and this trauma can surface or resurface during the college years. Older, returning adult students, particularly women, often face the difficulty of being solely responsible for the economic and psychological survival and growth of children.

Our students come to us in the midst of the AIDS epidemic. They are sexually active, yet large numbers of them do not protect themselves from HIV or other sexually transmitted diseases (Desiderato and Crawford, 1995). As the epidemic spreads, more and more heterosexual and homosexual students will have friends and relatives who are HIV-positive or who have AIDS or who die from AIDS-related complications. In students' romantic and sexual lives, a sense of caution and sometimes anxiety coexist with significant interest and pressure. Our society continues to give contradictory messages about sex. On the one hand, we sell everything from cigarettes to bread using sex as an underlying motivator, while, on the other hand, we are puritanical and have difficulty agreeing about how much we should talk about sex. These confusing and contradictory messages make it difficult for students to talk with each other about sex, a necessity in preventing the spread of the HIV virus, and in many cases these messages contribute to confusion and anxiety in the development of sexual identity and sexual values.

The widespread use and abuse of alcohol and other drugs in our culture is another potent influence on our students. Some use these substances as part of their own coping mechanisms, and many have grown up in homes where one or both parents were addicted to alcohol or other drugs. Students who have experienced parental drug or alcohol abuse or dependence and who may have increased genetic risk are more likely to have drug and alcohol problems of their own (Buelow, 1995), and those who have grown up in families rendered dysfunctional by abuse of alcohol or other drugs frequently have emotional, psychological, and relational problems. Returning adult students may have this history and may also be dealing with a spouse or child with an alcohol or other drug problem.

Female students must still deal with difficult sex-role issues. Although great strides have been taken, women still encounter many sex-role restrictions and stereotypes. Significant numbers of college women are affected by our society's continued emphasis on female appearance. The incidence of eating disorders related to anxiety about body appearance attests to this continued cultural pathology (Kurth, Krahn, Nairn, and Drewnoswski, 1995). Men in college also face gender difficulties. Many are faced with admonitions to develop their "feminine" side and to be more sensitive and relationship-oriented, yet they have often been raised with traditional views of masculinity, which are reinforced by many campus organizations and cultural norms. For male and female college students, then, there may be confusion and difficulty in incorporating gender roles into their identity structure.

It can, of course, be argued that the college years have always been difficult and that societal norms and expectations, the economic situation, and similar factors have always been confusing and uncertain. It has, after all, been "the best of times and the worst of times" for many generations. There does, however, seem to be compelling evidence that the end of the twentieth century is a period of transformation and rapid change and that society has an escalating number of significant social problems.

Clearly, the experiences that students have had and are having in all these areas affect their mental health and their psychological development and also what they make of a college or university experience. College counselors and mental health workers around the country report increasing demands for counseling as a result of the anxiety, depression, and developmental problems related to these and other issues (Stone and Archer, 1990, Gallagher and Bruner, 1994). The increasing demand for these services is also a result of a significant increase in public awareness of the types of trauma and psychological and psychiatric problems that people experience. One need only watch TV movies or the many daytime talk shows to see how public so many issues like sexual and physical violence have become. As a culture we have moved rapidly in our understanding and identification of many emotional and psychological problems that were previously not discussed, and many of our students are trying to understand the role that these experiences play in their own unhappiness. Also, counseling and psychological assistance has become more acceptable than it once was.

Thus, compared with students in the past, students today arrive on campus with more problems as a result of dysfunctional family situations, with more worries and anxieties about the future and about the serious problems facing them in modern society, with an increased awareness of their own personal demons, and with a greater willingness to seek psychological and psychiatric help.

The potential problems and difficulties students may experience on contemporary campuses should all be viewed in the context of learning and development. Although many problems may require individual, problem-oriented counseling, the more difficult challenge for counseling and mental health services comes from the need to find ways to contribute to a student's growth and development and to prevent dangerous and self-defeating behavior so that he or she can thrive in the college community and take advantage of the rich and varied educational opportunities available. Much of the discussion in this book focuses on challenges and solutions in the area of growth and development and in the area of the prevention of destructive behavior and on the balance between the two.

History of Counseling and Mental Health Services

In order to understand how college counseling services must approach the future and the many challenges it will bring, it is instructive to briefly examine the history of these services. The development of preventive and developmental services and struggles with the balance between these activities and individual, problem-oriented counseling are evident.

The notion that colleges and universities must be concerned with the mental health and character development of their students is not a new concept. Reifler (1990), in a paper honoring Robert Arnstein on his retirement as director of the Yale Division of Mental Hygiene, noted that Professor Edward Hitchcock was appointed college physician at Amherst College in 1861. Dr. Hitchcock championed the concept of "leading the physiological life," which was perhaps a precursor to the wellness movement. Reifler cites the appointment of James Angell, a psychologist, as president of Yale in 1921 as the beginning of a strong emphasis on a psychological approach to education. The first university psychiatrist was appointed at Yale in 1925.

It is interesting to note a kind of parallel development of counseling and mental health services. In a number of schools, such as Yale, Princeton, Harvard, and Stanford, counseling and mental health services for students grew out of the student health services and were generally staffed, at least early on, by psychiatrists. In other schools, including the University of Minnesota, the University of Illinois, Ohio State University, and the University of Florida, counseling services grew out of psychology departments or student personnel programs (or both). E. G. Williamson, an early proponent of the "student personnel point of view," wrote *How to Counsel Students* in 1936.

Stone and Archer (1990, pp. 541–542) summarized a history of counseling centers provided in an article by Heppner and Neal (1983):

1. Before 1945: The beginnings—Many different advisors, deans, and counselors "counseled" students during this period. The terms counseling, vocational guidance, and student personnel were essentially undifferentiated. During the later part of this period the need for specialized, "clinical counselors" was recognized.

2. 1945–1955: Transition and professionalism—This period saw the establishment of many counseling centers in response to the need for vocational guidance by veterans returning from World War II. Much of the emphasis was on vocational and educational counseling and money from the Veterans Administration was an important driving force. The role of counseling as a profession separate from student personnel work evolved.

3. 1955–1970: Expansion and consolidation—During this period the role of counseling centers expanded and personal counseling began to emerge as an important function, although centers continued to deliver mostly vocational . . . services. Consultation and outreach roles also began to develop and training became an important function in many centers.
4. 1970–1982: Broader scope and constricted budgets—This period was characterized by a further expansion of the counseling center role. The "cube" was introduced by Morrill, Oetting, and Hurst (1974) as a way of conceptualizing the expanded role of the counseling center. Center staffs began to see themselves as much more than individual counselors, with the entire campus environment as their client. Paradoxically, many centers had to deal with budget restrictions and threats to their resource base.

The period from 1982, not covered by Heppner and Neal (1983), might be characterized as *Increasing pathology, violence, need for outreach/prevention and limiting services.* Counseling centers [since 1982] have been faced with increasing numbers of students with serious psychological problems. At the same time the need and demand for more campus consultation and education to help universities deal with issues such as sexual violence, suicide, alcohol and drug abuse, and eating disorders has also increased. In addition, many campuses have had murder, rapes, and other forms of violence that have greatly disturbed their communities and have required community "trauma management" services by campus counseling and mental health services (Stone and Archer, 1990, pp. 540–541).

Historically, counseling and mental health services developed along somewhat different tracks. Counseling services, especially in the early years, included considerable academic and career counseling, while mental health services tended to be staffed by psychiatrists and to focus mainly on personal issues. As counseling services developed, they began to include more and more work related to personal issues. In the 1980s a significant number of these services transferred their career counseling special offices dealing with career development. In many cases academic support also developed as a separate service, and some counseling centers moved out of this service area. Counseling centers have also accepted more of a consultive, preventive role since the mid-1970s. In fact, a few centers have attempted to shift their emphasis from individual and group counseling to consultation and outreach work.

Mental health centers have also increased their preventive and consultive efforts. Health educators have taken on considerable responsibility for programs related to AIDS and other sexually transmitted diseases as well as programs for eating disorders, substance abuse, sexual violence, and other contemporary problems.

Though both counseling and mental health centers exist on many campuses, the distinctions that existed historically seem to have become blurred. In the 1970s, mergers between counseling and mental health services began. In 1972, Stanford University consolidated its counseling and mental health services into what was called the Counseling and Psychological Services Center (Talley and Rockwell, 1985). Numerous other colleges and universities have also reorganized and merged these services. Federman and Emmerling (1996) reported a survey of colleges and universities where the counseling and mental health centers had been merged. Of the thirty schools responding to the survey, ten reported the creation of one unit at the counseling center, ten reported the creation of one unit at the student health center, and ten reported some other alternative. Directors and clinical staff were generally more positive than negative about the mergers; however, no significant differences were found between responses indicating improvement and negative/neutral responses regarding utilization of services and funding and budget.

Need for Counseling and Mental Health Services

Current student needs for counseling and mental health services are great, yet the resources to provide them are limited. Waiting lists for these services are not unusual and are a result of increased demands for counseling and medication and an increasing awareness of how counseling can help. Serious problems seem to be on the increase, yet the need is immense for developmental and growth-oriented counseling that provides the support students require to effectively use the resources available to them.

The challenge is to help students move into leadership positions in a clearly changing and increasingly multicultural society, to allow them to experience the personal and educational growth necessary for becoming healthy and productive citizens, and to pass on a culture that is able to deal with developing ethical and moral challenges.

Students need specific education and counseling regarding drugs and alcohol, sexual violence, AIDS, racism, career development, stress, depression, planning for the future, changing gender roles, and a myriad of other issues. Public health issues such as AIDS, substance abuse, and sexual violence cannot be disregarded. University administrators are also faced with the practical need to encourage and develop a multicultural and multiracial environment. The demands of the campus community for consultation about how to handle mental health issues and how to provide a high-quality learning environment free of drugs and alcohol abuse, violence, and racism are also significant. These needs are so prevalent that they are difficult for college and university faculty and administrators to ignore even in the light of economic problems and philosophical opposition to a "whole-person" orientation in higher education.

An investment in college counseling and mental health services is enormously cost-efficient for society and for our educational institutions. In an era of limited budgets and increased focus on what it costs to educate each student, it is crucial to examine the quality of education that is being purchased. It is indeed short-sighted to ignore all the personal factors that affect this quality and determine how successful a student can be. Colleges and universities must provide personal help and environmental support for students to make use of the learning opportunities available. If students become educated in the truest sense of the word, they have a much better chance of leading productive lives that will enable them to raise their children in a healthy psychological environment and to create a society that can solve the many problems it will face in the twenty-first century.

PART ONE

MEETING THE NEED FOR BASIC COUNSELING SERVICES

In this part counseling services are discussed within the context of increasing demand and limited or decreasing resources. In Chapter One counseling needs and issues are examined. Chapters Two and Three focus on two preferred counseling models for college students: brief therapy and group counseling. Chapters Four and Five discuss faculty, staff, professional volunteers, and paraprofessionals in different counseling roles and propose alternatives and adjuncts to traditional counseling services. Chapters Six and Seven address the special needs of counseling programs and approaches for students with specific problems (such as substance abuse, eating disorders) and for students from minority and other special groups.

CHAPTER ONE

COUNSELING NEEDS OF TODAY'S COLLEGE STUDENTS

As discussed in the Introduction, higher education and societal contexts have a profound impact on college student needs for counseling services. The challenge to provide effective counseling service is daunting and requires all the creativity and energy that college counselors and administrators can muster.

Although dealing with more students with more severe problems is perhaps the central clinical concern in providing counseling services, a number of other complex and challenging clinical issues require attention. There is a continuing need to provide counseling for traditional-age students with "normal" career and developmental needs and crises (identity development, values clarification, sexuality and intimacy, death, relationship endings, parental divorce) as well as the need to attend to the special concerns of returning adult students (career and life changes, family and relationship issues, stress, time management). Providing specialized counseling for minority students and students from other groups is crucial and frequently requires extra time and effort as well as the cultural and technical expertise to be helpful. Counseling men and women regarding gender-related issues involves helping students confront conflicting values and definitions of what it means to be a psychologically healthy man or woman. A final challenge, and one that has become increasingly visible, is the need to provide counseling for the direct and indirect victims of campus violence.

In this chapter a number of the specific counseling challenges and issues related to the areas delineated above will be discussed in some detail. In Chapters

Two through Seven, models, methods, and specific counseling programs to address these challenges will be offered.

Complicated and Severe Clinical Situations

In the 1993, 1994, and 1995 *National Survey of Counseling Center Directors* (Gallagher, 1993; Gallagher and Bruner, 1994, 1995) directors rated the increase in students with severe psychological problems as their top concern (82.5 percent in 1993, 84 percent in 1994, and 82 percent in 1995). Stone and Archer (1990) reported this same increase in the numbers of students with severe problems. Because most of the needs-assessment surveys and assessment instruments given to college students have been limited to one campus and have not been replicated, there is little direct, empirical evidence that student problems are more severe than they were in the past. The perceptions reported by directors and other mental health workers are supported in several ways, however. Koplik and DeVito (1986) in a longitudinal study compared Mooney Problem Checklist scores of college freshmen in 1976 and 1986 and reported more distress in all areas of their lives. A number of large N-prevalence studies in specific areas such as substance abuse, eating disorders, and sexual abuse support the conclusion that significant numbers of contemporary college students have severe emotional, psychological, and developmental problems. Sharkin (1997), however, cautions against an overreliance on counselors' perceptions as evidence that problem severity has increased.

In reviewing several needs-assessment studies conducted since the 1970s, Bertocci, Hirsh, Sommer, and Williams (1992) report that one can make rough generalizations from the studies they reviewed: that a sizable minority of students, from 10 percent to 40 percent, suffer psychological impairment, and that from half to three-quarters have significant emotional difficulties. One problem in interpreting these studies is definitions. Just what constitutes "psychological impairment" or "significant emotional difficulties"? Only a few studies have attempted to use standardized instruments with specific definitions of psychological and psychiatric conditions. Johnson, Ellison, and Heikkinen (1989) evaluated Symptom Check List-90—Revised scores for 585 male and 1,004 female counseling-center clients and found that 65.1 percent of the males and 62 percent of the females had diagnosable psychiatric ailments when using adult norms and that 30.3 percent of the males and 26.5 percent of the females had psychiatrically diagnosable problems using adolescent norms. Of course, these data are for clients and not for the general college population.

Archer, Bishop, Gallagher, and Morgan (1994) reported a study combining general needs-assessment data from three universities (2,909 students) using the same survey. Their results followed a pattern seen in other assessments: career, relationship, and study problems were selected most frequently; but a significant minority of students reported experiences and symptoms often related to major psychological problems. Feeling depressed, feeling inadequate, feeling anxious and panicked, and fear of failure were among the top fifteen problems. Among the men 18.4 percent and among women 20.3 percent expressed a moderate to high fear of becoming an alcoholic; 28.3 percent of the men and 36.7 percent of the women, of having a nervous breakdown; and 14 percent of the men and 16 percent of the women, of killing themselves.

Compounding the issue of accuracy regarding perceptions of increased pathology and severity of problems is the fact that it has become increasingly culturally acceptable to admit to and confront mental illness and difficult issues like past physical or sexual abuse, depression, anxiety, and panic attacks. Negative feelings about seeing a counselor have declined, and more students are inclined to seek out help than in the past. Students with severe problems present themselves for counseling in great numbers, and counseling and mental health services are stretching and searching for ways to handle the demand.

Stone and Archer (1990) identified several problem areas that increased in the late 1980s: eating disorders, substance abuse, sexual abuse and sexual violence (stranger rape, date rape), dysfunctional families, and AIDS. This section examines the prevalence of and the needs and challenges presented by each of these problems.

Some evidence indicates that the prevalence of alcohol abuse may have leveled off or gone down somewhat. Gonzales and Broughton (1994), in a study of college students at Daytona Beach during spring break, reported a decrease in alcohol use from 1981 to 1991. In 1981, 90 percent of the males and 88 percent of the females indicated that they currently drank alcoholic beverages. In 1991, 82 percent of the males and 76 percent of the females reported drinking alcohol. The students they surveyed also had a decrease in the reported amount of alcohol consumed each month. These modest decreases are somewhat dwarfed by the prevalence data from the 1989–1991 Core Alcohol and Drug Survey (Presley, Meilman, and Lyerla, 1994). This study, which included 58,625 students from colleges and universities around the country, found that 16.1 percent of the males and 3.8 percent of the females reported having sixteen or more drinks per week. Of the men 51.2 percent and of the women 35 percent reported one or more binges in the previous two weeks, with 10.4 percent of the men reporting more than six binges during the past two weeks. Of the students, 26.4 percent reported using marijuana, 5.2 percent cocaine, 4.9 percent hallucinogens, and 4.9 percent amphetamines.

Presley, Meilman, and Lyerla (1994) quote Eigen and Quinlan (1991) on the future results of alcohol use. "Between 240,000 and 360,000 of our current student body of 12 million college students will eventually die of alcohol-related causes. It's as if the entire undergraduate student body of all the schools of the Big Ten is destined for death as a result of alcohol abuse" (pp. 12–13). Rivinus (1993) estimates that one in ten college students already has or will have a problem with alcohol or other drugs.

Substance abuse does not occur in a vacuum. A student's judgment in many other arenas is affected by substance abuse. "The college and university years (18–30 generally) are a time of extremely high risk for mortal accidents, rape, suicide, and other untoward events related to substance use and abuse" (Rivinus, 1993, p. 72). Among these potentially "mortal" accidents is unprotected sex.

Many students who are abusing alcohol or other drugs have not yet reached a stage where they can see how their life is being adversely affected by their abuse. Within the college subculture abuse of alcohol and other drugs is tolerated and considered by many students to be part of normal development and experimentation. Often, students who abuse substances get to a counselor because of mandatory referrals or because they have been persuaded to seek help. The counselor is challenged to help students realize and understand their abuse and dependence problems. Substance abusers, in part because of the impact of ethanol on memory encoding, are notorious for denying their problems, and counseling is often intermittent, punctuated with frequent regressions. Often some group support, such as that provided by Alcoholics Anonymous (AA) or Narcotics Anonymous (NA), is needed. In extreme cases detoxification and inpatient treatment are necessary.

The challenges of providing services for students with eating disorders are similar to those of counseling substance abusers. A large cohort of students have some eating problems (compulsive eating, dieting, obsession with body image and food), and a smaller number have bulimia and anorexia. Students in the early stages are hard to access, like substance abusers, and adequate treatment is really secondary prevention, often requiring major campuswide programs. The smaller number of diagnosable cases of anorexia and bulimia present difficult clinical situations. The condition of these students is sometimes life-threatening and necessitates considerable and comprehensive treatment. Cooper (1989) has argued that the treatment of chemical dependence and eating disorders requires a biopsychosocial perspective.

The treatment needs of students with substance abuse and eating disorder problems are an example of the complex challenges facing college counseling and mental health services. Here are two widespread and destructive behavioral problems with social, psychological, and biological components. Large numbers of students are in various stages of these problems, demanding preventive interventions and perhaps even short-term counseling. Smaller numbers require intense and comprehensive treatment. If not enough emphasis is placed on preventive efforts, even more serious cases will develop; yet the serious cases that do exist demand attention and resources. Assessment and treatment, particularly to sort out the substance abuse and eating disorder problems from pervasive personality disorders, are extremely difficult and require therapists with considerable expertise and special training.

Since the mid-1980s a greatly increased awareness of sexual violence among college students has resulted in a high demand for counseling services in this area. In 1994, 66 percent of counseling directors reported an increase in reports of childhood sexual abuse (Gallagher and Bruner, 1994). Aizenman and Kelly (1988) reported that 22 percent of the students on college campuses had been directly involved in an incident of date violence, and Koss, Gidyez, and Wisneiwski (1987) reported that 27.5 percent of the 3,187 college women in a national sample had been victims of rape since age fourteen. Berkowitz (1992) indicated that a review of studies of the frequency of sexual assault among colleges males showed that from 25 to 60 percent had engaged in some form of sexually coercive behavior.

Sexual violence is thus a major problem on our campuses. A large number of students bring a history of sexual abuse with them to college, and a significant number of women experience sexual violence while they are students. It is not unusual for students to have a history of abuse and then also become victims of date rape or some other kind of sexual violence on campus. Victims are much more likely to seek help now than in previous decades. Such victims, particularly victims of child abuse, present with other symptoms such as depression, anxiety, or interpersonal and self-esteem problems. Many are seriously disturbed, and some have dissociative disorders.

The basic challenge for counseling and mental health centers is finding and developing crisis and treatment programs that work but that do not necessarily involve long-term counseling for all students. Most specialists in sexual-abuse counseling have conceptualized the treatment as long-term, requiring considerable time for the client, whose trust has been betrayed (often by a relative or parent) in a most fundamental way, to learn to trust the therapist and to be able to confront the pain and sometimes repressed memories of abuse. Given the large number of victims, the severity of the posttraumatic stress that many victims experience, and the length of treatment, how can a campus counseling center or mental health center address the needs of these students?

Questions about how to organize sexual-abuse services are also significant. Should they be independent or separate programs? How much specialized training is required? What relationship should these services have to campus sexual-abuse adjudication policies and procedures? Should the counseling or mental health service also provide counseling services for perpetrators of sexual violence, typically male students? Should participation in counseling be a condition for their staying in school?

Although AIDS is clearly one of the great dangers to young people and college students today, large numbers of associated counseling cases have not yet been reported. In the Data Bank Survey covering 1992–1993, 252 counseling directors reported a total of 379 clients with HIV or AIDS. Recent estimates put the HIV seroprevalance on American college campuses at 3 per 1,000 to 5 per 1,000 for men and 0.2 per 1,000 for women, although it is potentially as high as 1 or 2 per 100 for all college students (Schneider and others, 1994). It is difficult to determine what the future demand for counseling students with AIDS will be; however, there can be no question that sometime in the reasonably near future increasing numbers of students will need help with this disease. Again, the type of counseling that can be offered must be determined and creative ways to help students dealing with being HIV-positive and having AIDS must be found. Also, the issues involved in "warning" actual or potential sexual partners of nondisclosing HIV-positive clients are particularly complex.

Families in the United States have been described as being under stress. One out of every two marriages ends in divorce; over one million children suffer from physical, sexual, or emotional abuse; 16 percent of couples experience domestic violence every year, with two million children, wives, and husbands punched, kicked, beaten up, or injured (Witchel, 1991). Use of the term *dysfunctional family* has become a popular way to refer to families that do not function in a healthy or ideal manner. And the designation ACOA (adult children of alcoholics) describes adults who grew up in families rendered dysfunctional, at least in part, by an alcoholic parent. Newton and Krause (1991) suggest that "the experience of dysfunction in the family of origin is a ubiquitous phenomenon that potentially is a concern if not an influence for the majority of college students" (p. 92). How, then, do counseling and mental health services deal with the counseling needs of students from all these problem families?

One significant challenge is to assess the needs of students from dysfunctional families. As Newton and Krause (1991) point out, not all students from alcoholic families need counseling; many have already developed healthy ways to cope with their past. Counseling services are caught in a bind. It makes sense to use the popular language and offer "ACOA" and "family-dysfunction" groups because they help troubled students gain access to services. But an overreliance on these popular terms tends to communicate a message to students that anyone from a family that had problems or a member who struggled with alcohol use needs counseling.

Career and Developmental Counseling

Although the need for counseling by students with severe problems exerts a strong pull on counseling resources, staff and administrators in counseling and mental health services must also attend to the many students who have problems related to normal developmental issues such as careers, relationships, and identity. The definition of "normal developmental problems" does become a bit problematic in light of the large number of students with histories of sexual, physical, and emotional abuse. Stone and Archer (1990) ask, "If 27 percent of the women in college have been raped since they were 14, is this becoming more of a 'normal' developmental experience?" (p. 546).

Nevertheless, typical developmental and college-adjustment problems must be addressed because these problems are the most immediately relevant to college success, at least from a superficial perspective. If students do not learn how to manage time, study for tests, handle their emotions, set goals, develop friendship groups, or achieve some successes on which to build a positive identity and self-esteem, they will not be successful in school. The majority of students expressing needs for counseling list these kinds of developmental problems. How can time be reserved for these counseling cases in the face of traumatic and pressing problems like previous sexual abuse and serious depression? The issue is further complicated by the fact that students with these seemingly "simple" developmental and adjustment problems often have complex psychological histories that clearly influence their developmental and adjustment progress. Consequently, even though most students and probably most faculty members and administrators imagine that counseling for these developmental and adjustment problems is relatively simple, it sometimes is not.

Clearly the counseling or mental health service must examine what it can and wants to offer. Should a brief-therapy, managed-care model be used by adopting limited counseling goals that focus on specific adjustment problems? How can the counseling be defined and seen as educationally purposeful and in tune with the primary mission of the institution? How many of the normal developmental and adjustment problems can be handled in groups or workshops, with self-help books and computer-assisted programs, or by paraprofessionals? Should the professional counselor be mainly a consultant to less-skilled personnel and faculty who work with students on these personal, career, and adjustment problems? Does it make sense to handle these concerns in specialized programs such as career resources and learning assistance?

Career counseling appears to be receiving less priority in counseling and mental health services than it once did. Stone and Archer (1990) identified this trend and suggested that a shift had occurred away from preventive, developmental counseling toward "clinical" kinds of therapy. This trend seems to be continuing, at least with regard to career counseling. In the 1994 survey of counseling-center directors (Gallagher and Bruner, 1994) only 30.3 percent indicated that career counseling was done primarily in the counseling center, and 51.9 percent reported that career counseling was done primarily in a separate career development office. One must understand the history of college counseling centers and their strong historic involvement in career counseling to fully appreciate the significance of this change.

Does this separation of personal and career counseling make sense theoretically? Pinkerton and others (1990) argue for an integration of psychotherapy and career counseling with college students. Essentially, they contend that often career issues cannot be separated from other developmental issues. For example, a student may not choose a career because he or she is not self-confident enough in interpersonal relationships or because of a sexual-orientation problem.

The basic challenge is to ensure that there is an integration of career and developmental counseling regardless of where they are provided on campus. How well can this integration be accomplished by separating offices for career and personal counseling? Staff in separate, comprehensive career services argue that they must have the resources and expertise to move a student from the early stages of decision making up through the interview and job-selection phase. Separate career centers typically have staff who are focused on and interested in career counseling, and comprehensive counseling and psychological centers sometimes do not. However, the emphasis in career centers can be on encouraging a focused, assertive, goal-oriented approach, which may not match the student's developmental readiness. Whatever organizational scheme is used, career services should offer developmentally appropriate career counseling by counselors who are well trained and who can recognize the interaction between personal developmental issues and career choice and provide appropriate counseling or referral regarding these related personal developmental issues. Political and economic questions are also involved in this issue. Are counseling and mental health centers moving away from the central mission of the institution when they stop doing career counseling? Is this movement primarily an economic necessity because additional resources can be made available through a separate career counseling agency? Does one organizational structure work best in the delivery of career counseling services?

Counseling for Minorities and Other Special Groups

Two issues are central to a consideration of counseling services for minority and other special groups: access and cultural barriers to counseling. Historically, ethnic and racial minority groups have not used counseling services in the same proportion as their majority counterparts. Also, college counseling and mental health services have generally recognized the fact that cultural differences and a lack of cultural understanding can make counseling difficult and lead to premature termination (Das, 1995). The most common attempts to solve this problem have involved providing multicultural training for staff and hiring diverse staff to represent campus populations.

Boesch and Cimbolic (1994) in a survey of counseling centers reported that black students were using counseling services more than nonblack students in general, especially for emotional and social concerns. They suggest that this finding, which is contrary to those in previous studies, may indicate a change in help-seeking attitudes and a change in access factors, and they recommend further research. Another explanation of their data might be less positive. Perhaps black students are encountering more problems than white students as a result of racism and related factors on predominately white campuses and therefore seek counseling in greater numbers, even though they are reluctant clients.

The degree of a student's cultural commitment has been identified as one variable that may determine attitudes toward counseling and therefore willingness to seek help. In a study of Native American college students, Price and McNeill (1992) found that those more strongly committed to tribal culture had more negative attitudes toward counseling. Atkinson, Jennings, and Liongson (1990) found similar attitudes in a study of minority students, with ethnic-identified students expressing a stronger agreement than other minority students with the view that the unavailability of culturally similar or sensitive counselors was an impediment to counseling.

The challenges of access and culturally effective counseling must be addressed, especially because the nature and type of ethnic minority groups vary from campus to campus. One of the solutions, supported by the studies just cited, is to develop counseling strategies for minority students at different stages of cultural-identity development. For example, some African American students and some Hispanic students may be highly acculturated to the mainstream culture and may not hesitate to use counseling services. But ethnically committed students may find it impossible to work with a white counselor. An understanding of racial and ethnic identity development, especially for traditional-age college students in the midst of rapid development, is probably a crucial aspect of multicultural understanding (Helms, 1990). This is not to say that this issue is not important for older minority and ethnic students. In fact, the issues of racial and ethnic identity can be even more complicated for adults who have already arrived at some understanding of their ethnic identity when they come back to a campus and are confronted with different kinds of racism and the often more radical views of younger minority students.

Recognition of oppressed groups other than the traditional minority groups (African Americans, Hispanic/Latino Americans, Asian Americans, and Native Americans) is growing. Gay, lesbian, and bisexual students have become a much more recognized and vocal group, as have disabled and physically challenged students. International student populations have increased on many campuses and offer unique counseling challenges. Although they are not currently a separate or identified group, the number of students who are biracial is increasing. Work has just begun on exploring identity and developmental issues for these students, and counseling them can provide unique challenges even for the counselor who has considerable multicultural training and understanding.

Access to counseling is related to composition of the staff, visibility on campus, and even to public and political positions. Practical issues, like how to provide a diverse staff when a service has only a small number of counselors to begin with, provide difficult dilemmas. Does a center director hire a part-time counselor to represent each minority group? Is this tokenism? Can the service afford to invest a large amount of time reaching out to specific groups? What if some staff members do not believe that they need multicultural training or do not agree that they need to be effective counselors for different student groups?

Counseling Women and Men

All students, including those who seek counseling, are struggling with what it means to be a male or female in contemporary society. We are clearly confused about this issue as a society. In general, sex roles, particularly for women, have been expanding, and many more opportunities are available to them than in the past. Many returning adult women are in college because of this role expansion. However, many of the traditional "feminine" messages are still communicated clearly to our female students—for example, that they must be thin and beautiful to find a man and to be worthwhile. College mental health workers see the pathology of eating disorders related to this set of socialization influences. In addition, women are subjected to a great deal of gender bias, which in its most virulent form includes harassment and physical and sexual violence. Almost all college women must contend with a "chilly" climate in the classroom and throughout their higher education experience (Pace, Stamler, and Yarris, 1992).

College counselors, then, must deal with some of the negative results of sex-role messages and with the confusion that both men and women experience. How can counselors provide counseling services to women when most of the theories on which their training is based were developed for males? For example, individuation and independence have always been central issues in college counseling. Healthy development has been viewed as moving away from parents toward self-reliance and independence. But does this assumption hold true for female students? Gilligan (1982) and others have suggested that female development may be quite different. Are college counselors able to respond to these differences? Is there a problem, as Pace, Stamler, and Yarris (1992) suggest, with providing female counselors for female clients who request a female therapist? Is providing a therapist of a certain gender ever contraindicated because of the nature of the student's problems?

In specific terms, how do college counselors help their female clients learn healthy attitudes about appearance, for example? How do they help men, who often wait to come in for counseling until they are extremely stressed and sometimes until they are dangerously suicidal, so that they can handle emotions and seek support from friends before their lives become so overwhelming? How do college counselors, who are typically supportive of expanding sex roles for both men and women, deal with traditional students who do not want to have their sex roles expanded?

And what about the form of counseling used for both sexes? Does it make sense to offer more groups rather than individual counseling for women, who generally operate on a more relationship-oriented basis and who may need support groups for problems such as sexual violence and eating disorders that generally affect women only? Should male students have their own groups? What about allocation of resources to male and female students? Do the gender bias and sexual and physical violence that women students experience justify putting considerably more resources into programs for women? Magoon (1992, 1993) reports from a survey that 67 percent of the large counseling centers and 57 percent of the small centers have special services for women. There was no question on the survey about special services for men.

Counseling Victims of Violence

From a clinical perspective, counselors must be available for crisis situations when students are victims of violence; they must also provide crisis services to students when a particularly public or traumatic violent event occurs on campus; and they must respond to students with a history of violence that is interfering with their current development and functioning. A distinction between direct and indirect victims of violence is helpful in conceptualizing the kinds of clinical challenges that exist in this area. These incidents often involve many indirect victims. Take, for example, the student murders at the University of Florida in 1990 (Archer, 1992) and the faculty murders at the University of Iowa in 1991 (Stone, 1993). Although the number of direct victims was small, there were thousands of indirect victims. Those who were related or close to the victims had to handle grief reactions and the loss of their loved ones. However, other students on these campuses also had intense reactions, sometimes related to previous sexual or physical violence, that required counseling and support. College counselors have an obligation to respond. This is difficult work and requires a well-organized crisis system that can mobilize many counseling services quickly. The long-range effects of violence must also be considered. Archer (1992) reported that requests for general counseling increased after the University of Florida student murders, and Stone (1993) reported increased requests for consultation by faculty.

Our campuses exist in what some have called a culture of violence. Whitaker (1993) reviewed some of the alarming statistics to support his conclusion that college students are coming from a violent society. From 1979 to 1989 the homicide rate for people from fifteen to nineteen increased 61 percent, with a 54 percent rise for black males from 1985 to 1989. Even domestic violence and physical abuse, usually perpetrated by husbands toward their wives, have come to campus in the form of "predomestic strife" (Puig, 1984). Stalking is also a campus problem. In a national survey (Gallagher and Bruner, 1993) 55 percent of counseling-center directors reported stalking cases in the previous year, with four students killed and thirty-four physically injured.

How can counseling services for all victims (direct and indirect) be provided with available resources? Should every campus have a crisis-intervention center available twenty-four hours a day? If so, how should it be funded and staffed? Can peer counselors provide counseling to victims of violence? Is it professionally sound and ethical to provide only crisis intervention to victims of violence when the experience of violence opens up deep emotional and psychological problems? What responsibility does the counselor have to counsel the perpetrator? Should special counseling services be set up for victims, and what are the implications of emphasizing victimization?

◆ ◆ ◆

College and university counseling and mental health workers are clearly faced with a number of difficult challenges concerning the delivery of counseling services. The remaining chapters in this part of the book will explore some of the issues involved in meeting these challenges; they provide examples of programs that have been developed on various campuses in the United States and Canada. The use of brief therapy with a strong group-counseling program is discussed and recommended as the way to most directly meet the challenge for clinical services. Many other alternatives to direct counseling that can meet some or all student needs are also examined. These include the use of nonprofessional counselors in certain roles, self-help technologies and adjuncts (including medication), and targeted programs for special problems and populations.

CHAPTER TWO

BRIEF THERAPY

The Model of Choice for College Counseling

Not all college counselors see themselves as being "mental health" providers, and in fact some have argued that counseling centers should provide only educational, career, and developmental counseling that is directly related to the academic mission. Stone and McMichael (1993) suggest that counseling-center professionals have not argued persuasively that clinical counseling services are an essential educational service. However, even if one accepts the more common view that personal or mental health counseling is critical to education and to student growth and development, it seems clear that such counseling will have to be rationed.

As resources for counseling and mental health services continue to be scarce and as counseling and mental health services are scrutinized for cost efficiency and effectiveness, college counselors will need to rely increasingly on research and the demonstrated effectiveness of their counseling efforts. The need for accountability and for cost-benefit analysis is not new to college counseling and mental health services (Bishop and Trembley, 1987; Stone and Archer, 1990), but demands for demonstration of the clinical effectiveness of specific treatments for specific problems are increasing, fueled by managed care and a general move toward standardized and research-supported treatment protocols (Hayes, Follette, Dawes, and Grady, 1995).

In these circumstances, brief therapy makes sense as the model of choice for college and university counseling for a number of reasons. First, there is growing research evidence of its effectiveness with a wide range of clients and problems. From a strictly clinical perspective, considerable evidence in the research literature supports the efficacy of short, targeted approaches to counseling. Bloom (1992) and Steenbarger (1992), in reviewing research on brief therapy, find strong evidence that planned, short-term therapy is effective for a wide range of problems. Second, the types of developmental, crisis, and situational problems often presented by students are particularly well suited to brief therapy. For example, students involved in relationship breakups may experience intense emotions and in extreme cases even have suicidal thoughts. Brief therapy, focused on helping them navigate the crisis and manage their emotions, will often produce a speedy recovery. Or, if the breakup raises personal issues for them (for example, inability to express emotion), brief, targeted therapy can take advantage of a "teachable moment" to help them learn, say, to be expressive. Because college students are often bright and insightful, the underlying assumption in brief therapy that a small change can trigger future growth is particularly applicable. Third, limited resources make it necessary to prioritize services and to provide as equitable a distribution as possible. Brief therapy allows the greatest number of students to receive counseling. Fourth, consultation on and prevention of serious campuswide problems such as HIV, sexual violence, and diversity demand time and attention from college counselors, as does the development of programs to help students integrate personal and classroom learning and to use their educational opportunities effectively. Consequently, counselors have less time to devote to individual therapy. Fifth, the previously mentioned growing demand for counseling has increased the number of students who must be served despite the limited time and resources available.

There is no standard definition for *brief therapy* (or *brief counseling*). It has been defined by different theorists and practitioners as encompassing anything from a single session to forty or fifty sessions. Discussing time limits for college counseling, Pinkerton (1996) suggested that two categories of brief therapy may be useful for college students: very brief (one to five sessions) and extended (six to sixteen sessions). Pinkerton and Rockwell (1994) also outlined several common college counseling situations where one, two, or three sessions were appropriate. For purposes of this discussion, the range will be one to fifteen sessions, with the average number of sessions between five and six.

In the process of setting limits and defining services however, college counselors should not abandon students with crucial needs. Counselors must, in fact, argue as persuasively as they can for counseling and mental health services for all students. There is a strong rationale for offering extensive counseling to students who need more than brief counseling (such as victims of incest or those with serious alcohol problems), particularly as an opportunity to address issues that may profoundly interfere with their development and subsequent success in school and in life. From a broad perspective, their contribution to society will be greatly enhanced if counseling is available when problems interfere with college performance and personal development. Ultimately, however, resource limitations will probably in general allow for only brief therapy with, perhaps, some extensive programs in targeted areas. Such programs, sometimes combining individual and group counseling, are most possible in areas like sexual abuse, eating disorders, and substance abuse—areas that may have campuswide support. Future legal actions based on the Americans with Disabilities Act may force universities to provide essential services to the emotionally disabled, but such cases have not yet occurred.

This chapter includes a discussion of brief, intermittent approaches to therapy (and the limitations of these approaches), single-session and very brief counseling, crisis counseling, therapist attitudes, initial assessments, and referrals. The need for planned and conscious decision making about clinical offerings is stressed as is the importance of acquiring a scientific basis for counseling services and treatment modalities. Later chapters will include a discussion of less traditional ways (using paraprofessionals, self-help books, computer programs) to meet the counseling needs of students.

Brief, Intermittent Counseling

Many college counseling and mental health centers currently use some version of brief therapy. They usually either set specific session limits or employ other methods to encourage brief counseling. Because colleges and universities operate on a term basis (semester, quarter), some natural limits are imposed at the end of the term. Sometimes exceptions are made when trainees are doing the counseling or for specific problems that require extensive treatment. College counseling and mental health centers are obligated to provide information on the treatment options and limitations prior to counseling and to specify referral procedures.

Cummings (1990, 1995) argued for a general model of brief intermittent therapy throughout the life cycle. He, and many other brief-therapy advocates, suggest counseling that is basically symptom-oriented; the primary goal is returning people to their previous level of functioning by emphasizing their strengths and helping them develop ways to overcome specific problems or developmental blocks. The goal of "curing" people is rejected in favor of providing brief and intermittent assistance for specific problems. On a superficial level, this "chiropractic" or "family-practitioner" model of counseling may seem to lack the educational or developmental goals that have been so much a part of college counseling. Close analysis, however, reveals that this model is not necessarily only remedial. The major goal of stabilizing the client can be expanded to include learning new skills, improving cognition, and overcoming developmental blocks so that the person can continue to grow and progress.

A number of approaches to brief therapy are available to the college counselor. These fall into several different categories. Several psychoanalytic approaches have been developed as brief therapies. Strupp and Binder's (1984) time-limited dynamic psychotherapy has been refined over many years as part of the Vanderbilt Psychotherapy Research Project. It is highly interpersonal and does not require an extensive evaluation of the past in order to focus on current problems. Mann's (1973) time-limited approach is interesting because it includes an absolute twelve-session limit. Cognitive-behavioral approaches that focus on specific behavior and cognition can be used in brief therapy. Ellis (rational-emotive behavior therapy) (1989), Beck (cognitive therapy) (Beck, Rush, Shaw, and Emery, 1979), and Meichenbaum (stress-inoculation training) (1985) all offer well-documented brief-therapy techniques. Yapko (1988), Zeig and Gilligan (1990), and many others have offered variations of Eriksonian, hypnotic, and other methods for use in brief therapy. Walter and Pelletier (1992) have developed a manual for using solution-focused therapy, a method that primarily emphasizes client strengths and inherent abilities to create solutions to problems. McFarland (1995) developed a method for applying this approach to eating disorders. Many other brief therapies have been described. Clearly, there is no dearth of approaches and techniques that college counselors can use.

The emerging brief-therapy literature indicates that change and psychological growth can take place after a brief intervention and that there is a maximally effective "dose" of counseling after which the benefits level off (Bloom, 1992). Bloom (1992), in reviewing studies and reviews since the early 1970s, concluded that brief, planned psychotherapies are, in general, as effective as time-unlimited therapy. It may seem suspicious to some that research supporting brief, targeted therapy is emerging in concert with strong economic demands for therapists to work quickly and to achieve specific results. In reality, the research on brief therapy has accumulated over a number of years and, although supportive of short approaches, should not be used to reinforce unreasonable and inappropriate demands for brief counseling. Miller (1996) in a critique of brief-therapy research argued that reviewers of such research have overstated the findings supporting these approaches. He strongly urged that the length of therapy be determined on a case-by-case basis with the needs of the client as the principal deciding factor. And, in fact, a large-scale survey conducted by *Consumer Reports* did find a correlation between length of treatment and amount of therapeutic gain as rated by the clients surveyed (Seligman, 1995).

Gelso (1992) also warns that some of the promising findings supporting brief therapy have evolved into what he calls "myths." He suggests that there is no clear evidence that brief therapy is more effective than long-term therapy or that changes are as durable for brief therapy as they are for long-term therapy. He also argues that just because the most change in counseling often occurs in the early stages, this does not mean that more therapy is not needed. He suggests that agencies and clients must decide how much of an effect is sufficient relative to agency resources, and college counseling and mental health agencies need to consider this question when developing brief-therapy systems.

Client selection and readiness is another factor that deserves consideration. Prochaska and DiClemente (1992) have developed a five-stage model of change: (1) precontemplation, in which the individual has not yet acknowledged the problem; (2) contemplation, a period of problem awareness in which the individual is aware of the problem and is deciding which actions to take; (3) preaction, in which the individual is specifying changes needed and is beginning to make them; (4) action, in which the individual is working on specific changes; and (5) maintenance, in which the individual consolidates previous gains. If one applies this theory to brief therapy with college students, a brief, intermittent approach makes good sense. For example, if a resident assistant has persuaded a student to come to the counseling service because the student studies excessively and has no social life, the student may be in the precontemplation stage and not yet ready to make any changes; the appropriate intervention for the counselor would be to talk with him about social and interpersonal needs and offer the services of the center to help him grow in that area when he is ready. This session may take only thirty minutes and does not waste valuable counseling resources on a student who is not yet ready to face a particular developmental need. This student may well show up in six months or a year in the contemplation stage, ready to at least consider his need for social relationships. Using this approach, the therapist then helps the student work toward the action phase, where there is real motivation for change.

This kind of brief, intermittent, non-cure-oriented approach is different from traditional therapy in several ways: in brief therapy, more students can be seen more quickly, therapists probably have fewer deep and ongoing relationships with clients, therapists have to assume that most client growth will take place outside of counseling, and therapists have to focus more on superficial or symptomatic problems and eschew work with underlying personality dynamics. In other words, therapists work less with clients about their past experiences, and therapy is more directive and focused. It may also involve strategic use of time, with sessions of varying lengths and intervals.

This model also requires quick and accurate assessment so that students who cannot benefit can be referred for other kinds of treatment. Assessment is usually done during the initial, or "intake," interview in college counseling settings. As Webb and Widseth (1991) point out, there is a risk in referring out students who are "relationally fragile" and who may experience referral as just another rejection. Counselors must make the most efficient use of the initial time they have with students, but how they present their assessments to prospective clients is extremely important. If effectively used, a brief, intermittent model of counseling can provide a student with a sense of caring and support even though the student may be seen only a relatively few times over the course of a year or a college career.

Single-Session and Very Brief Counseling

Although brief therapy consisting of more than five sessions may be optimal for resolving many problems, even very brief contact with clients, such as a phone call or an e-mail message, may be enough to trigger growth. Writers discussing single-session therapy emphasize the importance of short phone contacts even before therapy starts (Talmon, 1990; Bloom, 1992).

Very brief and single-session therapy appear to some therapists, including some college counselors, to signal the ultimate demise of the therapy process. Certainly, such therapy is very different from traditional counseling, which is an ongoing process where trust is developed over time and the therapist has a satisfying relationship with the client. In reality, however, much of the counseling that goes on in a variety of settings occurs in a single session. Bloom (1992) reports that a significant number of clients are seen only once. This is certainly true in a college setting, where waiting lists and semester and summer breaks mean that students coming in late in the semester cannot be seen more than once. A one-time session may also be appropriate from a therapeutic perspective, depending on the student's needs and developmental readiness.

Program Example: One-Session Counseling at the End of the Semester

At the Student Counseling Service at Texas A&M University a program was developed as an alternative to putting students on a waiting list at the end of the semester. When about four or five weeks were left in the semester, the waiting list was typically so long that any students requesting counseling could not be seen except for an intake session. With the new program, staff at the center informed students requesting services after a fixed date that they could be seen for a single session or they could be referred out. If students chose the single session, they received information on the purpose and limits of a single counseling session. Students on the waiting list were also given this opportunity. Staff reported that most students understood the reason for this system and accepted it. In the single session counselors were able to assess risk, problem-solve, and if necessary plan counseling for the next term or for the period before the next term. This method allowed the center to provide end-of-the-term services for all students who requested them.

Source: Stachowiak, 1994.

Crisis Counseling

In many respects it is difficult to differentiate crisis counseling from brief, intermittent and single-session counseling, particularly in a college or university setting. Many students come to counseling because they are in some sort of crisis (loss of a relationship, poor grades, parental divorce), and these crises are often opportunities for the student to address developmental needs and issues. More serious crises (suicide attempts, acute anxiety or depression, death of a parent, rape) are also frequent on college campuses. In many instances the crisis, although intense, can still be handled with brief counseling. The important assessment issue for the counselor is whether the crisis is related to any serious and potentially long-term psychological issues such as personality or affective disorders, psychosis, or other organic or developmental difficulties that have been chronic or pervasive.

If the counselor determines that the client has a disorder that is not amenable to brief therapy, a plan for support, crisis intervention, and stabilization is required. In some of these cases the counselor may make a referral once stabilization occurs. In a few crisis situations, particularly when the student is dangerously suicidal, inpatient treatment is called for, and the counselor must provide a referral; in extreme cases the counselor may have to execute a mandatory commitment for evaluation. These cases are often difficult to manage and take considerable time and emotional energy. Often faculty and administrators are involved.

The policies of a counseling or mental health center must include a set of procedures for handling serious crisis cases that require follow-up and stabilization. For example, a student may be referred to counseling by a faculty member or resident assistant because she has been behaving strangely and is upsetting many of her friends. The student comes to counseling and is quite agitated, telling the counselor that she has been addicted to crack cocaine for over a year. If the agency does not have a special program for drug addiction, the counselor is faced with trying to stabilize the student and deal with the problems that she is creating in her social environment and at the same time finding a referral or treatment facility for the student.

Counselors and counseling services have an obligation to help every student, at least with crisis intervention, even if that student is clearly not an appropriate candidate for counseling by the college agency. Crisis intervention can be time-intensive, and administrators need to understand that using a brief-therapy model for college counseling does not mean that the institution can simply deny counseling services to students whose needs do not fit the model. Counseling and mental health centers always have an obligation to provide crisis intervention, stabilization, and referral.

Therapist Attitudes

Brief counseling can be difficult for therapists and requires skill in assessment and the use of approaches that are focused and solution-oriented. If a center is to use a brief-therapy model effectively, staff counselors and psychologists must be involved in developing the model and must receive training in using it.

Pinkerton (1996) suggested that brief-therapy counselors must have the following characteristics: a belief in the effectiveness of brief therapy, comfort with being in a position of authority, comfort with modest goals, the ability to make rapid and accurate assessments, and the ability to rapidly establish a positive relationship (pp. 9–10).

Bloom (1992) and many other brief-therapy theorists and advocates contend that therapist attitudes are a serious impediment to an increased use of brief therapy. Although college counselors and mental health workers are often much more versed in brief-therapy methods than other counselors because of the academic calendar and the nature of student requests for help, many still view brief therapy as superficial and less interesting than traditional mental health models.

Assessments

One of the most difficult problems with brief therapy is assessing which students can benefit from it and which cannot. Criteria for inclusion vary considerably, depending on the theoretical point of view of the agency. This difficult assessment process, which was discussed earlier with regard to crisis intervention, is also vexing for students who are not in crisis. These guidelines should be followed in developing assessment procedures for brief therapy:

1. The clinical mission of the agency and criteria for receiving counseling services must be clear, and the assessment system should be well defined. Such a system could use DSM-IV criteria, specific behavioral criteria, or other established methods for identifying student problems and psychopathology.
2. The staff, college or university administrators, faculty, and students should all be involved in defining eligibility criteria for counseling.

3. The kinds of counseling services to be offered must be clearly communicated to the campus community. Brochures from the counseling and mental health center should not be overly expansive in attempts to encourage students to seek counseling.
4. Specific guidelines should be developed by the staff to ensure that assessment procedures are consistent with the best clinical and ethical practices and that there is consistency among staff in applying these guidelines.
5. The assessment process should be monitored, and staff should discuss their application of the agency criteria and guidelines on a regular basis.
6. Exceptions to agency guidelines to accommodate student and professional development (for example, exceptions to rules about the number of long-term clients counselors can see) should be made with great care.
7. Referral and emergency systems must be provided for clients who do not fit the criteria for agency treatment. Referring out students whose functioning has deteriorated while they are clients is particularly difficult and requires a consideration of legal, ethical, and therapeutic issues. Mandatory student health insurance or a requirement that other coverage include mental health benefits is extremely helpful in these referral situations. Unfortunately, most colleges and universities do not have such mandatory coverage.
8. Specific guidelines for absolute numbers of sessions allowed should be avoided. There is no solid evidence that specific session guidelines decrease the average number of sessions; in fact, the opposite may be true (Gyorky, Royalty, and Johnson, 1994).

As the following program example makes clear, Newton (1993) and the counseling staff at Kansas State University have done an excellent job of identifying the characteristics of clients and their problems that are necessary for achieving success in brief therapy. These characteristics are supported by current theory and research, and they would be a good starting point for any agency assessment system.

Program Example: Developing an Assessment Plan for Brief Therapy

At Kansas State University the counseling-center staff, after a merger of the counseling and mental health services, defined a mission that emphasized brief treatment for developmental concerns, crisis intervention, and managed supportive care, and decided that long-term and specialized treatment would be referred out. In order to fulfill this mission the staff held a retreat and developed an implementation plan. Part of this plan was to develop an intake system that would allow staff members to make sound decisions regarding suitability for brief therapy and referral out. They started with a set of "action markers" for brief therapy used at Colorado State University (Dworkin and Lyddon, 1991) and established criteria for these markers using a card sort, with each staff member participating. The following list describes the action markers they used and the four most frequently chosen criteria for each marker as determined by their staff card sort:

Action Marker #1: Nonseverity of prior treatment
1. No history of psychosis
2. Previous treatment for acute or developmental problems
3. No psychiatric hospitalization or unsuccessful substance abuse treatment
4. Previous treatment was not the result of client's presenting a danger to others

Action Marker #2: Positive use of prior therapy
1. Client able to articulate how prior treatment was helpful and evidenced in behavior
2. If previous therapy was not helpful, client able to show insight as to what happened and what he or she would do differently
3. Current presenting issue less serious than previous therapy issues
4. Client able to differentiate between therapy and life

Action Marker #3: High motivation for change
1. Client appears committed to change
2. Client shows ego strength to make changes and tolerate feedback
3. Client desires a basic shift in perspective, understanding, and behavior rather than just wanting to dump anger and frustration
4. Client shows enough pain to be motivated

Action Marker #4: Desire for symptomatic relief
1. Client exhibits specific symptoms
2. Client is willing to do homework
3. Client shows willingness to talk
4. Client is able to relate to own behavior

Action Marker #5: Presence of situational problem
1. Client presents issues around adjustment to a specific life situation or event
2. Client can identify stressor that motivated him or her to make an appointment
3. Client can identify problematic behaviors (nonproductive stress reactions, procrastination)
4. Client presents age-appropriate issues such as separation and autonomy from parents, career indecision

Action Marker #6: Ability to clearly identify a focal conflict or impasse
1. Client identifies problem specifics and shows some problem-solving capacity
2. Client's issues have a manageable theme

3. Client does not engage in excessive externalizing or vagueness
4. Client shows ability to take responsibility for conflict when appropriate

Action Marker #7: Ability to be introspective, monitor self, and experience feelings
1. Client shows appropriate affect connected with content as issues are presented
2. Client shows ability to recognize and reflect on his or her feelings
3. Client shows ability to observe and analyze self
4. Client shows ability to hypothesize reasons and solutions for current issues

Action Marker #8: Ability to develop trust, be open, and form relationships with therapist and others
1. Client able to appropriately interact with therapist in sessions
2. Client has history of positive interpersonal relationships
3. Client is able to talk about personal matters
4. Client has history of positive use of support systems

Source: F. Newton, director, Counseling Center, Kansas State University, Manhattan, Kansas, personal communication, 1993.

Brief, focused, and problem-oriented therapy can be particularly effective with many minority students, male students, and others who view counseling as a way of solving a particular problem. (Students who are more process-oriented may have differing expectations of counseling; these are sometimes students who have already had counseling or therapy.) Even though in many instances students who want to solve specific problems do not fully understand the underlying dynamics and causes of these problems, they sometimes do not want to spend a great deal of time exploring their past history and searching for insight and understanding. For example, an African American male student seeks out counseling because of a difficult situation with his family. He is reluctant to come in for counseling but feels anxious about his situation and wants some specific advice. Certainly, the counselor would want to attend to his anxiety and how it is affecting his life, but the real focus of counseling needs to be on his request for advice. If the counselor does not provide focused, brief counseling, the student is not likely to return and will probably be dissatisfied with his counseling contact. It is extremely important for the counselor to understand the student's request and respond to it. Brief therapy fits well with such student expectations for a practical and quick way to confront a problem or difficulty. The experienced and wise therapist can also help these students gain insight into and understanding of themselves and help them take away from brief counseling increased knowledge and problem-solving skills that they can use in other situations. Along with cultural understanding, effective and efficient brief therapy can be particularly important in establishing a good reputation with minority students.

Making the complicated decision about who is eligible for brief counseling is even more difficult when little time is left in a semester. A student who is graduating and comes in for counseling late in the spring semester cannot be referred or seen for more than a few sessions. In this case the brief approach is forced on the counselor; he or she must attempt to intervene positively and perhaps establish the expectation of later contact with a therapist wherever the student relocates.

Referrals

Because some students will not benefit from brief therapy, establishing a referral process and ascertaining the availability of other resources for these students are crucial. If a college or university counseling or mental health service has as clearly as possible defined what counseling services it can offer (crisis intervention and brief therapy, special treatment programs for those with eating disorders and victims of sexual violence) and if it has devised an effective and consistent assessment method, it must then attend to the problem of how to handle referrals of students who do not fit the criteria for counseling in the agency.

Criteria for referral need to be explicit and fair and clearly communicated to students. In some settings an absolute number of sessions is offered, so that it is possible to inform students that they can have, for example, six sessions to work on their problem but that they will need to be referred out after that. There are pros and cons as to providing a few sessions when one knows that more will be required. Sometimes it makes sense to directly refer the student out rather than open a discussion and establish a relationship that cannot be continued. As discussed previously, in a crisis situation there is often little choice because the counselor has an obligation to at least stabilize the student as part of a referral process. In less crisis-oriented cases a decision can be made during the first session about referral.

Availability of referral sources is critical. In some cases, especially when campuses are in isolated areas, few resources exist. And the matter of cost must be confronted. Some students have insurance through their parents (although they sometimes do not want to involve their parents); some may have insurance that covers additional visits through the counseling center; and some may be able to pay for service themselves or with their parents' help. A close liaison with area mental health providers and, when possible, arrangements for them to provide reduced-fee or pro bono counseling are important. Sometimes local therapists are willing to get involved with a campus counseling agency and provide service in exchange for an academic affiliation. Referrals can be tricky in that the campus personnel must follow ethical guidelines and give a student several choices. A referral directory that lists licensed mental health personnel, their specialties, and their fees is helpful.

Program Example: Using Pro Bono Community Therapists

The University of Florida Counseling Center asks licensed community therapists (mental health counselors, psychologists, psychiatrists, social workers) to volunteer each year to see one college student on a pro bono basis. The letter from the center requesting help explains that counseling services on campus are limited and that the demand for counseling often exceeds the resources available. A list of volunteer community therapists is kept at the reception desk so that counselors can refer students to therapists as appropriate. Approximately thirty private-practice therapists volunteer each year, and they are used for referrals of students who do not have insurance or the financial means to get private therapy. The center has maintained a cordial relationship with many local therapists, some of whom are graduates of one of the university's counseling or psychology programs. The center sends a thank you letter and a certificate of appreciation at the end of the year.

Program Example: Computer Data Bank of Referral Resources

At the University of Virginia the Counseling Center has developed a data bank for local referrals. A survey of local licensed practitioners includes information on whether they want to be listed on the center referral network, their degrees, licenses, theoretical orientations, charges, insurance they accept, competence with particular problems and populations, and areas of clinical experience. Therapists who return the survey are invited to visit the center for short, informal meetings with the staff.

Counselors can access the database on computer. This database is indexed according to therapist expertise, populations served, fees, and fee structure. This system allows a counselor to find, for example, therapists who work with sexual-abuse survivors with borderline personalities. The database is periodically updated.

Source: Clack, 1995.

◆ ◆ ◆

A brief-therapy counseling model fits well with a college population. Implementation of this model, however, requires a realistic view of the limitations of brief therapy and considerable thought about how it can be put into operation and explained to the campus community. Appropriate ethical and professional guidelines must also be followed in establishing referral and crisis-intervention systems.

CHAPTER THREE

GROUP COUNSELING

Treatment of Choice for Many Students

G roup counseling is the most appropriate counseling approach for many college students. Because most developmental issues for college students relate in some way to their interpersonal functioning, the opportunity to learn from a group experience can be extremely useful. College counseling and mental health centers have utilized group approaches for many years, but only a few centers have developed comprehensive group programs. Golden, Corazzini, and Grady (1993) in a survey of 148 counseling centers found that 83 percent of the respondent centers had fewer than 20 percent of their clients in groups. Much greater utilization of group counseling by college counseling and mental health programs is warranted.

Several types of groups are appropriate for college students: crisis-intervention groups, ongoing general therapy groups, theme-oriented process groups, and structured groups. Group counseling in a college setting is almost always time-limited because of the academic calendar. Groups are run over the semester, quarter, or year. Ongoing groups, which students enter and leave as their needs are met, tend to be the exception rather than the rule.

However, group counseling is not always an appropriate form of therapy. Some students are too anxious and afraid of groups to function well, and some problems, particularly those related to traumatic childhood experiences, often must first be dealt with on a one-to-one basis. Also, students who are in severe crisis and are dangerous to themselves or others need to be followed by an individual therapist until they are stabilized. A number of other types of clients may be difficult to work with in groups—for example, those with highly narcissistic personalities and those who are extremely hostile and angry; however, appropriate group composition may increase the likelihood that such students can function in and gain from the group.

This chapter includes a discussion of individual versus group therapy, time-limited groups, open groups, structured groups, general therapy groups, and information on developing effective group programs in college counseling and mental health centers. Discussion of structured workshops with fewer than several sessions is included in Chapter Eight.

Group Treatment Versus Individual Counseling

In addition to being the treatment of choice for many students, group counseling can be a more efficient therapeutic modality than individual counseling. This is not always the case, however, because considerable time is spent forming groups and groups sometimes do not reach a large enough size to make them more efficient than individual counseling.

MacKenzie (1993) reported a number of research reviews confirming the value of group therapy compared with individual counseling. Toseland and Siporin (1986), in reviewing thirty-two studies with randomized assignment to group and individual therapy, found that in 75 percent of the studies there was no difference between outcomes from group and individual therapy, and in the remaining studies group therapy was found to be more effective. Orlinsky and Howard (1986) reviewed fourteen comparative studies and found that in eleven there was no difference, in three individual therapy was more effective, and in two group counseling was more effective. In a meta-analysis of nine studies with 349 subjects Tillitski (1990) compared group, individual, and control treatments; the effects for group and individual were about double those for control subjects with little difference between individual and group treatment.

Group counseling can be an effective step after individual counseling. A group can be an opportunity for a student to try out some interpersonal behaviors or new ways of viewing self or others in a relatively safe environment. At other times an educational or structured group might be the first phase of a therapy program. For example, a group might be used to teach students some basic information about eating disorders, depression, or substance abuse prior to counseling. The group, in this case, might be used to help the students learn about the topic and also develop readiness for therapy. Participation in group and individual counseling simultaneously is not common for a variety of reasons, but it too must be considered as a viable alternative. Students in need of close supervision and support might be well served by such counseling during certain periods; students who use support groups, such as twelve-step groups, might also benefit from being in individual counseling.

The combination of treatments requires careful consideration as to how the two approaches can complement each other. The danger of combined programs is the perpetuation of the myth that individual counseling must always precede group and that a group is a kind of finishing off of individual therapy. This may be the case in certain instances, but in general group treatment can stand alone as a treatment of choice.

Time-Limited Groups

Although most college counseling groups are time-limited because of college calendars, group counselors need to be aware of the implications of time-limited groups. MacKenzie (1993, p. 425) suggested eight principles to be used in both individual and group time-limited psychotherapy:

1. There is an expectation that the time limit will increase the tempo of psychotherapeutic work and encourage rapid application to real-life circumstances.
2. Careful assessment and selection are used to rule out patients who might be at risk for harm from an active approach.
3. An explicit verbal agreement regarding circumscribed goals is openly negotiated between the patient and the therapist.
4. The therapist will intervene actively to develop and maintain a therapeutic climate and maintain a working focus on the identified goals.
5. From an early point in therapy, there is an expectation that ideas will be actively applied to outside circumstances.
6. The therapist will expect the patient to assume responsibility for initiating therapy tasks and will encourage him or her to do so.
7. There will be encouragement to mobilize the use of outside resources that can reinforce positive changes.
8. It is anticipated that the change process will continue after therapy terminates and, therefore, that the full range of problematic issues need not be addressed within the therapy context.

MacKenzie (1993) also emphasized the importance of preparation before the group meets and suggested a continuum between psychoeducational groups, which require less group interaction, and process groups, which require more interaction. He suggested that the optimal size for time-limited groups requiring more group interaction is between five and ten members, and the optimal size for more educational groups is between fifteen and twenty. MacKenzie (1993) reported that most time-limited groups that seek to develop cohesion and allow the members to do interpersonal work require twelve to twenty sessions. This range allows the therapist to facilitate movement through the typical group stages: engagement, differentiation and conflict, interactional work, and termination; and it allows the therapist to ensure that the group and individuals remain focused on their original goals. Time limits require that the therapist be active and focused and able to judge when to allow and not to allow digressions from primary therapeutic tasks.

Program Example: The Depression Group

The depression group at the Counseling and Testing Center of the University of Georgia was an eight-session, structured, cognitive-therapy group based on David Burns's work. Burns allowed drafts of what was to become *Ten Days to Self-Esteem* (1993a) and the leader's manual for it (1993b) to be used for the group.

Prior to the group meetings, prospective members were screened to determine whether they were appropriate. They completed a Beck Depression Inventory and an intake packet. Students who were so severely depressed they could not function in a group and those who had multiple problems with depression being a secondary problem were not included in the group. During the screening, the nature of the group and the importance of attending and participating in meetings and doing self-help activities between meetings were explained to the students.

The eight sessions of the group were each ninety minutes in length and were devoted to such topics as the cognitive model of emotions, the Daily Mood Log, the externalization of voices, and self-esteem. The leader's manual provided by Burns was followed closely. In addition, each week members completed the Burns Depression Checklist, the Burns Anxiety Inventory, and the Relationship Satisfaction Scale to monitor their progress. A point system was used to promote attendance and to encourage doing the homework activities.

Evaluations at the end of the group indicated that members found the sessions useful. Because of their busy schedules, they least liked doing the self-help activities between meetings. Overall, however, feedback showed that the group was a success. Access to the leader's manual significantly reduced the energy required by leaders to plan and conduct the group.

Source: S. Kaye, counseling psychologist, Counseling and Testing Center, University of Georgia, personal communication, 1996.

Open-Ended Groups

Open-ended groups can be organized in several ways. An ongoing general therapy or theme group, for example, can be run at a particular time, and clients can enter and exit the group as their needs require. Participants can be limited to a certain number of sessions to encourage them to participate and focus. These open-ended groups require a well-developed set of norms with an initiation-at-entrance procedure that is perpetuated by the group. The development stage of these groups tends to repeat and is facilitated by well-developed rituals and norms.

Crisis drop-in groups and groups for waitlist clients are run on some campuses as a way to respond quickly to students who need immediate help and support. The crisis groups can be intense and require leaders who can quickly assess students to determine whether participation in the group is appropriate. The leaders must be able to provide individual assistance and even intervention in some cases. Because of their intensity and the need for accurate assessment these groups cannot be too large and work better with two therapists rather than one. Noncrisis waitlist groups, which provide help while the student waits for counseling, must be designed to deal with a variety of problems and a varying group population.

Program Example: Groups for Life-Skills Enhancement as an Alternative for Waitlist Clients

C. A. Clark (1993), from the Counseling Center at Bowling Green State University, reports that the life-skills groups are similar to traditional content-oriented groups that deal with a single category of skills such as stress management or assertiveness training except that the life-skills groups are flexible and respond to the needs of a changing waitlist population. Students are screened at intake with the exclusion criteria including suicidality or homicidality, recent psychiatric hospitalization, active eating disorder, biopsychological disorders not yet stabilized on medication, high-risk or disruptive behavior, or affect-laden issues such as crisis, abuse, and grief. Students meet with the facilitator ahead of time for screening. The groups meet for ninety minutes, and the leader negotiates with the group at the beginning of every session as to which skills will be covered. The group uses a psychoeducational format, with formal instruction, group discussion, and demonstrations. Members are encouraged to share as a way of increasing self-efficacy and self-esteem.

One other variation of an open-ended group in use in some college settings is the group for "chronic" clients. These groups tend to serve as support groups, mostly for students with personality disorders or other chronic difficulties where the prognosis is guarded. The goal of these groups is to provide the periodic support that these students need to function in the university environment. Many college counseling and mental health centers refer these students out because of the potentially heavy demand on resources, but a chronic group is one strategy for providing support that is relatively less resource-intensive.

Structured Groups

Structured skill, theme, and population groups have been a mainstay of college counseling programs for many years. In addition to the fact that structure facilitates the development of group stages and provides individual and group focus, as pointed out by MacKenzie (1993), structured groups have a number of advantages for college students. Drum and Knott (1977, pp. 24–25), in their book on structured groups, emphasize several of these advantages:

1. Structure communicates goal-directedness and raises positive expectations.
2. Structured groups are relatively nonthreatening, and through carefully planned exercises they encourage participants to try out new behaviors.
3. They allow for both peer and professional feedback.
4. They are economical.
5. They encourage active problem solving.
6. They help participants understand that many others have the same problems.
7. They reduce the stigma of counseling.
8. By establishing boundaries they encourage a sense of safety.

Winston, Bonney, Miller, and Dagley (1988, p. 4) in discussing the advantages of what they call intentionally structured groups added that these groups focus on developmental areas where change may not be supported in the environment; they are enjoyable; and they are versatile with regard to population, problem, and developmental task.

Structured groups appear to be successful because they combine the advantages of process groups and more didactic learning experiences. Structured groups encourage the development of cohesiveness and interpersonal work along with using a focused and structured set of graduated learning exercises to achieve group goals. Therefore, a key to the successful design and implementation of structured groups is careful consideration of goals, methods, and the population. Winston, Bonney, Miller, and Dagley (1988) suggest an adaptation of the cube model (Morrill, Oetting, and Hurst, 1974) with three planes: (1) intrapersonal functioning, interpersonal functioning, information, skill development, (2) enhancement, prevention, remediation, and (3) student development (physical, social, academic). In designing a structured group to help students manage stress, for example, a counselor would make decisions about the design relative to each plane. Will the group focus on intrapersonal or interpersonal functioning, on the transmission of information, or on skill development? Will it be geared toward enhancement, prevention, or remediation, and will it target certain student development dimensions?

Drum and Knott (1977) and Andrews (1995) suggest a number of guide-lines for structured groups. These include attention to

Goals and major program elements

Objectives

Size and composition

Duration

Intake/screening

Marketing

Ongoing and final evaluation

Planning specific sessions and selection of exercises and techniques

Transition and transfer of learning outside the group

Program Example: Two-Phase Eating Disorders Program

A two-phase group psychotherapy program for college students with eating disorders has been reported as successful by staff at the University of Delaware Counseling Center. The first phase is an eight-session psychoeducational group. The goals of this group are to educate students about eating disorders and to help them decrease their symptoms (bingeing, purging). The second phase is a less structured insight-oriented group that moves beyond a symptom approach. Typical themes in this two-phase group are separation and individuation, family relationships, dating and friendships, managing emotions, self-esteem, body image, stress management, sexuality, and loss. Students may participate in both phases, or they may be placed directly in either one. Typically student clients with active symptoms that are not well controlled are placed in the first phase, and those with stabilized symptoms or previous treatment (or both) go into the second phase.

Source: Weiss and Orysh, 1994.

Program Example: Autonomy Training

Staff at the Kansas State University Counseling Service developed a structured group to promote knowledge, self-awareness, and change toward autonomy. It was specifically targeted at codependent students, who frequently came from alcoholic or dysfunctional families. Several established theories were used in developing the intervention including developmental, systems, and cognitive-behavioral theories, and the interventions included techniques patterned after reality therapy, rational-emotive therapy, dysfunctional-family treatment processes (ACOA, codependence, and AA), assertiveness training, values clarification, and psychodrama. There were four modules, each of which included three one-and-a-half-hour sessions. These sessions involved the following: education, personal awareness, preparing for change, and the change process. The final module emphasized personal change, and participants were offered a follow-up support group or an individual counseling appointment.

Source: Newton, Brack, and Brack, 1992.

The AUCCCD has established an extensive library on structured groups. This library, called the Clearinghouse, is currently housed at the University of Texas Counseling and Psychological Services Center in Austin. Materials from the Clearinghouse are available to all college counseling personnel.

General Therapy Groups

Although various kinds of structured, theme, and population groups have become popular and fit well in a time-limited model of group work, general therapy groups can also be effective in a college setting. Using either an open-ended model, with participants entering and leaving at various times, or a specific designated time (semester, quarter, or year), these groups can provide an opportunity for students with a variety of problems to work in a group setting. Although structured and theme groups provide ready-made cohesion because of similarities in problem or life experience, heterogeneous groups also have unique therapeutic and practical advantages. Therapeutically, these groups provide a wide range of experience and behavior from which participants can learn. For example, students who are having interpersonal difficulties with romantic partners might have the opportunity to learn from a variety of people of both genders about those relationships and how they might make positive changes. If these same students were in an assertiveness training group they might not get the range of responses and opportunities to model behavior. However, the time necessary to bring the heterogeneous therapy group to the work stage and through the cohesion and conflict stages might well be longer than in the structured, skill, or theme groups. Leaders in a general therapy group can certainly provide some structure at the beginning to facilitate the development of cohesion, although some group theorists would argue that if the group does not struggle to formulate its own definition of goals, effectiveness will be limited.

From a practical perspective general therapy groups offer an easy way to form groups from clients coming in for counseling. In many counseling and mental health centers, particularly at smaller colleges and universities, the pool of clients makes it difficult to form specific theme, skill, and population groups.

Developing Effective Group-Counseling Programs

Effective group-counseling programs require strong commitment to group approaches by the counseling staff. In addition to administrative, space, and scheduling difficulties, referral to group, particularly from intake, is still difficult for many college therapists. Yet their willingness to strongly recommend group or even to offer it as the only alternative is a significant factor in determining whether a comprehensive group program can be offered. Student clients are naturally inclined to want individual treatment or to be anxious about group treatment, and it is up to the counselor to help the client understand the value and in many cases the superiority of group treatment. Corazzini (1994, p. 3) suggested a number of staff beliefs that hinder the use of group treatment:

1. Individual therapy is the best form of treatment and should be preferred except when the agency has a waiting list.
2. Group therapy provides finishing skills for clients who have achieved success in individual therapy.
3. Clients must talk in group therapy if they are to improve.

Although Corazzini (1994) also indicated that a belief in grouping clients by presenting issue interferes with the development of a group program, numerous successful programs use theme, skill, and population groups: for example, African American women's groups, ACOA groups, incest survivors' groups, assertiveness training groups. As previously discussed, the homogeneous nature of a group can facilitate the development of trust and movement to the working stage, and a specific structure and time limits can provide a focus on specific goals. Also, students are sometimes more willing to participate in a theme or skill group than in a general counseling or therapy group. Theme or problem groups also allow the development of sequential treatment programs for students with specific difficulties, such as eating disorders. Such sequencing is advantageous therapeutically, and it allows a targeted approach to a particular problem area.

Program Example: Making Group Therapy the Treatment of Choice

At the Virginia Commonwealth University Counseling Service, a group therapy program that incorporates apprenticeship training is a major part of the counseling program. The center developed a group therapy model because group therapy is a preferred mode of treatment for many college clients and because group therapy can be more efficient, less expensive, and as efficacious as individual therapy. Client satisfaction scores for group clients have been close to scores for individual clients. A general group therapy model is used with heterogeneous groups rather than problem or population groups.

Students receive a brochure about the group therapy program that discusses the advantages of groups by answering the
following questions:

- Just what is group therapy?
- Why does group therapy work?
- What do I talk about when I am in group therapy?
- What are the common misperceptions about group therapy?
- What are the ground rules for my participation in the group?

Because this is a training program, the counseling service has significantly more group leaders than would otherwise be possible. Trainees from several academic programs gain valuable clinical experience and are able to observe and collaborate with experienced therapists. Trainees also participate in the screening process to determine who is and is not suitable for group therapy. Use of a general group therapy model as the treatment of choice for a significant number of students enables the center to maximize the counseling resources available.

Source: Corazzini, 1994.

Developing group programs that are effective and that provide services to a significant percentage of student clients can be difficult in college counseling settings. Counseling centers promote the development of such programs by following these suggestions. First, as mentioned, generate staff enthusiasm and support. Most counseling and mental health counselors are supportive of group counseling at some level. If a center wants to expand its group programs, a retreat can generate energy and ideas. Bringing in a consultant who is enthusiastic about group work can also be helpful. Discussion about the goals and possibilities of a group program will usually generate support. Allow staff time to talk about their own experiences and attitudes as well as the particular local concerns that might get in the way of implementing an extensive group program.

Second, staff must be adequately trained to lead and supervise group work. Once a decision is reached to upgrade and expand a group program, a series of training workshops should be offered. If funds are available, travel to various conferences and workshops can bring many new ideas to the staff. If funds are limited, it may be possible for a few staff members to go to specific workshops or conferences and then come back and present what they have learned to others.

Third, determine which kinds of groups should be offered and try to offer these groups every semester. Group programs develop a history, and if a particular group, such as a women's support group, is offered every term the word gets out, and expectations for the group are created. The type of groups to be offered—theme, open-ended, general therapy, population, time-limited—should be explored. Much of the data on need can come from an examination of the center's client population, although the center may also want to recruit from the student population in general for certain groups. Much of the value of group work is in the interaction among participants, but structured and time-limited groups, which tend to be skill-oriented, can also provide considerable opportunity for interpersonal learning. Students may be interested in a theme group or in a population group because they are less threatening than a general therapy group or because they imagine that they will be better understood if they have something in common with other students. Although one can argue the therapeutic merits of theme, population, and general counseling groups, the needs for each on a particular campus have to be determined.

Fourth, develop a mechanism for getting student clients into groups easily. One center places a note on every folder of students coming in for intake that says "THINK GROUP." Whatever mechanism is used to evaluate student clients for counseling, the availability of groups and a good description of what goes on in a group are important to potential members. Counselors need to advocate placement in groups and help students overcome their fear of and resistance to participation in a group. The mechanism for referring students to group leaders is important. Students can be lost in the bureaucratic hassle of getting a screening interview for a particular group. Also, staff must be aware of the current availability of slots in particular groups. In a college setting there are advantages to ongoing groups, where people move in and out, because referrals can be made throughout the semester as opposed to trying to fill all groups at the beginning of the term.

Fifth, provide appropriate facilities for groups. In many centers, especially smaller ones, it is difficult to find good rooms for groups. Creativity is the key word here. Counseling staff have been known to visit Goodwill and other inexpensive community outlets to get comfortable furniture and to furnish group rooms with rugs and paintings. Sometimes a group room can serve other purposes in a center; it can be a staff meeting room, seminar room, or trainee office in order to use the space efficiently. It is difficult to have an effective group program without a decent, designated group room.

Sixth, it helps enormously to have a coordinator who is enthusiastic about groups and who can help lead the staff and provide administrative support.

◆ ◆ ◆

A strong rationale exists for extensive use of group work in college settings. In fact, some group enthusiasts have argued that group counseling programs should be developed as the primary treatment modality for college students. Because so many of the developmental difficulties presented by college students are related to relationships and interpersonal issues, this argument makes considerable sense.

Many different kinds of groups are workable; and an overall agency effort, with the cooperation and enthusiastic support of staff, is necessary for a successful group program. Creativity and constancy are key in college group work. Constancy, in particular, is important. To be successful college counseling and mental health centers must develop a history of offering groups and of recommending group counseling to a high proportion of their clients.

CHAPTER FOUR

EXPANDING SERVICES WITH FACULTY, STUDENT, AND OTHER HELPERS

S tudents have always turned to friends, parents, faculty, staff, clergy, and others for help and advice. College counselors and mental health workers need to capitalize on this tendency and encourage people in the campus community to counsel and help each other. This requires campuswide efforts toward the creation of an actively caring community. Part Two includes an extensive discussion of the role of counseling and mental health centers in campus community development. The discussion here focuses on the kinds and levels of counseling that can be offered and encouraged by various campus personnel. This effort to encourage nonprofessional helpers was characterized as "giving psychology away" in the early phases of the community psychology movement. The climate of strong professionalism and increasing liability concerns make "giving psychology away" somewhat more difficult today, with more setting of boundaries and controls necessary. Three kinds of nontraditional counselors will be discussed: students as paraprofessionals, faculty and staff, and volunteer and part-time professionals.

Paraprofessional Student Counselors

Perhaps the most valuable resource available to our counseling and mental health staffs are our students. We know from research and from experience that students often provide counseling to each other regardless of whether it is in the context of a professionally supervised program. Peer counselor programs have been actively researched and used on college and university campuses since the 1960s (Archer and Kagan, 1973; Delworth and Moore, 1974). The notion of a pyramid, with counselors training and supervising a small group of students who then interact with and help a much larger number of students, was an exciting development, and it spawned many different kinds of programs. Many of these student paraprofessional programs have evolved into peer education programs, with students providing workshops and counsel in particular areas such as substance abuse, sexual violence, and eating disorders. Contemporary peer education programs in these areas are the cornerstone of efforts to positively alter the student culture as well as to provide information. For example, many of the efforts to develop a responsible attitude toward alcohol have come from student peer education and peer counseling groups.

It is helpful to differentiate peer counseling and peer education, even though these functions overlap in many campus programs. Peer education programs provide information on a particular campuswide issue. They can be combined with peer counseling programs to provide a focus on a particular area such as eating disorders. Peer counseling paraprofessional programs are often the legacy of the crisis-intervention phone lines of the 1970s; these programs provide counseling on any issue a student brings. Undergraduate resident assistants housed in residence halls continue to provide general counseling to students, and college counseling and mental health personnel have been heavily involved in training and supervision; however, the increasing professionalization of residence hall staffs has allowed counselors to move into a consulting role.

Because paraprofessional programs have a strong history and are operational on most campuses, counselors need to determine what kinds of programs are needed and will be most useful and what role they wish to play. A campuswide clarification of needs as well as an understanding of the different kinds of paraprofessional programs is crucial. A peer education program focusing on dissemination of information and advice about resources may be appropriate; a combined education and peer counseling program focusing on a target area such as gender relationships may be most appropriate; or a general peer counseling program providing crisis or first-level help for troubled students may be needed.

Program Example: General Peer Counseling Program

Hood College in Frederick, Virginia, has had a peer counseling program for many years. Peer counselors are selected and trained undergraduate volunteers. They live in residence halls, have single rooms, and although they have no specific hours, are generally always available to students. They have no noncounseling responsibilities. Students at Hood are bound by an academic and social honor code so these peer counselors do not have a regulatory function. They undergo preliminary training in March and April after being selected for the next year. They also receive a week of training in August before school begins and then meet for weekly supervision with Counseling Center staff. The training includes the following components: crisis management, conflict resolution (mediation), cross-cultural counseling, assertiveness skills, stress management, special topics (eating disorders, grief and loss, substance abuse, sexual assault, sexual abuse, gay and lesbian issues, and dating violence), and team building. During the 1995–96 school year, the most student contacts were related to relationships, decision making, academic stress, and self-esteem.

Source: T. Baker, director of counseling, Hood College, Frederick, Maryland, personal communication, 1996.

For counseling-oriented paraprofessional programs, certain key elements determine success: selection, training, supervision (clinical and administrative), program development, program culture, and evaluation. Selection may be the most critical challenge. Because training and supervision time are almost always limited, it is crucial that students who already have natural helping characteristics and potential for training and who are themselves reasonably well adjusted be selected. This kind of selection typically involves considerable time and effort; it includes extensive interviewing and may use performance-based criteria with a simulation component (role play and small groups). Current peer counselors are typically heavily involved in the organization and management of the selection process.

Training must include general counseling skills and background in the areas of concern in the program (for example, eating disorders, gay and lesbian identity development). General programs require some introduction to college student developmental issues as well as to common problem areas. Often the most effective training vehicle is a credit course so that students do not have to find extra time for training. Coordination and supervision of peer counselors must be done by a professional who has been assigned adequate time to carry out these responsibilities. Advanced graduate students in counseling and psychology can be helpful in this role.

Effective peer counseling programs develop a culture that helps the organization socialize new members into the ethics and expectations of the role. This socialization is particularly important because these programs are constantly adding and losing members as students graduate and new students replace them. An important side benefit for student participants in these programs is the opportunity for personal growth.

Underlying these programmatic and organizational challenges is the need to make these programs cost-effective; the primary goal should not be to bring even more students into the counseling or mental health center. This is the most difficult contemporary challenge. The outreach role of peer counseling has historically been an important one and may still be in many circumstances, especially in regard to minority populations, but in general college counselors must train student paraprofessionals to be helpful to students without necessarily referring them to a counselor for further work. Peer counselors need to be able to offer their fellow students brief counseling that will allow them to begin to take steps to overcome their problem or developmental difficulty, assuming that a small change or improvement will lead to further growth and change. College counselors should be circumspect about developing peer counseling programs designed to greatly increase referrals, because typically professional resources to handle these referrals do not exist.

Several guidelines may be helpful to college counselors working with paraprofessional programs in today's higher education environment. First, whenever possible, play the role of consultant to campus peer education and peer counseling programs. Counselors can most effectively use their expertise by helping faculty and other staff run and supervise programs. Basic training in counseling skills, common to many programs, can often be done by other staff and does not necessarily need to be done by counselors.

Second, serve as a catalyst for the development of new paraprofessional programs that meet campus needs and that can provide services that expand those already offered. Counseling and mental health centers cannot house all of the needed paraprofessional programs. For example, if it is determined that a campus needs a paraprofessional program to help students manage stress, it may be possible to find a faculty member or staff member from student affairs who would be willing to direct such a program, perhaps with the help of graduate students and a professional from the counseling center.

Third, consider developing new programs in high-priority areas. As part of the prioritizing and planning process, it may become obvious that a particular need cannot be met by professional counselors. For example, if a center cannot offer any special programs or counseling for male students, it might develop a peer counseling or peer education program for men dealing with issues like stress, managing emotions, and role strain.

Fourth, establish a coordinating council or some other mechanism to coordinate all campus paraprofessional programs. Such a group can encourage effective evaluation and development of existing programs and coordinate new initiatives.

Fifth, find ways to include paraprofessional training and experiences in the curriculum. Course credit for training and practicum and internship credit for participation can help support paraprofessional programs and help students with their own career development and in the practical application of classroom knowledge.

Sixth, encourage all counseling and mental health staff to participate in para-professional programs. Working with bright, energetic, and committed students who want to make a positive contribution to their campus can help revitalize counselors who have spent too many years in their offices seeing only students with problems.

Seventh, ensure that legal and ethical guidelines are well thought out and clearly articulated. These guidelines can be explicit without being too conservative and unnecessarily limiting what peer counselors do. A written contract for peer counselors and easy access to consultation will help establish that a "reasonable and prudent" standard exists. Also, considerable work with paraprofessionals about their limits and boundaries and the need to refer is usually required.

Program Example: Career Peer Counselors

A peer counseling program for career development has been operating at the University of Florida Counseling Center for several years. Peer counselors conduct initial individual and group interviews with students who come to the center with questions about careers or choice of a major. This initial session gives the students a general overview of the career development process and informs the students about different options depending on their needs. Some students are referred for individual counseling with staff; some are referred to the career resources center for specific information about career areas; and some complete the DISCOVER program (an interactive computer guidance program) under the tutelage of a peer counselor. Sometimes during the process of completing the DISCOVER program, students are referred to a staff counselor for additional inventories (SCII, MBTI). In these cases the staff counselor discusses the inventories with the student and helps provide additional career counseling. Peer counselors usually follow up with students after they complete DISCOVER to see how their choices of careers and majors are developing. Peer counselors also offer a variety of workshops throughout the campus, including a session on choosing careers and majors and also workshops on academic skills and attitudes.

This program is jointly funded by the student government and the university. It is housed in the counseling center and is supervised by a graduate assistant who is supervised by one of the staff members in the center. Students who are interested in becoming peer counselors take a training course offered through the psychology department. They receive instruction and practice in basic counseling skills and in the career development process, including the use of DISCOVER and career and personality inventories. Special attention is paid to helping the peer counselors assess when a student's blocks regarding a career or a major are related to personal or developmental problems that need to be addressed in personal counseling.

Using student paraprofessionals has been a viable approach in college counseling since the early 1970s, and it still offers enormous benefits to students. It also often has a significant positive effect on the growth and development of the peer counselors. New challenges for counselors—such as playing a consultive and catalytic role and developing programs that go beyond effective listening but do not exceed boundaries of competence—call for new and innovative ways to continue the effective work that has been done with paraprofessionals.

Faculty and Staff

It may seem naive to look to faculty and staff, who are being called on to increase their own productivity and to teach more students or manage more educational functions, for help in counseling and advising students. Although faculty and staff are in general busier than ever, they remain a great potential resource for giving help and counsel to students. In many cases, with training, encouragement, and backup, they can provide limited counseling. The campus culture as well as issues like promotion, tenure, and evaluation make a considerable difference as to how much time and energy a faculty member can and will spend in student counseling. In a large research university, faculty-student relationships are less likely to be counseling-oriented than at a small, teaching-oriented liberal arts college where greater value is placed on personal involvement by faculty. Certainly expectations about how much time faculty can spend counseling students must be tempered by many external factors. It is also important to understand that not all faculty members feel comfortable in individual discussions with students about personal or developmental concerns.

Many faculty and staff in contemporary higher education believe that any discussion of a personal issue should be done only with a professional counselor. Professional counselors sometimes support this perception when they encourage faculty to refer any students with problems to a professional. Counselors have sometimes used such referrals to reinforce the value of and to justify the need for their services. For example, if a student turns up in an English instructor's office crying, the instructor may immediately decide that the student must be referred to a professional. This may or may not be true. The faculty member may be able to listen to the student and provide advice and support that will help her negotiate whatever crisis she is experiencing. One could argue that professional counselors would be more effective and efficient and that the faculty member might even do harm to the student by trying to counsel her. However, on almost every campus professional counseling resources are stretched, and many students will not seek out a professional counselor at a counseling or mental health center. Also, many of our students would benefit from personal contact with faculty and an opportunity to get adult advice and feedback.

Archer (1991) in a book designed to provide advice to faculty and staff who counsel students but who are not professional counselors underscored the need for limited focus, for boundaries, and for faculty to be knowledgeable about referral processes and resources. If counselors want to encourage faculty to take on a limited counseling role, they need to provide workshops, publications, and consultation. Describing specific examples and cases is helpful to faculty. One case might show how a faculty member can be helpful to a student who is emotionally upset. For example, a student starts to cry when talking to his professor about course selection. With a few gentle probes the professor discovers that the student is not doing as well academically as he thinks he should. The professor chooses to talk with the student about his academic work and his life at school, makes some suggestions, and agrees to see him a couple of times in the next several weeks to encourage him and to see how he is doing. Another case, in which a student breaks down and tells the professor that she is depressed and has been having suicidal thoughts, might be used to illustrate the need for referral and follow-up. Clearly, training programs for faculty who are interested in being effective in their personal contacts with students are advisable; this kind of training is usually most feasible during the summer, when faculty and counselors may have time.

One issue that worries some faculty members is the potential of being accused of sexual harassment. Because of this possibility, encouraging faculty to counsel students is riskier than suggesting referral of all students with problems, but it also has the potential of opening up important resources for students.

Perhaps the most natural "counseling" role for faculty is in discussions with students about careers, life goals, and general philosophies. This mentor role may be easier for faculty to accept than the counselor role. And mentors can be trained to be good listeners and good counselors. These kinds of discussions can be significant. In the course of a few sessions, a sensitive faculty member can help a student sort out many of the factors that may be interfering with growth and identity development. Because such informal contacts seem to be scarce on large campuses, formal mentor programs, which include assignment of students to a specific faculty member and some training for faculty, may be necessary. Organized mentor programs can be particularly valuable to minority students, who might otherwise have a difficult time engaging in these kinds of conversations with faculty or staff.

College chaplains and local clergy are also potential sources of help for students. Counseling and mental health staff should encourage the use of counseling services provided by local religious groups. Staff members might help find space near campus for a religious counseling cooperative and provide consultation assistance for it. This option can pose difficult ethical problems for counselors, however, if clergy are not well qualified to provide counseling or when religious groups want to use counseling to proselytize and convert new members. One way of dealing with this problem is to help form a counseling cooperative of well-trained clergy with a student and community board. Less formal encouragement of qualified clerical counseling on smaller campuses is also possible.

Volunteer and Part-Time Professionals

Some academic departments have begun to use volunteer retired faculty to teach courses as a contribution to the department and the college or university. The use of volunteer retired therapists may also be a viable alternative for counseling and mental health centers. Particularly in medium-sized or large towns there may be retired counselors who are willing to work one day a week. The opportunity for professional association and the stimulation of counseling can be incentives for retired therapists to participate. A number of issues need to be addressed before such a program can be set up, including supervision and evaluation, integration and inclusion into the staff, liability coverage, need for an active state license, office space, parking (a major concern!), and crisis and after-hours responsibility. The easiest way to use volunteers is on an individual basis, particularly if the volunteer is someone the staff knows or has worked with on campus or at the counseling center. An aggressive approach, seeking out volunteers, requires a carefully defined system for applications, interviews, selection, and articulation of conditions of employment.

Using part-time counselors is an innovation that can provide needed and targeted services. College counseling and mental health centers can predict the times of greatest demand and can hire part-time counselors for those periods. Although there is a danger of taking advantage of part-time counselors because these positions often do not pay much and do not include benefits, it is often a mutually advantageous arrangement, especially for a person looking for work during a circumscribed period. In addition to the cost benefit, nontraditional part-time counselors (minority counselors, specialists) can help provide a diverse counseling staff. They may be especially helpful to small counseling and mental health services where few full-time positions are available.

Program Example: Swing Shift Counseling

At the University of Oregon Counseling Center community therapists are hired to work a swing shift from 4 P.M. to 8 P.M. on weekdays and from 8 A.M. to 12 noon on Saturday. This strategy was arrived at as a way to reduce the waiting list. Because students had begun to fund part of the center with activity fees, this was a way to provide service to student consumers who were partially paying for the counseling service.

Community therapists are hired on contract for limited periods, usually winter and spring terms. A selection process including interviews is held to select the therapists, and a staff member is assigned to supervise their work (both individually and in a group). These counselors are assigned clients directly from the waiting list. The center reports that client evaluations of these counselors are in line with those of other staff and that the original goal of reducing the waiting list has been met.

Source: G. Tistadt, University of Oregon Counseling Center, personal communication, 1993.

◆ ◆ ◆

This chapter has included a brief examination of the use of paraprofessionals, faculty and staff, retired volunteer therapists, and part-time counselors as a way to expand counseling services. The overall message here is that counseling centers need to be creative and flexible. Even though much of the work of counseling and mental health counselors seems to involve students with serious mental health problems, many students are dealing with developmental and adjustment concerns and can benefit from counseling contacts with faculty, staff, and other students.

CHAPTER FIVE

ALTERNATIVES AND ADJUNCTS TO COUNSELING

College counselors and psychologists must take the lead in developing and researching alternatives and adjuncts to counseling that will expand the therapeutic possibilities for students. Counselors have traditionally provided students with opportunities for educational and personal growth as alternatives to counseling. Part Two is devoted to these general efforts. In this chapter, the discussion centers around alternatives and adjuncts to counseling that provide help for specific problems.

Four major kinds of alternative and adjunct counseling approaches and programs are covered here: self-help materials, interactive computer counseling and guidance systems, self-help groups, and medication. Self-help materials, including books, manuals, tapes, computer bulletin boards, and other programs and methods, are widely available, and students use them with or without the help or sanction of their college counselor or psychologist. Because the quality of these materials ranges widely, college counselors can help provide guidance and access to materials for students. Little research is available, however, so the recommendations of counseling and mental health services must be based on clinical evaluation of materials, or centers must develop their own high-quality materials.

Interactive computer systems are now available for career and personal counseling. Most of the programs and systems are in the career area, but interactive personal-counseling systems are also being developed. Even virtual-reality technology has been suggested for certain counseling purposes. This is truly a "brave new world" for many counselors; although it is difficult to imagine any interactive computer system replacing the sacrosanct counseling relationship, the incredible popularity of "chat rooms" on the Internet (places where people can become involved in worldwide conversations, sometimes on a particular subject) requires a serious consideration of new technologies and new technological models of counseling.

College counselors must also continue to support the development of self-help groups and individual support systems such as AA and its many offshoots. These kinds of peer treatment programs have never worked for everyone, but they are an effective treatment for many college students. Other disciplines and practices, such as the martial arts and meditation, must also be considered as treatments that can help large numbers of students.

The use of medication in place of and as an adjunct to counseling must also be closely examined within college counseling. With the advent of antidepressants such as Prozac, which have minimal side effects, and the continued development of our understanding of the brain and its function relative to specific emotions and psychological and learning disorders, it seems safe to assume that the use of psychopharmacology with college students will increase.

Self-Help Materials

Self-help materials (brochures, books, manuals, tapes, computer bulletin boards, and other information sources) can be used as an adjunct to counseling or in place of counseling. The notion of self-improvement is not new. As Santrock, Minnett, and Campbell (1994) point out, people have used advice given in books since they first used the Bible. They note that Benjamin Franklin dispensed advice in *Poor Richard's Almanack:* "Early to bed, early to rise, makes a man healthy, wealthy, and wise." In the last few decades self-help books of all varieties have proliferated, and millions of people, including college students, have used these books and related materials. Considering the fact that college students are generally bright and verbal, the possibilities for self-help seem quite good. Students are often motivated to change and to develop the skills that they need in an environment where learning requires a great deal of individual effort.

The question for college counselors is how to help students access these materials in a constructive way. Of two possibilities, the more controlled approach is for a counselor to use a book or other material as an adjunct to counseling. For example, a therapist might be working with a student on high levels of stress. Rather than spend considerable time teaching the student how to meditate or practice some other form of relaxation, the therapist might suggest a particular book, other reading material, or tape, thereby saving the counseling time to discuss more complex issues related to the client's experience of stress. The other alternative is for a counseling or mental health center to make materials available to students to use to work on their own problems. The great advantage of the center's providing a library, bulletin board, tape service, or some other vehicle to dispense the information is the ability to provide some quality control and the ability to offer advice as needed. Because students find self-help materials on their own anyway, it seems reasonable for college counselors to guide this use if possible. Allan and Sipich (1997) discuss the development of a self-help brochure series.

There are unlimited possibilities for providing good self-help information and advice to students, particularly with current and developing technology. Libraries can include computer databases that make it easy to locate materials on a particular problem or topic. Automated telephone services can provide tapes on various subjects, and computer bulletin boards can provide a menu with information that students can download on their computers and, if necessary, print out for their use.

Expending the effort to provide all these services and to gain funding is based on the supposition that these materials are worth the effort. Although there is some evidence in the psychotherapy research literature that certain self-help treatments can be effective, little or no controlled research supports positive outcomes from most self-help books. Yet most professional therapists appear to agree that these materials can have great value, and the general public, by their purchase of these materials, attests to the fact that consumers believe this kind of material is helpful. Ellis (1993) cites several studies indicating that 90 percent of the samples of psychologists considered self-help books helpful, and 60 percent encouraged their clients to read them.

In reviewing the literature on self-help books, Ellis summarized the advantages and disadvantages of these materials. He listed the following advantages (1993, pp. 336–337):

1. Some people learn more by reading than by interaction with a therapist or group.
2. Some people learn more from audiocassettes and videocassettes than from books.
3. Using self-help materials may make therapy more effective and shorter.
4. Self-help materials are relatively inexpensive.
5. Some people who refuse counseling or oppose it on religious or philosophical grounds find self-help materials acceptable.

6. Self-help materials offer more choices than therapists can regarding methods of change.
7. Self-help materials are available when therapists are not.
8. Self-help materials can be referred to many times.
9. Many people who are turned off to therapy may return after being encouraged to by self-help materials.

Ellis listed the following as disadvantages (1993, pp. 335–336):

1. Many self-help materials are dogmatic, antiscientific, and unsound.
2. Interpretations of self-help material can vary greatly.
3. Self-help materials sometimes give the impression that personal change is simple and easy.
4. Many self-help materials are designed mainly for profit and lead users to expect miracles.
5. Some materials discourage needed therapy.
6. Self-help materials cannot be individualized for each person.
7. Disturbed individuals may treat themselves for the wrong problems because of an inability to diagnose their difficulties accurately.
8. Many users of these materials are inactive and antisocial and need the contact of a therapist or a group.

Many of these disadvantages can be minimized in a self-help program developed on a college campus. Perhaps most important, the materials can be selected by a professional. Guidance in how to use the materials and opportunities for consultation and asking questions can also be provided. For example, a counselor might field questions about self-help materials and progress through their use during certain telephone hours or by electronic mail or via written responses. Alternatively, student paraprofessionals might be trained to help others access and use materials. Counselors can also provide their own self-help pamphlets and brochures in areas that are particularly relevant to college students. Commercial pamphlets are also available.

The Authoritative Guide to Self-Help Books (Santrock, Minnett, and Campbell, 1994) reports the results of a survey of five hundred counseling and clinical psychologists that asked them to rate self-help books in a variety of areas, such as abuse and recovery, anger, divorce, communication. This book is an invaluable resource in selecting good self-help books. Also, several journals, such as the *Journal of College Student Development,* have enlarged their book-review sections to include some self-help books. Although it takes considerable time, another way to select materials is for professionals to review them. A committee of counselors or graduate students or both can be formed to take on this task for a particular campus.

In selecting materials, counselors should choose those that help students solve specific problems as well as those that help with general personal growth and development. The library, phone system, or local Internet site can then be used by students who are having a crisis and want some immediate help. For example, students feeling stressed can call and hear a tape on stress management, or they can visit a self-help library to read about relaxation methods; students having problems with romantic partners can visit the campus mental health computer site to get materials on effective relationships. A counseling or mental health center can thus provide materials at a fairly low cost to help achieve two of its primary missions: helping individual students solve problems and helping students develop and grow as human beings. Centers should be aware also that these materials can be valuable academic resources for the institution because of their usefulness for papers, reports, and readings in academic courses such as psychology, health education, counselor education, and social work.

These libraries, computer sites, and phone-in systems can generally be funded on a one-time basis, and they have minimal upkeep costs. This aspect helps with fundraising and budgeting. Often money is available for setting up programs and buying equipment but is not available for ongoing programs.

Program Example: Self-Help Library

The University of Arizona Counseling and Mental Health Service has developed an extensive self-help library. They created the library with several goals in mind: to reach out to students by providing mental health information, to use the materials as an adjunct to therapy, to reach out to faculty and staff, and to have videotapes and bibliographies available for workshops and presentations. The library is supplied with a computer and printer; it contains approximately five hundred books, two hundred audiotapes, and thirty videotapes. Materials were indexed by computer and are organized by topic (anxiety and stress management, sexual abuse, love and intimacy, gay and lesbian issues). The library is staffed by student assistants and is open at designated periods. From forty-five hundred to five thousand students, faculty, and staff use the library every year. The counseling center's professional library is run as a part of the self-help library to take advantage of available staffing.

Source: M. T. Velez, director, counseling, and psychological services, University of Arizona, Tucson, Arizona, personal communication, 1993.

Program Example: Self-Help Center

The Self-Help Center (S-HC) at the University of Missouri in Columbia opened in 1991 with an initial grant from the Student Fee Capital Improvements Committee. The S-HC was dedicated to Dr. John F. McGowan, a retired staff member who made extensive use of self-help materials. Books, videotapes, audiotapes, pamphlets, and other handouts are listed under one of four categories: mental health, personality development, career development, and educational development.

Students can access materials and print them out from the mainframe university computer or from off campus or residence halls with a modem or through Binet. Identification numbers and passwords are not required. The S-HC is open the same times as the counseling center.

Students have listed the following reasons for their visits to the center: to get information for class, to pass the time while waiting for a counseling appointment, referral by a counselor, self-referral, because of needing a work area, to search for resources and quotes regarding specific psychological topics (mentioned by reporters for the student newspaper), curiosity, and to refuel from the candy jar.

Source: R. Caple, director, Counseling Center, University of Missouri, Columbia, Missouri, personal communication, 1995.

Program Example: Internet Site

The SUNY Buffalo Counseling Center has developed a home page that offers a great variety of information about counseling and personal development topics. The initial menu has twenty-one possibilities, including topics such as the counseling center and its staff, what counseling is, relationships, stress and anxiety, alcohol and drugs, workshops, software, and Internet resources. After the user selects one of these topics, another menu is provided. For example, the menu for relationships includes the following:

- So you want to have a relationship
- Common questions about relationships
- Starting a new relationship
- Communication: from fighting to loving
- Coercion, rape, and surviving
- For and about men
- For and about women
- For and about lesbians, gays, and bisexuals
- Breaking up and letting go: relationship endings

Further topics are offered for each of these areas. If the selection "breaking up and letting go: relationship endings," is picked, a new screen offers information on either "coping with death and grief" or "feelings at the end of a relationship." One example of the creativity in this home page is the listing of "UB Real Men," which contains pictures of and short statements by various campus men about the male role in ending sexual violence. David L. Gilles-Thomas, who is responsible for this home page, has also created a directory of counseling-center home pages.

Source: Gilles-Thomas, 1996, 1997.

Interactive Computer and Writing Counseling Systems

Interactive counseling systems using computers, telephones, and writing are considerably more complex than the topic-oriented self-help systems discussed above. Several kinds of interactive systems merit attention: computer, telephone, and other systems where a student can contact a professional (or in some cases a paraprofessional) to seek advice or to ask questions about a particular topic (sex, relationships, eating disorders); letter writing and "journaling," where students reflect and write about important life issues; computer testing and scoring programs; interactive computer systems that provide counseling and guidance, usually in particular areas (career guidance, stress management); support "chat" rooms and bulletin boards. Little formal research has been done on these interactive systems except for computer guidance systems,

All these computer communication modes are particularly helpful to commuter students, who are not always on campus. In fact, with the advent of distance learning and the possibility of taking college courses and earning degrees via computer, long-distance communication systems may be essential aspects of counseling services in the future. It is not too speculative to imagine a counseling office with a live video hookup that makes counseling available to students far away from campus. Some forms of counseling and therapy are already available on the Internet, and there is considerable exploration and discussion of the ethical, legal, and other implications.

Interactive systems using phones, computers, and brief writing are not new. Phillips, Gershenson, and Lyons (1977) reported a study on writing therapy with undergraduate students. Students exchanged comments with a counselor via a notebook. Also, telephone counseling and advice lines have been used in college counseling for many years. The modern equivalent is a computer question-and-answer system conducted by e-mail. There are several advantages to a "Dear Abby"–type computer system:

1. Students who would not come in for counseling can receive help and advice.
2. If the program is appropriately set up, students can ask questions anonymously.
3. Students who want concise or specific advice can be helped quickly without needing to come in for a counseling session.
4. Counselors have an opportunity to provide advice to students who may be in serious trouble and perhaps can direct them to appropriate face-to-face counseling help.
5. If the questions and answers are posted on a public board, many students can profit from the advice given.

Program Example: Uncle Sigmund

At the Appalachian State University Counseling and Psychological Services Center a computer counseling system called Uncle Sigmund has been developed to answer student questions about personal matters. The advertisement for the program contains a picture of Sigmund Freud inside a computer screen and states that advice is available on stress, substance abuse, personal problems, and relationships. The introductory screen describes the service and allows the student to ask questions or to read questions and answers. Students are also instructed to seek professional help at the Counseling and Psychological Services Center or the Health Center if they have a serious emotional or health problem. An additional screen describes the commands and tells students not to worry about matters like spelling and punctuation. The student makes up an anonymous name and can find an answer within three days by keying in that name. Students at large can also access the questions and answers.

Typical topics have included: alcoholism ("I am scared I might become an alcoholic"), depression ("What does it mean when a person finds it physically impossible to cry?"), roommate conflicts ("My roommates don't do a very good job of keeping our apartment neat and tidy"), and relationships ("A few minutes ago my girlfriend and I were playing around in her room. I accidentally slapped her"). Some of the counselor responses include a referral for counseling, some provide advice, and some recommend self-help books. In any system like this there are also whimsical questions that can be answered with humor. "Q. Is Uncle Sigmund a virgin? A. Uncle is 135 years old and has been married 110 years. What do you think?"

Source: D. Sanzs, director, Counseling Center, Appalachian State University, Boone, North Carolina, personal communication, 1995.

Although there appear to be many advantages to these kinds of systems, Rosser (1995) cautions against on-line counseling for personal issues. She offers the following cautions to college counselors who are setting up on-line services (pp. 4–5):

1. Is confidentiality guaranteed on your network? Even if the answer is yes, you must be able to determine for sure whether and how the system might be invaded and take precautions if you plan to discuss any personal issues.
2. Do you have the time to respond to the number of questions and comments you are likely to receive given the population you serve?
3. How will you respond if someone threatens suicide or harm to another or reveals a threat to the community?
4. If you attempt to start a "Dear Abby"–type forum and you will be using licensed professionals, how will you go about ensuring informed consent and so on? How much responsibility for "clients" will you be taking on once they have access to a licensed professional over the network?

5. How does your institution feel about your reaching students through the computer? If you are asked about university or college policy, can you respond without potentially putting the administration in a difficult spot?

These caveats exemplify some of the difficulties in providing innovative, technological approaches to counseling. The legal and professional standards of the day seem to encourage a conservative and cautious approach to innovation. College counselors need to balance the need to be creative and offer innovative and technologically based services with the need to protect themselves, their centers, and the institution. The other pressing and difficult question concerns evaluation and research support. Research and evaluation efforts should accompany these new technologies.

Generally used by therapists, the term *journaling* denotes a process of introspection and personal growth through journal writing (Baker, 1988; Heinze, 1987). Although not new, the use of extended writing as a technique for personal growth and problem solving has great potential for college students. Many college classes and workshops use journals to encourage self-reflection and analysis, and many students enjoy this kind of writing and reflecting. Although the technique is often used as an adjunct to therapy, it can be adapted as an alternative to counseling. France, Cadieax, and Allen (1995) used "letter therapy" with a thirty-five-year-old female client who could not make regular office visits. The client was given specific instructions: opening up, focusing on life themes, redirecting toward strengths, reinforcing actions, and affirming a positive attitude. This model appears to be somewhat different from the writing therapy of Phillips, Gershenson, and Lyons (1977) in that the responses are in letter form rather than in a counseling dialogue format.

Many of the same cautions mentioned earlier regarding advice-giving computer programs apply here also. Certainly, counselors will feel that some letters require intervention. The advantage is that services can be expanded without requiring additional face-to-face counseling. This kind of letter writing and journaling is different from the earlier described question-and-answer systems in that a significant part of the treatment effect appears to come from the writing itself and subsequent insight and self-analysis.

Computer testing and scoring programs are available for most standard psychological instruments, including diagnostic instruments. Computer testing and scoring programs are useful for counseling agencies where enough tests are given to make them cost-efficient. Computer programs for precounseling assessment and information are in use on some campuses and hold considerable promise for the future. However, most college counseling and mental health services still try to make access to counseling relatively easy and to include a large number of students, so long and involved diagnostic computer systems, which are not much different from extensive test batteries, generally do not make sense for them. However, pressure to document outcomes of counseling may increase the use of such assessment systems in the future.

Some computer counseling and guidance systems have been developed that go beyond the question-and-answer format previously discussed. Computer guidance programs such as SIGI Plus and DISCOVER have enjoyed widespread use on college campuses. These programs have become more sophisticated over time and provide career services for a large number of college students. Sampson and Krumboltz (1991) noted, however, the lack of computer-assisted instruction regarding personal, social, and family issues. In their view, counseling involves a learning process, and computer-assisted instruction in the personal realm has great merit.

Few campuses have interactive counseling programs that offer students an alternative to personal counseling similar to what Sampson and Krumboltz (1991) describe as personal learning programs. One such program, called TLP (Therapeutic Learning Program) (Gould, 1990), provides computer-assisted counseling aimed at helping clients deal with the following questions about their stress: (1) What hurts, and what could you do about it that you are not now doing? (2) Would taking this action be a wise and safe thing to do? (3) What deeper fear stops you from doing it? The program has ten structured lessons, which take the client through the following steps:

1. Personal stress survey
2. Building an action plan
3. Anticipated dangers
4. Exploring more fears
5. Negative feelings
6. Identifying self-doubts
7. The self-doubt system
8. Origins of self-doubt
9. Perpetuating the self-doubt
10. Review and assessment

The program is intended to be used in conjunction with ten half-hour sessions with a counselor individually or in a small group. The client gets a printout of each lesson to discuss with the counselor. An early version of TLP was used with a group of college students at the University of Minnesota. A pre-post test, with no controls, showed that student clients increased their level of perceived control and self-concept (Mark and others, 1988). This program and others like it have great potential for college populations, and research on such populations is clearly needed. College counselors need to take the lead in promoting this research so that programs such as TLP can be evaluated for potential use on college campuses.

Chat rooms and bulletin boards are computer discussion groups where students can interact with others who are working on a similar problem. These discussion groups can be on line, where a student engages directly in a conversation with someone else, or they can be bulletin boards, where people make comments and then others respond. These groups can be sponsored or monitored (or both) by counseling centers.

Self-Help Groups

The notion of using a support group to help one overcome a problem and change behavior was formalized with the AA movement. The idea that one can gain strength and motivation from others for change and coping is now well accepted by the public and by mental health professionals. Support groups for a myriad of problems and concerns are listed in most metropolitan papers. On college campuses AA and derivative groups for family members, narcotics users, adult children of alcoholics, and others are popular. Many counselors refer students to these as part of counseling, particularly as a way to help them stop using and abusing drugs and alcohol. Other kinds of support groups—for gay and lesbian students, older-than-average students, students recovering from eating disorders—are also available on many campuses. Some groups operate totally on their own; some are sponsored by churches or national organizations; and some are sponsored by college and university counseling and mental health services.

College counselors need to decide when to use such groups as an alternative or adjunct to counseling or as the step after counseling. Several guidelines are appropriate:

1. Conduct a careful assessment of the student's needs and determine how well those needs can met by a support group.
2. Have a working knowledge of the groups available on or near campus and how they generally function. Appointing someone on the staff as a liaison is a reasonable method.
3. When making a referral, be positive and hopeful (which requires that the counselor have some confidence in the group and some appreciation of its value).
4. Provide an opportunity for students to reaccess counseling if the group is not helpful or if they need to discuss progress. If a student is referred to a group with no adjunct counseling, a check after a month or two is in order.

5. Prepare students for being in the group and help them understand their right to control their participation level. One of the dangers of unsupervised groups, particularly if they do not provide a support system outside the group, as AA does, is the possibility of causing harm by moving too quickly with an issue or a person.

If a counseling or mental health staff believes that support groups can be a valuable therapeutic tool, they can take an active role in supporting and developing such groups. This role may be limited to helping a group get started or to finding a place for it to meet. It is helpful if the group has a connection with a national organization or another ongoing group. A more active approach is to start support groups and to supervise them by assigning a professional counselor to monitor them and to provide guidance and supervision to the leaders or conveners. This is a difficult responsibility and may pose legal and liability complications. A more viable approach is to offer consultation services to support groups on a one-time basis so that the counselor does not assume responsibility without having control.

Medication

In considering alternatives and adjuncts to college counseling, one must examine the role of medication in treatment programs. Most college counselors and mental health workers are not advocates of a psychopharmacological approach to mental health, although, many have come to see the value of drug treatment for depression, anxiety, obsessive-compulsive disorder, schizophrenia, anorexia, bulimia, and other disorders.

Although the majority of college counseling centers are not directly affiliated with a medical facility, most student mental health centers are part of a student health service that is housed in a medical facility. Consequently, counseling centers must use outside psychiatric consultants to prescribe medication, while mental health centers may have a psychiatrist or general practitioner on site who can be used for this purpose.

Given our increased understanding of the value of certain kinds of psychoactive medications, college counselors must be able to make this kind of treatment available to students. The U.S. Public Health guidelines for the treatment of depression, for example, recommend medication as a primary treatment for major depression, and they include a statement that if no improvement in depressive symptoms is evident after six weeks of psychotherapy, "a reevaluation and a potential switch to, or augmentation with, medication should be considered" (quoted in Schulberg and Rush, 1995, p. 38). They also recommend that in the continuation and maintenance phases of treatment "full dose medication should be maintained indefinitely for patients in whom depression is a chronic, recurring illness" (p. 39). Large-scale studies of depression sponsored by the National Institute of Mental Health (1990) have found that cognitive and interpersonal counseling are equally as effective as medication, while augmentation of counseling with medication may be effective for rapid symptom relief. Certainly, medication for depression should be available when needed for student clients who do not respond to counseling alone. As new psychopharmacological treatments are developed and researched, guidelines such as these may be developed that strongly suggest the use of medication for other kinds of psychological problems.

Attention-deficit disorder, which we are finding increasingly in college students, is also frequently being treated with medication. Javorsky and Gussin (1994) reported that 70 percent of adults with attention-deficit disorder have been successfully treated with medication. This is not to say that other treatments and accommodations are not important with these students, only that this behavioral disorder has been identified as involving a brain dysfunction that responds well to medication.

The issue of medication, particularly for traditional-age college students, is a complex one. Most students do not like the idea of taking medication for depression, stress, or other personal problems, and most counselors are hesitant to begin students on a psychopharmaceutical road to adjustment so early in life. However, medication is in order and is probably the best approach for some. Assessment is crucial. College counseling and mental health centers may need to develop special additional assessment protocols for students who might benefit from medication, along with having expert psychiatric consultation easily available. An accurate assessment will also help determine which kinds of cases can be handled through psychiatric consultation at a nonmedical site and which need extensive laboratory and other medical support typically not available in college counseling operations.

◆ ◆ ◆

This chapter has explored alternatives and adjuncts to counseling as a way for college counselors to expand their counseling services in the college community. Although many of the alternatives discussed can also be viewed as personal-growth opportunities, the focus in this chapter was on problem-oriented counseling alternatives. It will no doubt be difficult for college counselors to embrace counseling alternatives that do not involve an actual counseling relationship, but it seems clear that new technologies and communication systems will challenge traditional notions about counseling and will demand creativity and openness to new therapeutic approaches.

CHAPTER SIX

MEETING THE SPECIFIC CHALLENGES OF SERIOUS AND DEVELOPMENTAL PROBLEMS

A number of problem areas demand special attention from college counselors. Traditional-age and returning students are pursuing new goals, are typically involved in significant life transitions, and are learning to cope with a competitive and stressful environment. The already complex challenges of emotional, social, and occupational adjustment noted by Chickering and Reisser (1993) often become exacerbated. Although there are a number of important developmental issues, three seem to come up most frequently: stress management, career choice, and relationship issues. Several other more serious counseling issues are also often seen in college students and require special attention: depression and suicidality, substance abuse, eating disorders, sexual violence, and AIDS. Each of these special counseling issues will be discussed in this chapter.

One perennial challenge is the concurrent need for prevention and developmental programs in these areas. The theoretical basis for preventive and developmental programs as well as a general discussion of the challenges and approaches will be discussed in Part Two. However, it is important to note here the connection between treatment and prevention in these specific areas as the question of allocating limited resources becomes salient. The tension regarding the balance between counseling and prevention always exists and is played out in specific terms in these areas. For example, nearly every campus has problems with alcohol and other drug abuse, and almost every campus has some kind of special programs in this area. How are resources allocated for prevention versus treatment? Some would argue that because of the educational context, resources should be put primarily into prevention. This argument has considerable logic but contains several serious flaws. First, one cannot simply ignore the needs of students who have problems that are beyond prevention and who are in need of individual or group counseling. Second, a good deal of counseling, particularly brief counseling, is preventive in nature; the counseling intervention, particularly with traditional-age college students, prevents a further deterioration or the development of serious physical and psychological consequences. Another part of the argument that has been made for focusing on prevention and development to the exclusion of remedial counseling treatment is that with enough prevention and environmental change the need for remedial work will disappear. This may be the ideal, but we are a long way from the knowledge and technology that would be required to achieve this objective.

These issues are mentioned here only to underscore the importance of managing special programs, like the ones to be discussed, so that counseling and prevention can be coordinated, usually under the same program umbrella. For example, a counselor who is an expert on eating disorders in a counseling or mental health center should be involved in both treatment and prevention efforts. Resources that are made available to target these special problems and special groups can be used most effectively if a synergy is created between treatment and prevention. Although counseling and prevention programs are discussed in different parts of this book, in practice they are usually closely connected.

Suicidality

The national data on counseling centers collected by Gallagher and Bruner (1994, 1995) indicate that moderate or severe suicidal ideation is common among college students and that suicide attempts and completed suicides are not atypical. One of the best longitudinal studies was conducted by Silverman (1993). His ten-year comprehensive investigation revealed an on-campus suicide rate half the national average for the same age cohort. Still, every death due to depression-associated suicide is likely to be needless and perhaps avoidable. What these data do not show is the substantial personal distress and academic interference that suicidal feelings and actions cause, both for the students themselves and for the many people on campus who are connected to them.

A large number of journal articles exist on this topic. Some (for example, Westefeld, Whitchard, and Range, 1990) lament the serious problems that the absence of a rigorous national data-collection system creates. Others focus on enhanced assessment (for example, Range and Antonelli, 1990), intervention (for example, Firestone and Serden, 1990; Foreman, 1990), and prevention (for example, Trimble, 1990). A special issue of the *Journal of College Student Psychotherapy* was devoted to college student suicide in 1990.

Jobes, Jacoby, Cimbolic, and Hustead (1997) established the usefulness of a six-item instrument (the Suicide Status Form) designed to assess suicide risk. The six items, based on the most current knowledge from suicidology, assessed levels of psychological pain, external pressure, agitation, hopelessness, self-regard, and overall risk of suicide. Despite the almost exclusive reliance by most clinicians on using interviews to assess suicidal students, the study found that clients and their therapists do not independently rate these six items the same. Moreover, as with other similar discrepancies, the client ratings were both more accurate regarding the clients' subjective reality and more predictive of their subsequent behavior than were the therapists' assessments. In addition, the questionnaire was useful in distinguishing between "acute resolvers," those whose emotions are situationally based and who work their feelings through fairly quickly, and "chronic unre-solvers," those whose problems are long-term and pervasive and who demonstrate less coping ability. Such a distinction has important treatment ramifications. It seems likely that the quality of suicide-risk interviews can be augmented by dialoguing with the client about his or her responses on this instrument. This step, along with the development of specific counseling-center policies and procedures regarding assessment and intervention, is recommended.

A research foundation is being built that supports the success of cognitive, interpersonal, and psychotropic interventions for persons who are depressed and suicidal, particularly those who are acute resolvers (Jobes, Jacoby, Cimbolic, and Hustead, 1997). For example, Watson and Tharp (1992) discussed how self-monitoring of positive thoughts can be useful with depressed and suicidal persons. Rational-emotive therapy (Ellis, 1989) emphasizes the importance of changing irrational beliefs leading to intensely painful feelings. Two of the most popular approaches to alleviating suicidal feelings and the concomitant depression are Beck's cognitive therapy (Beck and Weishaar, 1989) and interpersonal psychotherapy (Klerman, Weissman, Rounsavile, and Chevron, 1984). Cognitive therapy emphasizes the etiological importance of cognitive dissonance in producing depression and suicidal ideation and actions and suggests the use of decatastrophizing, reattribution, redefining, and decentering to weaken them. Interpersonal therapy attends to grief, interpersonal role disputes, role transitions, and interpersonal deficits as the principal means to improve the quality of the interpersonal context hypothesized to underlie the depression and suicidality.

Medications, especially the antidepressants, are a common treatment component for suicidal students (Seligman and Moore, 1995). Some suicidal individuals show elevated risk factors for misuse of such medications by overdose. In these cases, consulting or staff psychiatrists will often prescribe a less toxic (but perhaps less powerful) substance if such alternatives exist, or the counselor may work with people in the environment to control access to the medications. An additional advantage of working with family and friends is that it removes obsessing about abuse of the medication as a worry for the patient. The other potential hazard with medications is that students who are suicidal and also deeply depressed may lack the energy to engage in self-destructive acts, but as they begin to recover, the combination of continuing to experience highly negative affect plus having increased energy may lead to such acts.

However, these techniques can be used only with those who come or are sent for counseling, and they do not work for everyone. Most college counseling and mental health centers function under the assumption that a systemic approach is needed. Such an approach typically involves building campus and community referral networks, providing staff development, developing policies and procedures, and establishing accountability (Trimble, 1990). As an example of staff development, resident assistants are often trained to recognize, evaluate, and refer students at risk, and to limit their overinvolvement. Recognition involves being aware of the verbal, behavioral, situational, and depressive warnings a suicidal student may give, with consultation being available to help the resident assistant provide support without becoming overly enmeshed. While continuing, systemic follow-up is needed for those who are severely depressed and suicidal or who attempt suicide, counseling-center postvention in cases of completed suicide is also often required. Postvention can include providing services to the victim's family and friends and meeting with other students, the residence staff, and college officials. Evaluation of suicide potential in others is particularly important in cases of extensive media coverage or memorials.

Program Example: Suicide Prevention and Aftermath Teams

The Suicide Prevention Team and the Suicide Aftermath Team were instituted at the Counseling Center and McKinley Health Department, University of Illinois at Urbana-Champaign. Students are especially at risk of attempting suicide again in the weeks and months following an original attempt or threat. The university has addressed this increased risk by mandating that all students who have attempted or threatened suicide receive four sessions of professional assessment and counseling starting within a week of the threat or attempt. The Suicide Prevention Team administers this policy by receiving reports on suicide incidents and working discreetly but firmly to get suicidal students to meet with a mental health professional. The Suicide Prevention Team is staffed by professionals from the Counseling Center and McKinley Health Department. The team is available during normal business hours.

The Suicide Aftermath Team is a resource for students, faculty, and staff following the suicide of a student. Typically two members of the team go to a residence hall, apartment complex, or department meeting and facilitate a group discussion to address feelings and issues that significant others may have regarding the person or event. They might also meet individually with students before or after the discussion. Although the focus of the Suicide Aftermath Team is working with survivors of actual suicides, team members occasionally meet with students after particularly traumatic attempts and threats. The Suicide Aftermath Team is staffed by professionals from the Counseling Center and McKinley Health Department and is available both during and after business hours.

Source: Joffe, 1995.

Working with suicidal students can be particularly stressful for staff counselors. Mandatory consultation with other senior staff, depending on the degree of lethality of a suicide attempt, can provide support and consultive help as well as liability protection.

Substance Abuse

Presley and Meilman (1992) authored a report to college presidents entitled *Alcohol and Drugs on American College Campuses.* The data in this publication, based on responses to the Core Alcohol and Drug Survey of well over one hundred thousand students, presented a disturbing picture. Not only did most students drink and many use illicit substances, the level of abuse was quite high and correlated with a host of other problems such as residence hall damage, sexual assaults, fights, drunk driving, and impaired academic functioning. Additional connections between level of use and other consequences such as negative physical symptoms and memory loss were also evident.

Etiologically, substance abuse (particularly alcohol abuse) appears to result from the complex interaction of genetic predisposition, psychological vulnerability, and sociocultural influences (Cooper, 1994). In an individual, each of these factors may range from high to low. Does the student have an extensive family history of addictions? Does the student have poor self-esteem, negative emotions, and few coping skills? What are the values and behaviors of the student's peers?

Several counseling programs are available. The On Campus Talk about Alcohol program incorporates current research on alcohol abuse and dependence to assist students in determining their own safe drinking level (Daugherty and O'Brien, 1995). Connections to other illicit substances are made as well. For most, moderate use of alcohol is appropriate, but for some any use carries a risk; and with illegal drugs all use carries criminal consequences.

Research studies generally support the effectiveness of behavioral techniques in reducing or eliminating substance abuse problems. Specific interventions that often produce positive outcomes are behavioral self-control training, relaxation training, modeling, contingency contracting and management, systematic desensitization, covert imaging, and social skills and assertiveness training (Miller, 1985).

Counselors working in college and university settings are experiencing particularly good outcomes from empowering substance abuse clients through group work (Vannicelli, 1992). A highly collaborative style that incorporates tools such as goal setting, behavioral analysis, coping skills, and problem solving seems to work well whether a group or individual format is employed (Lewis, Dana, and Blevins, 1994). Establishing substance-free on-campus residential opportunities may also help students who wish to abstain from or reduce their use of alcohol and other drugs.

Awareness of the different dimensions of the problem is important when providing substance abuse counseling on campus. Prochaska's multistage process of change in clients with smoking addiction can be applied to substance abuse (Prochaska and DiClimente, 1992; Prochaska and Norcross, 1994). Those stages are precontemplation, contemplation, preaction, action, and maintenance. His research suggests that matching intervention to stage is correlated with treatment success or failure. Another dimension is whether the goal of treatment should be abstinence or controlled use. Although abstinence is clearly required in some cases (inability to stop use, severe medical problems), most students who obtain substance abuse counseling will have a higher level of motivation to meet a controlled-use goal. Another dimension, level of treatment, will vary with severity of abuse. Students with nonproblematic use will likely benefit from brief psychoeducational approaches. Students with mild or moderate abuse problems might find outpatient work sufficient. Those with severe abuse and dependence problems often require adjunct support such as AA, NA, group therapy, or intensive outpatient programs. Students who evidence dependence with life and health problems may need inpatient programs (Cooper, 1994; Lewis, Dana, and Blevins, 1994).

As described above, therapists can employ many different individual and group techniques with students with substance abuse difficulties. More important is the recognition that the motivation for change can be developed in most students (Lewis, Dana, and Blevins, 1994). Thus, the type of strong therapeutic alliance typically desired for assisting with other clinical issues is also desirable whether abstinence or controlled use is a major counseling goal. Moreover, relapse-prevention activities (Marlatt and Gordon, 1985) should be used with almost all clients with substance abuse and dependence issues. A number of substance abuse counseling programs involve a mandatory referral component. These kinds of involuntary counseling programs are discussed in Chapter Seven.

Program Example: Chemical Awareness Responsibility Education (CARE) Program

The Valparaiso (Indiana) University Office of Alcohol and Drug Education (which is part of Counseling Services) established the Chemical Awareness Responsibility Education (CARE) program to serve students referred by the local court and the campus judicial system. In three two-hour sessions (available once a month), students address topics relevant to their use of alcohol and other drugs. Students are admitted to the class following an individual, confidential screening appointment with the program coordinator. The primary purpose of the CARE program is prevention of further substance abuse. Educational sessions provide students with information and skills designed to help them make responsible decisions about alcohol and drug use in the future.

The sessions are designed to help students obtain accurate information about alcohol and other drugs and their effects on the human body; to allow students to explore and identify their own behavioral patterns, feelings, attitudes, values, family histories, and the social and environmental factors that influence the decision to use and abuse substances; to increase understanding of how the misuse of alcohol or other drugs can be detrimental to friendships, to a sense of personal worth and value, and to the overall healthy functioning of the individual; and to promote positive peer pressure through discussion and confrontation, which facilitates low-risk use of alcohol or the decision to remain alcohol and drug free.

Referrals to the CARE program come from the county court system as well as from judicial and administrative sources on the campus. Further, other concerned students can refer an individual to the CARE program. Individuals referred may be policy offenders, students arrested, or those displaying out-of-control behavior such as frequent drunkenness, aggressive behavior, or inability to meet academic requirements.

The CARE program has four rules. The first is attendance; each of the classes must be attended consecutively. The second is punctuality; all classes begin promptly at the designated time. The third rule is confidentiality; what is shared within the group that is of a personal nature is to stay within the group. The fourth is participation; students are expected to be honest and cooperative and to apply positive peer pressure through confrontation.

The topics in the first session include the physiological effects of alcohol use on the body and strategies for making low-risk decisions and reducing the risk of having alcohol-related problems. Connections with abuse of other drugs are made. The second session has two major topics: drinking and driving and the abuse of drugs other than alcohol. The third session emphasizes alternatives to using and abusing and methods of confronting a substance abuse problem (including training in assertiveness, peer support networking, and responding to impairment). A thirty-page workbook includes self-assessments, information on the physiological effects of alcohol, a rating of one's problem-solving ability, drug information, information on the interactive effects of alcohol and drugs, problem situations, legal considerations, coping techniques, crisis-intervention techniques, and techniques for caring confrontation.

The cost for the CARE program is three hundred dollars annually, which covers the workbook and other incidental costs. Income is derived from a fifty-dollar fee for each student attending; the local court waives collection of its fifty-dollar fee and routes that money to the CARE program.

A pretest is conducted at the beginning of the sessions, while evaluations are completed at the conclusion of the CARE program. Results of the evaluation are positive. Several students have become campus peer educators and student leaders as a result of their experience. These activities serve as a support network and bolster referred students' efforts to make positive changes.

Source: J. Nagel, coordinator, Office of Alcohol and Drug Education, Valparaiso University, personal communication, 1995.

Eating Disorders

The prevalence of eating disorders (or at least its detection) increased significantly in the late 1980s and early 1990s. Levels have remained high; many counseling-center staff report that today's clients tend to be aware of their dysfunction and yet often have serious or dangerous levels before they seek counseling. Peers are also much more aware of these disorders than they once were and are likely to seek assistance from staff in supporting and confronting a friend.

Like substance addictions, eating disorders appear to result from a complex interaction of biological, psychological, and sociological factors (Abraham and Llewellyn-Jones, 1989; Scarano and Kalodner-Martin, 1994). A family history of eating or mood disorders is not uncommon. Many psychological correlates such as anxiety, depression, and fear of sexual maturation have been hypothesized. So-cioculturally, reading any popular magazine or viewing many TV shows quickly reveals the dual message of "slim women as successful, attractive, healthy, happy, fit, and popular" and "the provision of food . . . as a major sign of caring; and sharing food . . . as one of the prime social contacts" (Abraham and Llewellyn-Jones, 1989, pp. 26–27). Zraly and Swift (1990) describe six core symptoms common to many clients with eating disorders: dependence on parents, problems with problem solving, trust and intimacy concerns, problems with anger and assertiveness, overvaluing external evaluations, and need for control. Scarano and Kalodner-Martin (1994) further developed an eating disorders continuum that ranged from normal to weight-preoccupied to chronic dieter to subthreshold bulimia to full bulimia. A patient's location on this continuum has important implications for tailored assessment and treatment.

The treatment for anorexia and bulimia on campus optimally involves a collaboration of health and psychological services with the decision to pursue hospitalization based on factors such as medical dangerousness, failure of outpatient counseling, or client preference (Cooper, 1989). Studies support the use of both individual and group counseling for students with eating disorders. The first order of change typically includes a cognitive component, to change how one is thinking about food and weight, and a behavioral component, to change actions or environments. The second order of change usually includes an identification of developmental, interpersonal, and emotional issues and their resolution through therapy rather than through the eating disorder. The additional use of psychotropics, especially the select serotonin re-uptake inhibitor (SSRI) antidepressants, has demonstrated effectiveness with most eating-disordered clients. This fact has led some researchers to hypothesize that depression underlies eating disorders in many people. The addition of nutritional counseling is often desirable and is available at many universities.

Regarding the use of group counseling, some authors (for example, Abraham and Llewellyn-Jones, 1989; Brouwers, 1994) suggest that clients should be moving toward recovery before they participate in such an experience. To use Prochaska's model (Prochaska and DiClemente, 1992), they should be in the preaction or action stage of change, because group members may describe techniques and abuses that those in the precontemplation or contemplation stage might add to their own behavior. Others (for example, Zraly and Swift, 1990) hold that group therapy is beneficial for such persons because they can see that recovery is a real possibility for persons like themselves.

Program Example: Treating Eating Disorders by Using a Multidisciplinary Team

In order to address both the educational and the treatment issues related to the problem of eating disorders on campus, the Eating Disorders Task Force was established at Northern Illinois University in 1991. The task force is composed of individuals representing various professions and offices that have an interest in the student with an eating disorder; the group has changed in membership over the years as interested staff learn of its existence. Members have included psychologists, predoctoral interns, athletic trainers, physicians, a psychiatrist, support-group leaders, nutritionists, physical and health education faculty, housing and food-service staff, the Greek affairs adviser, athletic-counseling programming staff, and an exercise physiologist, as well as interested graduate students in related disciplines and student athletes.

As part of its coordinating role, the task force developed guidelines for the outpatient management of individuals with eating disorders in the university setting. Some of the guidelines provide systematic approaches and procedures for assessment and psychological treatment, while others evaluate and monitor physical, nutritional, and dental health. Two sets of guidelines refer to specific populations: student athletes and students in group-living environments. The exercise guidelines provide general parameters for individuals with eating disorders.

The task force provided the basis for the development of various treatment components as well as the foundation for a strong multidisciplinary treatment team. Bimonthly meetings are held by this treatment team, which consists of treating therapists, the support-group leader, a physician, a psychiatrist, a nutritionist, and an athletic trainer; these meetings enhance communication among the various caregivers and allow them to serve as consultants to each other in the management of these often complex students.

The task force has also sponsored educational efforts on campus, including Eating Disorder Awareness Week and the National Eating Disorder Screening Program; these efforts include showing educational videos, classroom presentations, campuswide events with outside speakers, and the training of graduate students in eating disorder assessment.

Source: K. Hotelling, director, Counseling and Student Development Center, Northern Illinois University, personal communication, 1996.

Sexual Violence

The results of a number of major surveys on sexual violence on campus indicate its pervasiveness (Roark, 1993; Simon, 1993). Statistics showing that one in four or one in six college women will be the victim of an attempted sexual assault, typically by an acquaintance, served as foundations for national legislation mandating that campuses have sexual-assault policies and procedures (Carter, 1997). The growing cultural rejection of sexual harassment has also resulted in legal and campus initiatives designed to provide redress for these experiences, which are often damaging psychologically and cause significant academic interference (Burkhart and Fromuth, 1991).

Campus sexual-violence cases are often controversial and difficult. A number of intense reactions can emerge. Some students experience escalated levels of fear and insecurity. Other students may side completely with either the victim or the alleged perpetrator. The myths that most people hold about rape often come out. Administrators may voice strong concern about negative campus image and the possibility of civil law suits. Many of these reactions create additional problems for those trying to recover from the experience of sexual assault.

Counseling services for survivors have received attention from the profession (Frazier and Cohen, 1992). Authors such as Burgess and Holmstrom (1979) have developed a conceptual framework for the treatment and the recovery process. They differentiate between an acute, or disorganized, phase and a long-term, or reorganization, phase. During the acute phase, college students may be emotionally depressed or controlled. They may experience a variety of physical reactions (for example, soreness, sleep disturbance, problems with eating) and emotional reactions (for example, fear, emotional lability). During the long-term phase, college students often have intense dreams and nightmares, develop phobias, have difficulty at work or with academics, and experience problems with resuming their previous sexual activities. McCann, Sailheim, and Abrahamson (1988) wrote a particularly helpful article on the psychology of victimization. Their model posits that one's personal schemas of safety, trust, power, and self-esteem are adversely affected by the experience of sexual violence. These altered schemas, in turn, lead to maladaptive coping in the form of dysfunctional behavior, cognition, emotions, relationships, and biology. In employing this model, therapeutic work with college student victims alternates between normalizing these reactions and developing positive underlying personal schemas and enhancing adaptive behavior, emotions, and relationships in the immediate environment and life situations. Those clients who had inadequate schemas before the trauma (often as a result of abuse earlier in life) typically have greater problems and greater difficulty in returning to adequate functioning than those who started out with adequate schemas. Burgess and Holmstrom (1979) labeled this a "compounded reaction."

Program Example: Date-Rape Survivors as Peer Counselors

This program at Fordham University originated from a discussion among members of a group for date-rape survivors. Group members found that being with others who had similar experiences was helpful. Several had heard of other survivors of date rape whom they felt could benefit from the group experience. The Counseling Center staff member leading the group indicated that she was seeing other survivors individually who might benefit from talking to the group but who were reluctant to join at present. Some group members volunteered to speak individually with survivors regarding their shared experiences. The group leader took the names of these students and provided them with supervision.

Counseling Center staff members, members of the residential life staff, and others in the university community contact the group leader about survivors. The group leader sees each survivor and arranges contact between the survivor and a peer counselor. The students generally meet in a private room in the Counseling Center, but they sometimes meet outside the center. The goals of the contacts vary. If the survivor is not in counseling, counseling is encouraged. If the survivor is in individual counseling and wants to join the group, the peer counselor facilitates the process. One peer counselor did outreach work by speaking at floor meetings and at meetings during Rape

Awareness Week. She spoke of her experience and provided information to others regarding the help available both on and off campus.

The program has not yet been evaluated, but administrators and students view it positively. It is small, with only four peer counselors.

Source: G. Tryon, director, Counseling Center, Fordham University, personal communication, 1994.

University policies that stipulate that a finding of sexual assault must result in suspension or expulsion have both benefited and complicated treatment of sexual-assault survivors. The positive effects of having such policies are that a finding of guilt may be more likely to occur on campus than in a court of law, as the level of evidence required by campus judicial boards is limited to a "preponderance of evidence" rather than the extensive "beyond a reasonable doubt" level needed in court. As an additional plus for such policies, although many victims of acquaintance rape want some consequences for the perpetrator, most do not feel comfortable with the court's mandatory sentence of several years in jail (which is the typical minimum sentence for a rape conviction). But such policies are not without negative effects. Women who pursue campus adjudications often experience adverse reactions from members of their peer group (some of whom are usually friends of the alleged perpetrator as well). Considerable social stigma sometimes is attached to women who report acquaintance rape. Also, many women who go through these procedures talk about the violations of trust and control that can occur during the campus investigation and adjudication processes.

AIDS

Universities are no safe havens from the transmission of and infection by the AIDS virus. Estimates are that one in every 250 college students is HIV-positive with the number increasing (House and Walker, 1993). Moreover, surveys assessing the health concerns of college students indicate up to 90 percent expressing concerns about HIV/AIDS and other sexually transmitted diseases (Ascher, 1994). Despite these facts and despite the deadliness of AIDS, levels of safe-sex practices continue to be alarmingly low (Keeling, 1991; McLean, 1994).

The *Journal of Counseling and Development* special edition on AIDS/HIV included an article entitled "Counseling in the Era of AIDS" by Dworkin and Pincu (1993) that specifically addressed the needs of college students:

Because most students are in the early 20's, it is important to recognize that this is an age [in which] one's personal and social identity are established, and one

still has a sense of invulnerability. Physical appearance and sexuality are important issues, and these are emotional areas for those dealing with HIV and
AIDS. The counselor in a college setting must provide information and referrals, help students meet intimacy needs, and enable students to learn to express
intimacy. An important role for the counselor is that of sex educator. The counselor must also be aware of the campus climate for the acceptance of gay and
lesbian students and for the acceptance of those who choose to disclose their
HIV status, AIDS status, or both. Counselors must help students who are
considering disclosure weigh the costs and benefits (Dworkin and Pincu, 1993).

Two helpful resources for college counselors are "AIDS Issues and Answers for
University Counseling Center Staff" (Johnston, 1989) and *AIDS on the College Campus* (Keeling, 1989).

Hoffman (1991) provides a helpful model for working with the HIV-positive
and AIDS clients. She suggests that the individual's responses to the illness are
produced by the interaction of four components: special characteristics of seropos-
itivity including stigma, progressivity, and timing; interpersonal and institutional
social supports; situational aspects such as illness stage, source, and onset; and
client characteristics including psychosocial competence, attributional and ap-
praisal style, gender, gender identity, race and ethnicity, social class, state of health,
and life-style. Collectively, where clients are on these factors gives rise to a number of needs that can be addressed in therapy. Counselors can play important
roles in assisting clients to manage emotions, to build social supports, to engage in
health-promoting behaviors, to explore their spirituality, to rethink life goals,
and to develop coping strategies.

Hoffman includes a discussion of how her psychosocial model could be
adapted to college students. She argues that university counseling centers are
likely to see increasing numbers of students who have just learned that they
are HIV-infected and are in crisis. Many of these clients initially want only time-
limited counseling to decide whom to tell and to find out about available resources. These students then take a break from counseling and return when symptoms are negatively affecting their lives. Other students want an ongoing
counseling relationship.

Most important in college settings, however, are the limitations of extent and
time. The need for support services is likely to far exceed what most college counseling and mental health centers can provide, and the typical duration of the
illness makes it highly probable that the needs for counseling will continue and increase once the student leaves the academic environment. Gluhoski (1996) in
a summary of psychotherapy research with HIV-positive clients suggests that
cognitive-behavioral techniques (including stress management, problem solving,

relaxation training, and cognitive modification) seem to be effective in decreasing symptomatology and enhancing coping ability. One study (LaPerriere and others, 1991) reported a prophylactic effect in preventing depression through the use of cognitive-behavioral methods with persons awaiting notification.

One other important factor in the response of college counseling and mental health centers is the dramatic effect on staff working with this clientele. Farber (1994) argues that work with HIV-positive and AIDS clients can be meaningful, enriching, and rewarding, but that because of the biopsychosocial complexity of the illness some counselors can experience great depths of helplessness, hopelessness, and despair. These feelings are created by the discrepancy between the counselors' expectations for their therapy and the reality of HIV/AIDS clients' deterioration. As certain maladaptive psychodynamic and existential issues may intensify these feelings, Farber suggests that therapists obtain supervision that focuses on the underlying dynamics.

Ethics represents another major component when college counselors work with HIV-positive or AIDS clients. Specifically, the ethical dilemmas faced by professionals attempting to balance core priorities of confidentiality with duty to protect require Solomonic skill (Kain, 1988; Kelly, 1987; Lynch, 1993). Several articles on AIDS law for mental health professionals, such as the one by Wood, Marks, and Dilley (1990), have been published, but the case laws have not yet been adjudicated to provide much guidance. Also, there appears to be little uniformity across states on this issue.

Stress

Stress and anxiety problems are endemic among university students. Students with stress problems typically fit into one of three groups: those with a predisposition for anxiety reactions, those with a specific anxiety or phobia, and those coping with an intense external stressor. Cognitive-behavioral treatments have generally received the most support for use with all three populations, with different studies highlighting various individual or group and manual-type or tailored interventions.

In the first group, students evidencing substantial stress reactions in the face of normal stressors often show a history of high-arousal responding. At times, the adjunctive use of medication can be helpful. For example, the use of antidepressants by students with panic disorder often accelerates improvement when used with behavioral techniques such as relaxation training and with cognitive strategies such as cognitive refutation. For other clients, exercise, relaxation, dieting, and thinking about their situation in new ways lead to significant improvement. The top ten strategies to enhance coping with such stress are to face problems directly, exercise, talk out your worries, plan your work, have realistic expectations, get enough sleep and rest, take occasional work breaks, develop a positive perspective, eat nutritiously, and practice physical and mental relaxation techniques (Cooper, 1990).

In the second group, students sometimes seek support for overcoming specific anxieties like test anxiety, math anxiety, computer phobia, and speech anxiety. These problems present opportunities for counseling centers to do work that is directly related to academic success. Common treatments are systematic desensitization, anxiety-management training, discussion of negative feelings, and assertiveness training. As an example of an individual-counseling approach, a student with test anxiety could participate in six to ten sessions of cognitive-behavioral treatment combining deep muscle relaxation and relaxed breathing with use of an anxiety hierarchy, thought stopping, and coping techniques. Beginning goals should be easy to achieve, and progress should be gradual to ensure success. As an example of a group-counseling approach, students with interpersonal anxiety might be assisted through a twelve-session assertiveness training program. A combination of functional analysis, modeling, practice, feedback, and social support could be employed to help group members identify assertiveness skills requiring work and to reduce cognitive barriers to behaving assertively (Rubin and Feeney, 1986).

Program Example: Stress Lab

Psychologists working at the Counseling Center at the University of California-Irvine, created a lab to support the increasing numbers of students having problems with academic and personal pressures. Students who experience stress or anxiety are provided a room stocked with books, videotapes, and pamphlets that teach relaxation, coping, and perspective. A computer and biofeedback machine are planned additions. Being in the lab removes students from the source of their distress and gives them new knowledge and skills. All those who want to utilize the lab are screened by staff to ensure that this treatment is appropriate. Sometimes using the lab is enough, while other times the person requires follow-up counseling as a supplement. Center therapists also refer their own clients to the lab for specific problems such as inability to relax, family stress, or roommate conflict. The lab allows certain groups of students, such as ethnic minorities, whose comfort with traditional counseling is low, to receive assistance. An institutional grant, space in the Counseling Center, and gifts from a number of individuals enabled the lab's development.

Source: Murray, 1996.

The third type of stress reaction is due to a severe individualized stressor such as death of a family member, divorce of parents, loss of an intimate relationship, major car accident, significant illness, or a campus mega-incident such as the murders at the University of Florida or the shootings at the University of Iowa. Clients' symptomatic reactions to personal stressors are highly idiosyncratic, so therapy needs to be tailored to the individual (Pruett and Brown, 1990). Whether the treatment is one-to-one or group depends on factors such as the size of the campus, the number of other students with related stressors, and the commitment of the counseling center to group modalities. The utilization of groups becomes essential when dealing with stressors that affect a large group of students (Farberow and Frederick, 1990). For example, during the Florida murders, staff from the Counseling Center joined with staff from mental health, the campus police, and the county crisis center to meet with groups of students, faculty, and staff. Some of these meetings were requested, but many were initiated by the crisis-response teams (Archer, 1992).

Program Example: Critical-Incident Stress Debriefing

The Mitchell Critical-Incident Stress Debriefing (CISD) model (Mitchell and Everly, 1993) used at the Counseling and Testing Center, Northern Arizona University, is a seven-phase process that helps the individual work through an extreme crisis by relieving the acute stress and emotional reactions and reducing the development of delayed reactions such as posttraumatic stress disorders. Mitchell suggests that the primary CISD facilitator be a professional counselor or mental health professional. In addition to providing group facilitation, trained facilitators must be able to identify group members who may need additional intervention beyond the debriefing session. Crisis-response team members assist the facilitator in supporting distraught members and acting as doorkeepers, ensuring that the debriefing occurs without distractions. It is suggested that debriefing sessions occur in a facility other than a counseling or mental health center in order to support the normalization of the stress experience and to distinguish debriefing from counseling. Debriefing should occur between twenty-four and seventy-two hours after the critical incident.

Serious consideration should be given to choosing individuals who will attend a debriefing session. Debriefing is appropriate for those who were exposed to a critical incident or had a relationship to or common identification with a victim. Attendance at a debriefing session is inappropriate for primary victims of severe trauma, individuals intimately involved with a victim, individuals with psychopathology that might interfere with their participation, or anyone who could be implicated as a cause of the incident.

Source: DeStefano, 1995.

Career Counseling

The research of the noted theoretician of college student development Arthur Chickering (Chickering, 1969; Chickering and Reisser, 1993) has consistently demonstrated that selection of an occupation is a central developmental task for this group. Subtasks include establishing educational goals and plans, specifying career choices and directions, and determining life-style preferences and objectives. Knefelkamp and Slepitza (1976) developed a multistage model to identify development of career choice among college students. The common patterns were dualism, a belief that there is only one right career; multiplicity, a recognition that several career possibilities exist, yet with limited personal recognition; relativism, a shift to an internal and more complex view of decision making; and commitment with relativism, where the student clarifies and affirms his or her own values, purposes, goals, and identity.

In 1992, the National Occupational Information Coordinating Committee (NOICC) elaborated three career competencies and associated indicators for college students (National Occupational Information Coordinating Committee, U.S. Department of Labor, 1992). For *self-knowledge,* the indicators are having the skills to maintain a positive self-concept, the abilities to maintain effective behaviors, and an understanding of developmental changes and transitions. For *educational and occupational exploration,* the indicators are having the skills to enter and to participate in education and training, the skills to participate in work and lifelong learning, the skills to locate, evaluate, and interpret information, the skills to seek, obtain, maintain, and change jobs, and an understanding of how the needs and functions of society influence the nature and structure of work. For *career planning,* the indicators are having the skills to make decisions, an understanding of the impact of work on individual and family life, an understanding of the continuing changes in male and female roles, and the skills to make career transitions.

A number of implications for career guidance programs in institutions of higher education are associated with the NOICC competencies. Zunker (1994, p. 247) summarizes them:

> College students should be assisted in systematically analyzing college and non-college experiences and in incorporating this information into career-related decisions. In addition, career-guidance services should help students select major fields of study and relate these to career fields. Career life planning that focuses on factors that influence career choices over the lifespan is a valuable concept to incorporate in career-guidance programs. . . . Career-guidance activities in institutions of higher learning must provide assistance in helping each

student understand that career development is a lifelong process based on a sequential series of educational and occupational choices. Each student should be given the opportunity to identify and use a wide variety of resources to maximize his or her career development potential.

Historically, university counseling centers devoted significant resources to career counseling, and much of the counseling-psychology literature remains focused on career issues (Fitzgerald, Fassinger, and Betz, 1995). However, as the demand for personal counseling, outreach programming, and psychoeducational consultation increased, the commitment to career counseling decreased (Stone and Archer, 1990). Simultaneously, many universities that had separate job-planning and placement centers relocated career counseling from counseling centers to these sites, particularly if there was a merger with a separate mental health service.

The seven contemporary approaches to career counseling are trait and factor, person-centered, psychodynamic, developmental, social-learning, social-psychological, and computer-assisted (Walsh and Osipaw, 1990). In the early 1980s, Crites (1981) developed a still-used schema that compares and contrasts these approaches by diagnosis, process, and outcome and by interview technique, test interpretation, and use of occupational information. Elwood (1992) writes that most counselors doing career counseling today are encouraged to develop an integrated approach to their work.

The research on outcomes in career counseling is positive, typically showing that relatively brief interventions lead to valued outcomes in occupation-related decisions. Of equal importance, a number of studies (for example, Super, 1990) have shown that gains made through career counseling often benefit the personal side of life as well. In fact, overly differentiating between career and personal counseling probably limits the positive benefits that can accrue to students when these two are provided concomitantly. This may be an unfortunate secondary impact of the increased separation of counseling and psychological services from career development. The investigations also demonstrate that a straight test-and-tell method does not work for college students (Katz, 1993).

Zunker (1994) described a number of factors that can complicate the career development process: faulty cognition, such as the belief that "there is only one vocation in the world that is right for me"; maladaptive behaviors like poor communication skills; and, less likely with college students, problems with memory and persistence. Zunker adds that conflicts among life roles such as between work and leisure or between personal advancement and community service may also be a source of career-choice difficulties for some counseling-center clients. Consequently, counselors must use all their knowledge and skills to do career work; counselors and counseling psychologists remain the best-trained professionals to conduct career counseling. In addition, the current emphases in higher education on enhancing educational outcomes and on increasing the interface between academic affairs and student affairs create a political atmosphere where such work will likely be viewed positively by the administration. Although such activity may be precluded at large universities with comprehensive career centers employing their own counselors, the opportunity for such work continues to be available or expected in many other institutions.

Program Example: Providing Career Counseling Services at a Separate Career Center

Full-time and practicum staff from the Student Counseling and Development Center at Valparaiso University provide career counseling services to students at the Career Center, which is a separate office at the university. The change to delivering career work at a separate office has resulted in a tenfold increase in the number of students seeking career counseling, many of whom (for example, international students and non-traditional students) would not likely have come for such assistance to a "mental health unit." The career counseling services include normative and ideographic assessment, use of a computerized vocational guidance system, utilization of career-choice and occupational information in the facility's in-house Career Resource Library, and career counseling using whichever of the seven approaches (or a combination of them) is most appropriate. The full-time counseling staff also supervises peer educators, who maintain the career-choice and graduate studies sections of the Career Resource Library. In addition, counselors, practicum students, and peer educators conduct outreach programs.

Relationships and Intimacy

Chickering and Reisser (1993) emphasized the importance for the college student of developing mature interpersonal relationships. Specific components of this life task include increasing tolerance for others with differing views, attitudes, and behaviors; establishing mature relationships with peers accompanied by openness and trust; developing interdependence with others where mutuality is high; and engaging in intimate sexual relationships. Counselees receiving services at college and university counseling centers typically spend part and sometimes most of their session time on these issues. Attention to intimate sexual relationships is perhaps the most intricate of the four areas. The combination of love, sexuality, and commitment required is often made more difficult by significant time limitations, conflict with career development, and the need for personal differentiation common in college students.

Relationships and intimacy are areas where myths (or faulty beliefs) create many difficulties (Corey and Corey, 1997). Examples of relationship myths are that love means constant togetherness and that one "falls" in and out of love. Many destructive beliefs also surround the issue of sexuality, including that men can prove themselves only through sexual conquests and that one's partner is responsible for sexual decisions and for one's sexual satisfaction. And if challenging these myths were not difficult enough, college students' transition from child-parent to adult-adult interactions is a major theme for many of these intimate relationships.

College counselors can help their clients in a number of important ways. First, the therapeutic relationship can function as an important model for close relationships. Openness, vulnerability, empathy, support, and facilitative communication skills are often part of the therapeutic relationship. Second, the session acts to enhance the relational problem-solving abilities of clients and fosters the acquisition of productive relationship-related attitudes and skills. Third, the sessions assist students in reflecting on this aspect of their development and in making some of the many choices involved (Grayson and Cauley, 1989).

Although all these outcomes can and do result from individual therapy, a strong case can be made for group therapy as a more effective and efficacious approach to this area of functioning. The group modality offers the valuable additional benefit of gaining the perspectives and feedback of peers as well as many of the other positive aspects of groups, as described previously (MacKenzie, 1995).

◆ ◆ ◆

Although many serious and developmental problems may deserve special attention, this chapter focused on three common developmental problems—career choice, stress, and relationships and intimacy—as well as on a number of serious and sometimes life-threatening problems. Special programs for students with these problems and issues often include a counseling component, as discussed here, and a preventive or developmental component. Each counseling or mental health center must determine which problems require a special focus on its campus.

CHAPTER SEVEN

COUNSELING WITH SPECIAL POPULATIONS

A number of special populations need and deserve special attention by college counselors. Being a member of a minority group, a woman, a gay male, a lesbian, a bisexual woman or man, or someone with a disability often makes negotiation of the college environment particularly difficult. Racism, prejudice, and stereotyping affect students in these groups both developmentally and in their everyday campus interactions (Mooney, 1989; Weinstein and Obear, 1992). Disabilities may create additional academic challenges. College counselors need to reach out to these groups and to understand their unique needs for counseling.

Another special category of clients are students who are referred to counseling by the campus or local judicial system. These students, who are in trouble for difficulties such as substance abuse and relationship violence, are often moving along a path that will be costly to themselves and to society. Mandatory counseling interventions for them may well be cost-effective in the long run even if difficult to conduct in the present.

Presenting different types of needs are adult learners, the so-called nontraditional students, who are the most rapidly growing constituency in higher education. Adult learners often have far greater environmental or familial pressures than do traditional-age students and many have quite intense personal issues.

Minority Students

Students of color often underutilize the services offered by university and college counseling centers (Leong, 1992) and are more likely than majority students to prematurely terminate counseling sessions (Richmond, 1992). Because of the need to provide effective counseling to minority students and in response to the growing diversity both within U.S. society and on college campuses, a number of theorists (for example, Ivey, Ivey, and Simek-Morgan, 1993; Cheatham, Ivey, Ivey, and Simek-Morgan, 1993; Pederson, 1994; Sue and Sue, 1990; Ibraham, 1991) have proposed a multicultural perspective as a much needed fourth force of counseling theories, the first three being psychodynamic, humanistic-existential, and cognitive-behavioral.

A major hypothesis is that sociocultural factors, including race and ethnicity as well as gender, socioeconomic status, religion, sexual orientation, place of birth and upbringing, and age, have a profound influence on both the individual's and the counselor's attitudes, values, perspectives, and behaviors. More important, counseling will be less effective or even destructive when the therapist and client do not attend to this dimension, as is particularly likely when therapists impose their values and expectations, when they stereotype, or when they use only one counseling approach. Because there are almost always some salient cultural differences between client and therapist, most counseling is inherently multicultural.

Research and services to minority students have tended to focus on racial and ethnic diversity. Many of the early articles, in the mid-1980s, discussed ethnic and racial characteristics of minority students (see Taylor, 1986; Parham and Helms, 1985; Patterson, Sedlacek, and Perry, 1984; Tomlinson and Cope, 1988). The emphasis in this area began to expand in the late 1980s and early 1990s with attention to ethnic and racial groups' use and views of counseling services (for example, Sanchez and King, 1986; Price and McNeill, 1992; Boesch and Cimbolic, 1994; Atkinson, Jennings, and Liongson, 1990). More recently, the literature has attended to training issues and the counselor as a person (Hills and Strozier, 1992; Bishop and Richards, 1987; Mehlman, 1994). The American Psychological Association developed specific guidelines for providers of psychological services to ethnic, linguistic, and culturally diverse populations in 1993 (American Psychological Association, 1993). All the other major mental health provider groups (American Counseling Association, National Association of Social Workers, and American Association of Marriage and Family Therapy) specifically mention adjusting services to racial and ethnic minorities in their current ethical guidelines.

Sue, Arrendondo, and McDavis (1992) articulated three requirements for those providing multicultural counseling. The first requirement is awareness of beliefs and attitudes about differences and acceptance of diversity as a salient factor in life. The second requirement is knowledge, both of one's own racial and cultural heritage and of important cultural facets of one's clients. The third requirement is having a repertoire of skills and intervention strategies modified to accommodate cultural differences, such as differences in nonverbal communication, expression of affect, and worldviews.

Another important aspect of multicultural counseling is lessened reliance on traditional counseling and outreach techniques and increased use of the roles outlined by Atkinson, Morten, and Sue (1993). Their model is based on the premise that a number of different helping roles must be assumed by an effective cross-cultural counselor depending on three factors: the locus of the problem for the client (internal or external), the goals of the intervention (remediation or prevention), and the degree of client acculturation (high or low). Many situations involving minority students at colleges and universities call for environmental and preventive community-oriented work. Within this model, some of the most efficacious roles are change agent or consultant, adviser, advocate, facilitator of within-culture-group support systems, and facilitator of traditional healing methods. Following is a description of each of these roles and the related determining factors as outlined by Sue (1993):

The role of *change agent* "is characterized by an action oriented approach to changing the client's social environment. Like the consultant . . . in many respects, the change agent goes further in assuming responsibility for making changes which may be oppressing the client or clients" (external problem, high acculturation, remedial) (p. 20).

The role of *consultant* "is characterized by a professional but collegial relationship between the consultant and the consultee working to change or impact a third party. The effective consultant should possess knowledge and experience in organizational change" (external problem, high acculturation, preventive) (p. 20).

The *adviser* makes suggestions to clients "about how to solve or prevent potential problems, informs them about available options, and may share with them actions they themselves or others have found effective in ameliorating problems. For example, low-acculturated immigrants who have minimal experience with U.S. society may need someone to advise them about potential sources of stress due to culture conflicts" (external problem, low acculturation, preventive) (p. 19).

The *advocate* "may literally represent the best interests of clients to other individuals, groups, or institutional organizations. For example, limited English-speaking groups who do not understand institutional policies or practices nor their rights may need persons who 'speak for them,' encouraging or demanding appropriate and fair treatment" (external problem, low acculturation, remedial) (p. 19).

The *facilitator of within-culture-group support systems* recognizes that "many clients may respond better to indigenous support systems such as extended family, community elder, religious support groups in resolving their problems. In essence, the counselor must know what kind of support systems [are] available in the client's culture, and . . . facilitate their use" (internal problem, low acculturation, preventive) (p. 20).

The *facilitator of traditional healing methods* can refer clients "to healers (*currandismo*—Mexican folk healer, tai chi chuan instructor, and so on) knowledgeable about the original home culture" of the client or can use "indigenous healing methods [with] culturally different clients. This latter role, however assumes that the counselor is trained and skilled in those healing arts" (internal problem, low acculturation, remedial) (p. 20).

Research and conceptual work on multicultural counseling is continuing to receive significant attention. Steenbarger (1993) argued that it is possible and desirable for college counselors to integrate brief, multicultural counseling paradigms by expanding the goals of counseling and the roles the counselor takes on to support them. Thus, being a multiculturally competent therapist is not a negation of traditional counseling knowledge and skill but involves both an expansion of awareness and flexibility in action. Ridley, Mendoza, and Kanitz (1994) articulated a five-level multicultural-counseling training model that emphasized learning associated content and skills through a combination of didactic instruction, experiential exercises, supervised clinical work, reading and writing assignments, participatory learning, modeling, technology-assisted training, and introspection. Trevino (1996) emphasized the importance of counselors' attending to culture and change by adopting an anthropological perspective, paying special attention to different worldviews. Smart and Smart (1997) commented on the rise in attention to culturally sensitive diagnosis from DSM-III to DSM-IV. Separating reality from rhetoric, however, Essandoh (1996) issued a challenge to clinicians to catch their practice up to where theory says they should be. He argues that while multicultural psychology has been touted as the "new paradigm," its application has been limited and much is needed to actualize its possibilities.

Program Example: Retention of Minority Students

At Baruch College Counseling and Psychological Services Center, a set of counseling interventions was developed to improve retention and graduation rates for minority students. Data driving this development were the disproportional numbers of minority students who were the first in their families to attend college or who had deficits in their academic preparation. Four services are included. (1) Students on academic probation are offered assistance in planning and executing efforts to improve their academic performance. (2) Workshops on study skills and test taking are provided. (3) An ongoing data-collection project allows the Counseling and Psychological Services Center to assess specific counseling concerns of various groups. These data, in turn, are used to guide clinical interventions and to foster advocacy efforts. (4) Career counseling projects are given high priority, with data collected to demonstrate the connection between carefully made major and career decisions and academic and personal success. The program's positive outcomes are largely due to its integration with an institutionwide approach to retention.

Source: Ruffin, 1990.

As is obvious from Sue's (1994) listing of roles for college counselors who wish to enhance services to minority students, reaching out to the different minority communities is extremely important. Chapter Twelve focuses on the outreach mission counselors have to promote diversity and to help improve the learning environment for minority students. Other specific activities can enhance the provision of counseling services to these students:

- Providing effective training in multicultural counseling (see discussion in Chapter Fifteen). College counseling and mental health staffs must make ongoing training in this area a priority.
- Hiring counselors with diverse backgrounds, which allows minority students to identify with a member of the staff. However, although minority counselors may see a number of minority students, it is not useful to identify these counselors as the only ones for their minority group. Having a diverse staff is useful because it allows the staff to learn about people from different cultural backgrounds and because it signals to campus minority groups the fact that the center values diversity.
- Communicating with campus minority organizations to develop referral networks and to exchange ideas on the counseling process and how to access counseling. It may, for example, be important to offer creative counseling services for students from minority groups (such as counseling in different locations, different names and titles for groups, incorporation of music, literature, and art).
- Developing strong and ongoing relationships with minority peer and advising groups on campus. These liaisons help maintain a line of referral and communication with minority students on campus.
- Displaying at the counseling facility artwork and representations of different cultures (African American art, art and literature by minorities, posters for ethnic festivals and music shows). Such displays demonstrate a commitment to diversity.

- Offering peer counseling and education programs that include students from all campus minority groups.
- Providing one-session, drop-in counseling that does not require paperwork and an extensive counseling commitment. This kind of counseling can be helpful to minority students for whom formal counseling has little validity.

Leong (1996) commented that unidimensional models of cross-cultural counseling are inherently limited and that an integrated, sequential, and dynamic approach better fulfills the diverse counseling needs presented. The specific components of Leong's model include out-group homogeneity effect, cultural schema theory, complementarity theory, science of complexity, and mindfulness. Specifically, *out-group homogeneity effect* refers to the tendency for people to perceive greater similarity in out-groups (for example, "all people from Hispanic cultures are hot-tempered"). *Cultural schema theory* posits that underlying schemas play an important role in interpersonal perception and relations (for example, "men are emotionally constricted"). *Complementarity* has to do with the role reciprocity between counselor and client. When the roles are reciprocal, complementarity is high and the resulting therapeutic alliance is likely to be stronger. Low complementarity, which results from role conflict and competition, contributes to a weak therapeutic alliance. The *science of complexity* is most often associated with chaos theory. The notion is that the individual is a complex adaptive system composed of universal, group, and individual unique elements. Finally, *mindfulness* refers to the need for the counselor to comprehend the complexity and uncertainty of the cross-cultural context. Leong (1996) writes, "the effective cross-cultural counselor is one who recognizes the complexity of the enterprise and accepts the uncertainty created by this complexity. Yet, the mindful counselor is one who approaches the challenge of this complexity and uncertainty with a high level of creativity" (p. 207). Leong's approach is receiving a good deal of attention and may be quite fruitful for guiding interventions and directing future research in cross-cultural counseling.

Female Students

During the 1980s and 1990s, a plethora of empirical investigations and theories of women's development and of therapy with women emerged. The central criticism of the dominant theories in the field was that they were based on male models of development and communication and valued masculine characteristics more highly than feminine ones (Gelso and Fretz, 1992). Career development and socialization are two areas where the needs of many women are more complex than those of men (Betz and Fitzgerald, 1987; Luzzo, 1995). For example, the tension between work and home responsibilities is often great, particularly in dual-career families and in single-parent families, the overwhelming majority of which are headed by women (Gilbert and Rachlin, 1987). Many authors refer to these and related issues as "multiple-role considerations," and such concerns are likely to be significant among women. The paradox among college students, especially traditional-age college students, is their gross underestimation of the difficulties involved. Consequently, few students would attend a program on, for example, the problems of dual-career families.

Staff in college and university counseling and mental health centers need to be aware of a number of important factors affecting the counseling of women. First, many people punish women for exhibiting characteristics that are valued in males, such as being competitive or highly assertive (Goelyan, 1991). Second, our societal structures are based on masculine models of power and hierarchy (Schaef, 1992). Third, and most directly harmful, are the biases among helping professionals themselves, which are manifested when they support traditional sex roles, have rigid gender expectations, use sexist language, or relate to female clients as sex objects.

Fitzgerald and Nutt (1986, pp. 180–216) outlined the thirteen traits of good counselors for women:

1. Counselors and therapists are knowledgeable about women, particularly with regard to biological, psychological, and social issues that have an impact on women in general or on particular groups of women.
2. Counselors and therapists are aware that the assumptions and precepts of theories relevant to their practice may apply differently to men and women. Some may proscribe or limit the potential of women clients; others may be particularly useful for women clients.
3. Counselors and therapists continue throughout their professional careers to explore and learn about issues related to women, including the special problems of various female subgroups.
4. Counselors and therapists recognize and are aware of all forms of oppression and how these interact with sexism.
5. Counselors and therapists are knowledgeable about and aware of verbal and nonverbal processes as these affect women (particularly with regard to power in the counseling relationship). So that counselor-client interactions are not adversely affected, responsibility is shared by clients and counselors.
6. Counselors and therapists are able to use skills that are particularly appropriate for women in general and for particular subgroups of women.
7. Counselors and therapists ascribe no preconceived limitations on the direction or nature of potential changes or goals in counseling for women.

8. Counselors and therapists are sensitive to circumstances where it is desirable for a woman client to be seen by a female or male professional.
9. Counselors and therapists use nonsexist language in counseling, supervision, teaching, and writing.
10. Counselors and therapists do not engage in sexual activity with their clients under any circumstances.
11. Counselors and therapists are aware of and continually review their own values and biases and the effects of these on their women clients. They understand the effects of sex-role socialization on their own development and functioning and on their values and attitudes. They recognize that behaviors and roles need not be sex-based.
12. Counselors and therapists are aware of how their personal functioning may influence their effectiveness with women clients. They monitor their functioning through consultation, supervision, or therapy so that it does not have adverse effects.
13. Counselors and therapists support the elimination of sex bias in institutions and individuals.

These suggestions are congruent with the feminist development theory of Gilligan, Rogers, and Tolman (1991) as well as the central tenets common to all feminist counseling and therapy as espoused by Enns (1993). Feminist developmental theories emphasize sociopolitical, cultural, and historical influences on women's life experience, while feminist therapies focus on empowering and enfranchising women personally, socially, economically, and politically.

Counseling women effectively requires a heterogeneous perspective. In their book *Educating the Majority: Women Challenge Tradition in Higher Education,* Pearson, Shavlik, and Touchton (1989) call attention to the special cross-cultural effects of race, religion, and sexual orientation on gender. They argue for substantive changes within the structure and activities of higher education and the classroom. Many of their recommendations echo those given in the widely disseminated publications "The Classroom Climate: A Chilly One for Women?" (Hall and Sandler, 1982) and "Out of the Classroom: A Chilly Campus Climate for Women?" (Hall and Sandler, 1984). Unfortunately, recent research (for example, Terenzini, Pascarella, and Blimling, 1996) continues to document a chilly campus climate for many women.

Current research with women in college and female counseling-center clients continues, yet now tends to be microfocused. For example, many studies focus on specific clinical issues such as eating disorders (Johnson and Petrie, 1996; Kashubeck and Mintz, 1996) or career development (Juntunen, 1996; Lucas, 1997; Schaefers, Epperson, and Nauta, 1997)—topics that have been receiving attention for some time. Other articles exploring various types of violence against women (for example, Carden, 1994) highlight what has come to be a widespread sociocultural problem.

Program Example: A Group for Raising Women Graduate Students' Self-Esteem

The graduate women's self-esteem group was started in 1988 at the University of Wisconsin–Madison Counseling and Consultation Services. The group was established to address the needs of graduate women, including finding support, connecting with other students, being mentored, and learning to accurately assess their strengths and accomplishments.

The group is based on five fundamental assumptions about women. The first assumption is that many women work most effectively if they can listen to their own voices and make choices based on their own self-interest. The second assumption is that many women do not have much experience in identifying their own needs and asking to have these needs met. The third assumption is that women are skilled at identifying the needs of others and often attend to these before their own. The fourth assumption is that women need to learn certain assertiveness, networking, and self-promotion skills to be able to effectively and successfully complete graduate school. The last assumption is that women as a group have the resources to learn adaptive skills associated with these preceding assumptions and that the most powerful way for them to learn these is through helping and teaching each other.

The group is process-oriented, with leaders serving as facilitators rather than teachers, information providers, or advice givers and is semistructured. The first session includes making personal introductions, reviewing brainstorming guidelines, and generating a list of topics to discuss. In subsequent sessions, all participants (including the facilitators) start off by giving two adjectives that describe their current feelings, and they elaborate on them if they desire to. Then participants have the freedom and responsibility to ask for time during that session, with the content they bring up and the needs they express varying considerably. The facilitators' role is to build group cohesiveness through open-ended questions that bring in other group members' experiences. Finding creative ways of enhancing connections among members is a priority. The facilitators are also there to intervene if a group member's personal concern is emotionally overwhelming for other group members.

Source: J. Fulwiler, staff therapist, Counseling Center, University of Wisconsin–Madison, personal communication, March 12, 1997.

Male Students

The emerging interest in the psychology of men can be viewed as complementing the work with female students. Evidence of this interest can be found in the creation of a division with this exclusive focus within the American Psychological

Association and in a growing body of scholarship (see Levant, 1996). Researchers have identified a cluster of male socialization traits that are purported to underlie several significant male and societal problems: avoiding all things feminine, demonstrating restricted emotion, being tough and aggressive, being self-reliant, being oriented toward achievement and status, having nonrelational attitudes toward sexuality, and being homophobic. Knowledge of these traits and their contrast with feminist psychology can further the effectiveness of counselors of both genders. Specifically, these traits can be employed as stimuli for discussion in both group and individual counseling (Pollard and Whitaker, 1993).

The psychology of men as a discipline has emerged since the early 1980s and has resulted, in part, from the interaction of men's and gender studies. A basic focus is examination of traditional masculine roles. Two of the most well known concepts that have emerged are the notion of gender-role strain (discrepancy, dysfunction, and trauma) and the notion of a more androgynous masculine identity (Blazina and Watkins, 1996; Good and Wood, 1995; Levant, 1996; Marshall, 1993; O'Neil, 1990). Connections to earlier work by C. G. Jung have been made (Enns, 1994), and alternative helping formats have been explored that are more congruent with male socialization processes than counseling is (Robertson and Fitzgerald, 1992).

Viewing men from a positive framework, Heesacker and Prichard (1992) and others have discussed the mythopoetic view of masculinity, which includes the concept that men do express emotion but not in the direct verbal ways more common to women. Rather than training men to adopt a feminine emotional style, the goal is to enhance both men's and women's awareness and acceptance of male modes of expression. Using myths and archetypes, storytelling, showing feelings through action, and knowing when to be silent are all emphasized.

Gay, Lesbian, and Bisexual Clients

The American Psychological Association has been public in its official support for persons with homosexual orientations (Burnette, 1997; Welch, 1990). Its document *Answers to Your Questions about Sexual Orientation and Homosexuality* (American Psychological Association, 1994) states that homosexual orientation is not a choice or a mental illness or an emotional problem and is not amenable to change by psychotherapy. The document defines sexual orientation as "one of the four components of sexuality . . . distinguished by an enduring emotional, romantic, sexual, or affectional attraction to individuals of a particular gender" (American Psychological Association, 1994, p. 1). The answers given in the document are based on extensive research findings; the questions include: "What causes a person to have a particular sexual orientation?" "Can lesbians and gay men be good parents?" "Why do some gay men and lesbians tell people about their sexual orientation?" "Why is the 'coming out' process difficult for some gays and lesbians?" "What can be done to help lesbians and gay men overcome prejudice and discrimination against them?" "Why is it important for society to be better educated about homosexuality?"

Homosexuality is found in about 10 percent of the population, a figure that is surprisingly constant across cultures, irrespective of different moral values and standards. Moreover, the incidence of homosexuality in a population does not appear to change when moral codes or social mores change. Both these facts support an argument for a strong biological predisposition for sexual orientation. Yet research on this subject reveals that sexual orientation is a product of a number of factors, possibly including genetics, prenatal hormones, key developmental experiences, familial dynamics, and learned experiences; the strength or weakness of any or all of these factors varies considerably within individuals. Some individuals reveal patterns indicative of strong same-sex biological orientation, while others appear to develop a gay life-style only after high school or college sexual experiences. The research findings are of sufficient clarity to suggest that efforts to "repair all homosexuals" regardless of whether this sexual orientation is or is not ego dystonic result from social prejudices garbed in psychological accouterments, as do other forms of homophobia.

Psychologically, sexuality and sexual orientation form one of the most basic bedrocks of personality. Not only do they shape attitudes and passions, but they are so fundamental to personality structure that they, in large part, determine one's sense of personal cohesiveness and level of comfort in the world. They are a driving force behind how we love, work, and create (Gonsiorek, 1988).

During the 1995 American Psychological Association convention, the Psychotherapy Task Force of Division 44 disseminated a set of suggestions for affirmative counseling with lesbians and gay men. These suggestions cover the domains of special assessment and intervention knowledge and skills for working with lesbians and gay men, of helping develop a positive gay male or lesbian identity, of the diverse nature of lesbian and gay male relationships, and of psychotherapist education and training issues for working with lesbians and gay men (American Psychological Association, 1995b). The specifics within these domains flesh out the attitudes, knowledge, and skills needed by college counseling-center professionals to work successfully with members of this population. These guidelines strongly support the need for therapists employed in college and university mental health centers to go beyond the counseling role. Many of the alternative strategies noted in the section on minority students are useful in working with gay and lesbian students as well as affiliated campus organizations. In these alternative roles, counselors need to be aware that reactions to gay and lesbian students and groups vary on the basis of institutional factors such as valuation of diversity, geographical location, and religious affiliation, as well as on the basis of individual factors such as student attitudes toward and tolerance of homosexuality. Few gay and lesbian students would say that the diversity they offer is prized, and most would say they have experienced open oppression and even violence.

A special issue of the *Journal of Counseling and Development* (Dworkin and Guiterrez, 1989) and a feature article in *The Counseling Psychologist* (Fassinger, 1991) were devoted to counseling lesbian women and gay men. Browning, Reynolds, and Dworkin (1991) call attention to three specific domain concerns for lesbian women: identity development, identity management (including coming out), and unique interpersonal issues (including couples' concerns). In addition, the high incidence of substance abuse, domestic violence, and previous sexual abuse in this population often requires counseling. Use of feminist therapy as the guiding paradigm and the need to advocate for individual clients are extolled. Shannon and Woods (1991), in a parallel article concerning affirmative counseling for gay men, also emphasize the areas of identity development, identity management, and special interpersonal issues. The specific concerns of gay men that they discuss differ, however, and include the impact of aging, antigay violence, and spiritual and existential issues.

In line with some of these issues, Slater (1993) writes about violence against lesbian and gay male college students, while Burke (1995) calls attention to the high rate of suicide among gay, lesbian, and bisexual (GLB) teens, who are estimated to account for one in every three adolescent suicides. Perhaps for both external and internal reasons, gay individuals seek counseling at two to four times the rate of heterosexuals. Burke makes five specific recommendations for meeting the needs of GLB students:

1. The college counseling-center environment should be welcoming to GLB clients.
2. College counselors should be patient and take time to help students work through the pain, fear, self-loathing, and harassment trauma often present among those in this group.
3. Clients who voice a desire for networking should be assisted in locating friendship and support systems within the gay community.
4. Clients should be helped in addressing ambivalence about coming out to others.
5. Gay men and lesbians may need assistance in doing grief work about their situation given the homophobic society within which we live.

Beyond developing productive attitudes and orientation as well as knowledge and skills relevant to the GLB population, effective college counselors (whether they are straight or gay or lesbian) have to come to terms with their own homophobia (Kite, 1994). McHenry and Johnson (1993) suggest that denial of these biases often leads to negative treatment outcomes by producing nonproductive collusions at different points throughout the treatment process. They give strong arguments for including GLB issues in training and education, having ongoing dialogue about homophobia among practitioners, directly questioning GLB clients regarding their homophobia, and relying on an affirmative psychotherapy approach.

Many of the writers in this area suggest the positive potential of group work with GLB students. One key issue is whether the counselors themselves are GLB or heterosexual. As the gay community in all but the largest cities is often quite small, the counselor's being a part of this community raises some unique ethical issues of confidentiality and multiple roles. These two ethical issues are even larger on campus, where only a few people may be openly gay or lesbian. Different client-therapist issues arise when the counselors in GLB groups are heterosexual (McKee, Hayes, and Axiotis, 1994). Two such groups have been described in the counseling literature (Holahan and Gibson, 1994; Chojnacki and Gelberg, 1995) along with discussion of many of the associated issues. Evaluations document that such groups are effective.

Three questions of particular relevance to college counseling and mental health centers connect to the politics of conducting groups for GLB students. First, if heterosexual counselors can "successfully" offer such groups, will administration use this possibility to fend off pressures to hire GLB professional staff? Second, how will various campus and external constituencies view the counseling center if it provides such a group? And, third, what personal changes might staff undergo as they are transformed into GLB allies? These topics will be discussed further in Part Four. Suffice it to say that GLB groups facilitated by heterosexual counselors, while helpful, cannot compensate for the absence of staff who are GLB-identified.

Students with Learning Disabilities

Learning disabilities are the largest category of disabilities on college campuses. Access to a substantial resource network is available through clearinghouses such as the Association on Higher Education and Disability, and the National Clearinghouse on Postsecondary Education for Individuals with Disabilities. Many of these resources assist students and their families in demanding the academic and nonacademic accommodations and technology they believe are essential to their succeeding in college.

Counselors often provide psychological support for students with learning disabilities (Dinklage, 1991). These students face the normal developmental issues of students without handicaps, but many may experience a great deal of additional stress because of the great change from how their earlier educational environments responded to their disability. Specifically, the higher education environment demands a great deal more initiative and assertiveness from the student and does not provide the systematic support services integrated into most K–12 special education programs. At some college counseling centers staff provide additional services for students with learning disabilities, including conducting assessments to determine eligibility, serving as advocates to obtain accommodations or technical support, and providing expert opinion on the law to administrators and faculty. Each institution determines the relative amount of resources it allocates to these services and the structure by which they are provided. Counseling and therapy should remain the principal activities of counseling-center staff, and it may be necessary at some institutions for counseling and mental health centers to argue for the centrality of counseling.

College counselors can assume multiple functions, but they should be aware of the possible problems and issues and should educate the university community about them. Providing these extra services means that counselors are placed in new roles, which may diminish the focus on therapeutic material. Faculty and administrators may also be perplexed when counseling-center staff function as active advocates for classroom accommodations or technical support instead of limiting their services to the mental health and career development areas. The center may need to educate the campus community about the implications of the passage of the Americans with Disabilities Act (ADA) in 1990, which greatly increased pressures on colleges and universities to provide academic and nonacademic support to disabled students. For example, prior to the ADA, few violations of Section 504 of the Rehabilitation Act of 1973 were taken to court. The current legal statutes and educational environment, combined with the fact that this generation of students was identified early in elementary school, have drastically changed the incidence of litigation. Expectations have risen among individuals with disabilities regarding the nature of the services and opportunities that must be provided to them, and their willingness to use advocates and the courts has also increased.

Program Example: ADA Support Program

Since the founding of the Learning Access Program (LAP) in 1988, Richard Stockton College has set high standards for accommodating all its students with disabilities and making all their programs accessible in compliance with Section 504 of the Rehabilitation Act of 1973 and the ADA. The LAP, under the auspices of the Counseling Center, provides comprehensive services from planning the curriculum for the student with learning disabilities to providing all services for the student with physical and psychological disabilities. Services are available on a case-by-case basis. Examples of services are assessment, personal counseling, career development and job placement, tutoring, finding housing, providing faculty contacts, suggesting testing alternatives, and finding note takers. The knowledge and skills of a learning-disabilities consultant and other professional staff are available as needed. Since its inception in 1988, the LAP has experienced an increased demand for services. In the past, service demands were mostly for students with physical disabilities, but now students with learning disabilities are the largest population.

Source: T. Gonzales, director, counseling services, Richard Stockton College, Pomona, New Jersey, personal communication, 1994.

Program Example: Assessment of Neuropsychological and Learning Disabilities

Florida International University has close to thirty thousand students with diverse cultural backgrounds. The Student Counseling Center began providing neuropsychological assessments to students in 1994, after securing funding for resources, expertise, and space. Once testing materials had been obtained, criteria were established for eligibility for testing. Liability, ethics, and time constraints were carefully scrutinized and potential risks were balanced with student needs.

Potential clients are seen by referral only. Students without resources are given primary consideration, as are students who may have neuropsychological concerns that specifically affect their current ability to achieve academically. The primary goal of the neuropsychological testing is to identify cognitive strengths and weaknesses and to formulate specialized recommendations that will improve the quality of the students' lives and enable them to achieve their academic potential. Feedback sessions are of utmost importance. Findings are shared in a sensitive manner that empowers the student.

The Student Counseling Center took time to train the staff in various departments about neuropsychological testing and what to look for when making a referral. Staff in the Office of Disability Services and Health Services were initially identified for training, which led to new relationships between those departments and the Student Counseling Center. The provision of consultation services regarding neuropsychological matters resulted from this initial training.

Documents specific to neuropsychological problems were developed, including a separate "neuro-psychosocial" form, referral forms, an informed-consent form for testing, and an application. The informed-consent form was brought to the attention of the university attorney, who made appropriate recommendations.

Clients are given an extensive initial interview along with several neuropsychological screening tests to ascertain appropriateness of services. Potential clients are educated about the process of testing, and a commitment to using the services is secured. Community medical, supportive, and neuropsychological services are provided, as are fees, with appropriate alternative options and additional support available should the need arise.

Providing neuropsychological services to students through the Student Counseling Center is a unique and valuable way for the university to meet the needs and facilitate the success of the rapidly changing "average" college student.

Source: P. Telles-Irvin, director, and H. von Harscher, psychologist, Student Counseling Center, Florida International University, personal communication, 1995.

Students with Psychological Disabilities

Schepp and Snodgrass (1995) facilitated a discussion of counseling-center involvement with students with psychological disabilities at the 1995 AUCCCD convention. Their perspective was as follows (pp. 121–122):

> Counseling Centers vary widely in their involvement with students claiming psychological disability as protected by the [ADA] and Section 504 of the 1973 Rehabilitation Act. Requests for service are increasing rapidly, since special education and mainstreaming have succeeded in preparing more students with emotional and behavioral disorders for college, and people with controlled or chronic mental illness are expected to prepare for work. Also, young adulthood is a time when a number of first-incident acute and serious psychological problems may reach the level of disability.
>
> Many myths exist about what the ADA "requires" when in fact the following are of necessity subject to interpretation which is always evolving: "may not discriminate . . . against any person who has a mental or physical impairment which substantially limits one or more of such person's major life activities," "reasonable and necessary accommodations" and "without undue hardship to the institution." Directors need to understand the core of the above concepts, while realizing that different interpretations are made constantly in various courts, cases, and jurisdictions.
>
> Research shows the strong possibility of success in higher education for students who are qualified as eligible for psychological disability status, but there is little available on specific accommodations for OCD, depression, PTSD, etc. Factors that are highly correlated with success for the entire group are (1) skills, and (2) support. In many instances, the Counseling Center is inclined to advocate for the student who is asking for changes in the academic, residential or other areas, but meets heavy resistance. Often a neutral stance is more effective and helps inform/educate faculty, staff and sometimes students (while mediating for necessary accommodations, without undue hardship to the institution).
>
> The shadow of litigation is ever present, especially if there is any possibility that a student [is] not admitted to a program, or is dismissed, punished, or

treated negatively in any way which could be related to a psychological disability. (Active alcohol and drug abuse is not protected as a disabling condition, but recovering alcoholics are.) The costs to an institution are very high if a court finds flaws in a process. Once an institution is put on notice about a qualified disability, they must respond to the student's needs. Confidentiality is very important, but communication must occur with faculty, advisors, etc. Most Centers find that psychological disability work is very time consuming, even if the assessment/testing/certifying are required outside the institution, and the primary therapist is also referred out. What remains are the accommodations, communication, problem solving, and counseling related to campus issues. Some of these students are "high profile" and have parents with demanding expectations, and very often a number of people become involved with each case.

Students with psychological disabilities are a complex population that can put heavy demands on college and university counseling and mental health centers. In the past, many colleges used dismissal policies to separate students with severe emotional problems from the university (Pavela, 1985). A direct consequence of the ADA and subsequent cases is that people with these disabilities are entitled to reasonable accommodations and support under the law. Bodensteiner and Levinson (1997) summarized the relevant case law. Generally disability-related laws and the associated cases provide greater regulation and pressures at the elementary and secondary levels than they do at postsecondary institutions. Early case law placed little responsibility on universities and colleges to provide assistance to such students. Since the passage of ADA, however, case law is requiring that institutions of higher education must provide "reasonable accommodations" as long as these do not "fundamentally change the curriculum" or cause an "undue hardship" in their implementation.

Even before ADA, Hoffmann and Mastrianni (1989) made the case for keeping such students on campus in an article entitled "The Mentally Ill Student on Campus: Theory and Practice." They pointed out that when troubled individuals identify themselves as students, their sense of self and long-term prognosis improve. They argued that providing the needed support for these students would also enrich the institutional environment because other students, staff, and faculty would have a real-life experience in humanitarian and ethical issues. If colleges are to continue moving in this direction, efforts are needed to work through the biases against mental illness that have shaped policy and practices in this arena.

The addition of counseling resources is not likely in the near future so most college counseling and mental health centers must make a commitment to meet the needs of students with emotional disabilities in the face of significant limitations. Major institutional commitment, including high-level administrative support, and a broad awareness of relevant issues among residence hall staff, student affairs staff, and involved faculty and administrators are necessary for a comprehensive and successful approach to these students. Such support should not in any way alter normal academic and disciplinary programs (Amada, 1993).

Effective systemic approaches required to support students with psychological disabilities typically include five components: counseling services to the student; consultation with connected students, staff, and faculty; establishment of "safe" alternative places to sleep if staying alone is too risky; access to short-term psychiatric hospitalization; and knowledge of longer-term psychiatric centers with expertise in the specific area of emotional dysfunction. An ideal arrangement for a student with a chronic mental illness might be for the campus counseling or mental health center to provide support but not be the primary treatment provider.

Program Example: Support Group for Multiple Personality Disorder

The group for students with multiple personality disorder (MPD) at the Counseling and Testing Center, University of Kentucky, was started with some trepidation by a therapist who had some experience with MPD clients. This group was difficult to get started because it was hard to identify people with this diagnosis who also wanted to be in a group. The nucleus of the MPD group was two women who had been in a sexual-abuse group the previous semester. Ads were placed in the school newspaper, and fliers were posted all over campus. After a lengthy period two other women with MPD were located who were in individual therapy at the time and whose membership in the group was supported by their therapists. All the members had accepted MPD as being an accurate description for the group even if they were uncomfortable with that label. All of them had been in individual therapy for considerable time. This was a special population of MPDs in that they were functional enough to be in a higher education setting and were far enough along in therapy to be able to tolerate a group experience.

The group was seen as a supportive and safe environment where members could talk with each other about the experience of being "multiple" and attempting to get college degrees. At times it became a process group because interpersonal issues between members had to be addressed. The members all requested some structured time and exercises geared to their child alters. The group was not seen as the appropriate place to deal with sexual-abuse memories. In the first, organizational meeting the "internal self-helpers" emerged and generated a list of possible topics: love, trust, friendship, anger, appropriate boundaries, and physical touch. The members insisted on a check-in format for starting the group where each member gave the highlights of the week. Many of these highlights became discussion topics. The length of the group was two hours. The members usually wanted additional minutes because it took them all considerable time to get used to the group and to feel somewhat comfortable.

They all became accomplished in quickly recognizing each other's different alters. They requested certain alters to make appearances as well. The freedom to "switch alters" and the normalization process seemed beneficial for all the members.

Attendance was good, with members being quite committed to the group, especially as time went on. An absence usually signaled a crisis for a member. The group met for about a year. Continuation was not possible because new members were difficult to locate.

Source: C. O'Neill, associate director, Counseling and Testing Center, University of Kentucky, personal communication, 1996.

A brief-therapy approach is particularly difficult to implement with students with emotional disabilities. In most cases, their needs are chronic and sometimes intense. Gilbert (1992) discussed the ethical issues involved in initiating treatment with students with severe psychopathology. He emphasized the importance of institutional agreement on the role of the counseling center in such cases. He also indicated that the lack of research on long-term curative treatment versus short-term stabilization counseling increases the difficulty of making decisions about initiating treatment. Small centers, particularly those without a health center with infirmary facilities or those without access to psychiatric hospitalization, may not be able to offer services because of ethical problems.

Mandated Clients

College counseling-center directors are reporting a significant increase in the demand for "disciplinary counseling." Causes of this increase include a movement in higher education toward the concept of being disciplined communities, increased concern about liability, a perception that personal problems may be associated with disruptive behavior in some students, and pressure from the ADA to serve rather than sever students with behavioral problems resulting from psychological disabilities.

Historically, Williamson's (1961) student-personnel approach specifically included connecting counseling with disciplinary action within higher education. However, most helping professions since the early 1960s have expressed discomfort with doing mandatory counseling, sometimes viewing it as an oxymoron because the essential ingredients of successful therapy—confidentiality, administrative neutrality, and volunteerism—do not exist. A national survey by Stone and Lucas (1994) demonstrated the mixed sentiments held by university and college counseling-center staff. Responses from 115 counseling-center directors out of 200 AUCCCD members were 52 percent yes and 48 percent no to the question "Should university and college counseling centers do disciplinary counseling?"

Moreover, many of the directors whose centers engaged in disciplinary counseling wished they did not, and the majority of respondents felt that disciplinary counseling raised serious ethical concerns.

Some type of mandatory counseling is requested by almost all colleges and universities. For example, disciplinary leverage is typically utilized to get students in violation of alcohol policies to attend assessment sessions or educational classes or both (Meilman, 1992). Mandating that students at high risk for academic failure attend academic-skills and support groups is also common (see Schwitzer, Grogan, Kaddoura, and Ochoa, 1993). College counseling centers and mental health services have a number of options. Some staffs refuse to take mandated clients. Other centers take them only for certain issues such as sexual harassment or alcohol education. Still other units carry out a single-session assessment but provide follow-up therapy only if the student chooses it voluntarily. Regardless of the option selected, counseling center staff may experience a conflict of interest between what is best for the student and what is best for the institution (Gibbs and Campbell, 1984).

Stone and Lucas (1994) offer a useful distinction between "disciplinary education" and "disciplinary therapy." Most college centers are invested in education, and providing a session or more of education tailored to a particular violation of campus policy can be viewed as an extension of this education. Doing so is not without problems because it is a deviation from what is usually expected of college mental health staff. In addition, some would argue that providing mandatory education generates a negative feeling toward counseling services. However, if done correctly, disciplinary education can receive positive feedback.

The issue of mandatory therapy is more complex than that of mandatory education. When the primary concern is the student, rather than the student's impact on others or the institution, then free collaboration between client and counselor and the absence of significant role conflicts are essential. Forcing a student to receive ongoing counseling is probably counterproductive. At present, the best approach for college and university counseling-center staff is first to educate others about the difference between mandatory education and mandatory counseling and then to offer disciplinary education while resisting providing mandatory ongoing counseling. Some college counseling centers and mental health services provide a single mandatory assessment session followed by optional continuation of counseling. Students often choose to continue therapy once they are empowered not to return if they do not wish to. This choice may tie in to issues of autonomy and independence. Thus, giving control back to the students may eliminate the need for them to resist exploration of their behavior, feelings, thoughts, and situations. Such an approach may not be possible with students who are particularly unstable.

Program Example: Mandatory Assessment with Recommendations

At the University of North Carolina at Wilmington the hearing officer may refer students with alcohol and other drug-related violations to the Student Development Center for an assessment with recommendations. These steps are followed:

1. The purpose and importance of the referral are explained by the hearing officer.
2. The student is given the date by which the appointment must be initiated with the Student Development Center and the date by which the assessment must be completed. Typically, three weeks are allowed.
3. A copy of the Consent for Release of Information form is given to the student and mailed to the Student Development Center.
4. If the student does not show up for the appointment, the Student Development Center notifies the office of the dean of students. The dean's office contacts the student, and the student meets with the dean or a designee. If no extenuating circumstances for missing the appointment are offered, the student is referred to an off-campus agency at the student's expense. If that option is not acceptable to the student, the student pays thirty dollars to the Substance Abuse Education and Prevention Fund and is given another appointment at the Student Development Center.
5. If the student is given another appointment, the dean notifies the Student Development Center. The student is also required to bring the receipt for payment to the Student Development Center.
6. The counselor provides the hearing officer with a summary or recommendations from the substance abuse assessment within two days of the appointment. The recommendation can be that no further counseling is necessary or the student can be referred to the Substance Abuse Education Group or the student can be given an individualized program for counseling.
7. The counselor notifies the hearing officer by letter if the student is not following through with recommendations and on completion of the requirements.

Source: P. Johnston, director, Student Development Center, University of North Carolina at Wilmington, personal communication, 1995.

A role conflict can occur when staff at college counseling centers conduct assessments to determine whether a mandatory withdrawal is necessary or whether a student who has been withdrawn for a specified period should be readmitted to the institution. In this situation the solution that is healthier for the individual can be different from the solution that is less stressful for the institution. When a student with emotional handicaps is involved, the student's legal rights and the liability issues described earlier can become paramount. Many schools have changed their policies so that the evaluation must be conducted by outside, nonaffiliated personnel. Mandatory counseling rather than dismissal for this group of students creates a particular challenge because resources are usually already overstretched.

Additional discussion of various ethical dilemmas involving involuntary assessment, mandatory counseling, and psychiatric withdrawal is included in Chapter Fourteen.

Adult Learners

Because of decreases in the number of eighteen-year-olds, many predicted a major enrollment crisis would hit higher education in the mid-1980s. This decrease did not occur because of two factors. First, the percentage of traditional-age students going to college increased, and, second and more important, more adult learners (or nontraditional students) are attending college than at any previous time. Adults are in college for many reasons, including to prepare for new occupations, to change careers after losing a job, and to earn an income subsequent to a divorce.

Adult learners often bring to their studies an intensity and seriousness that are lacking in many traditional students, who are simultaneously focusing much of their energy on nonacademic endeavors. Nontraditional students have a wealth of experiences to share with others. They may also bring along significant psychological or interpersonal baggage acquired after many years of life; this baggage can cause significant difficulties in academic performance. College counseling staffs are often challenged to learn new techniques and to adjust their therapy for these students, a number of whom are first-generation students (Chartrand, 1992).

Program Example: Women's Reentry Counseling Workshop

A one-day intensive counseling workshop was put together by staff at Oregon State University to help reentering women meet various needs: for example, to identify a support group, to find time to fulfill personal responsibilities, to feel academically competent to succeed in college, and to deal with their expectations of themselves. This structured counseling session included activities to help the women network, reduce stress and manage time, deal with health issues, be assertive, manage finances, and become familiar with the campus and its resources. The women were also encouraged to contact a counselor at mid-term to talk about current stress, family situation, finances, and academic issues and to bring up unexpected problems they had encountered.

Source: Flynn, Vanderpool, and Brown, 1989.

◆ ◆ ◆

Clearly, providing effective counseling services to special groups of students requires an understanding of both their developmental experiences and their experiences within the campus environment. Racism, prejudice, and stereotyping make counseling diverse groups of students especially challenging; providing such counseling requires training in skills and awareness. Also, making counseling appealing to diverse groups requires effective outreach to the different campus communities and a strong commitment to providing special and if necessary flexible kinds of services. Counseling students who are involuntarily referred is difficult and somewhat controversial; however, the possibility of preventing further problems for both the students and society makes the challenge worth pursuing.

As is evident from the brief discussions of several different special populations, these groups present many needs and challenges to college counselors. Traditional counseling models often do not apply or do not work, and counselors must make special efforts to understand the developmental obstacles, sometimes involving racism and other insidious forms of discrimination, that students who are members of these groups face. Counselors must also focus on environmental issues; they cannot disregard the social, political, and cultural changes that are necessary to make the college or university a productive environment. Prevention, in this sense, is part of the treatment.

PART TWO

STRATEGIES FOR OUTREACH AND SYSTEMIC INTERVENTIONS

In this part of the book the emphasis is on prevention and outreach to the campus community. Chapter Eight includes a review of prevention and developmental theory as applied to college students, and Chapter Nine describes an activist, initiator-catalyst approach, a logical extension of previous outreach models. Chapters Ten, Eleven, and Twelve discuss applications of this activist model with a focus on faculty and student development, campus public health issues, and promoting diversity on campus. The prevention, outreach, and community-development material presented in this part complements some of the material on counseling services in Part One but has a distinctly different focus.

CHAPTER EIGHT

PROMOTING PREVENTION THROUGH OUTREACH AND CONSULTATION

Advocates for counseling and mental health outreach programs often use the following story to illustrate the need for prevention:

> One day a great healer was called from his village to the side of a stream to assist a man who had fallen into the stream and was near death. The healer worked furiously to revive the victim, to keep him warm, and to nurse him back to health. The next day he was called again to deal with another victim who had fallen into the stream. He was called more and more frequently to help people who had fallen into the stream until finally he just didn't have enough time to minister to all the victims. Finally, a wise woman in the village asked him whether he knew why so many people were falling into the stream. With a great flash of insight the healer realized that he ought to go upstream to see whether he could stop the villagers from falling into the stream rather than expending all his resources trying to heal them after they almost drowned.

The message in this story is simple: put your effort into stopping the problem before it occurs. There is great wisdom in this parable and its application to psychology and to counseling and mental health services in a college community.

Unfortunately, the reality of prevention is considerably more complicated! Counselors cannot always help people avoid falling into the stream. We have not yet devised strategies for attitude and behavior change that will consistently convince people to avoid harmful and self-destructive behavior. Sometimes the self-destructive behavior (falling into the stream or maybe jumping in) feels good, at least for the moment. At other times the destructive behavior appears to be a result of social and economic forces that the counselor has no power to change. Consequently, it would appear that for some time to come there will be a need for new and creative approaches to prevention.

In addition to the ever-present demand for counseling and crisis services, college counselors are faced with a myriad of preventive and developmental needs. They must help the campus prevent a number of serious and sometimes life-threatening events—HIV, rape, other types of violence, suicide—and at the same time work toward becoming a positive educational force within the institution by helping students to grow and develop so that they can be successful in the institution. Students must, for example, develop the interpersonal skills and self-confidence that enable them to participate in classroom and independent academic work, and they must develop a sense of purpose and direction in order to actively pursue their educational goals.

This dual outreach mission of prevention and development can be overwhelming to a counseling or mental health center. Certainly counselors cannot take on the major responsibility for all prevention and development. In many ways the growth of what might be called an outreach-consultation philosophy in college counseling has been hampered by the inability of counselors both to narrow down the preventive and developmental tasks to which they can attend and to involve the whole campus community in large-scale preventive and developmental activities. A number of relevant suggestions regarding needs and approaches will be presented in the next several chapters, which focus on an activist approach to the campus community.

This chapter addresses some definitional issues and comments on the growth of outreach approaches in college counseling. Terms such as *consultation, outreach, prevention, development,* and *environmental design* are frequently used but often with little precision. Although real precision is not possible because of the overlap and interrelatedness of the terms, it is important to work toward clear definitions and an understanding of how these terms are applied. The chapter will specifically include a consideration of outreach and consultation, prevention, development, and environmental assessment and design. A brief consideration of the historical context and development of general community outreach and consultation is also included.

Outreach and Consultation: The Methods

The terms *outreach* and *consultation* are used in a general way to identify any activity by college counselors that is focused outside the counseling or mental health center. The activities may be direct or indirect, preventive or developmental (definitions are given later). Stone and Archer (1990, p. 557) used a simple, common-sense definition of consultation and outreach. Consultation is "any activity where a staff member provides advice and assistance based on psychological principles to a clearly understood client (group, office, department, club, and others)." Outreach is "any organized program, workshop, media effort, class, or systematic attempt to provide psychological education—includes systematic attempts to modify the campus environment."

In one sense the basic difference is in the relationship to the consumer or target of the service. In most consultation activities the client is clearly defined and the service is requested; these activities are similar to counseling, where the user of the service makes a request. Outreach is usually a more targeted educational activity that may or may not be requested by the consumer. Complicating the simple definitions is the fact that consultation may be a part of outreach (counselors may consult with a fraternity as part of a larger outreach program to decrease substance abuse) or outreach may be a part of consultation (counselors may offer an educational or training workshop on substance abuse as part of a consultation with the office of the dean of students on campus substance abuse). The nuances of the definitions are not important, but an understanding of the two different approaches and how they fit into an overall community outreach effort and into a specific approach (such as the initiator-catalyst approach advocated in the next chapter) is important.

Gerald Caplan (1970) popularized mental health consultation in his book *Theory and Practice of Mental Health Consultation;* his four types (client-centered case consultation, consultee-centered case consultation, program-centered administrative consultation, and consultee-centered administrative consultation) are still regarded highly by professionals in the mental health field. Mendoza (1993) presented a cogent review of Caplan's consultation types. "In client-centered case consultation, the consultee approaches the consultant for assistance with a difficult client case." (The consultee is the direct service provider; the goal is prescriptive; the target is the student client.) "The primary focus in consultee-centered case consultation is the elucidation and correction of the consultee's professional shortcomings that have a deleterious effect on his or her functioning with regard to a particular case." (The consultee is the direct service provider; the goal is educative; the target is the consultee.) "In program-centered administrative consultation, the consultant is invited by an administrator (or group of administrators) to help with problems in program development, [or] the planning and implementation of organizational policies." (The consultee is the administrator; the goal is prescriptive; the target is a program.) "In consultee-centered administrative consultation, the consultant is called by one or more members of the administrative staff to help them effectively carry out their duties, such as program development, the implementation of policies, and personnel management." (The consultee is the administrative staff; the goal is educative; the target is the consultee.) (pp. 530–535)

Several theorists have expanded on Caplan's work in ways relevant to college counseling and mental health. For example, while Caplan advocated that consultation should be done with individuals, Altrocchi (1972) argued that group consultation with paraprofessionals and adjunct personnel offers particular additional advantages. Parsons and Meyers (1984) have reconceptualized some of Caplan's work for school settings. They have introduced a set of common conflicts surrounding authority, dependence, anger and hostility, and overidentification. Pryzwansky (1977), also writing about educational settings, advocates that where joint responsibility is possible, collaboration is better received within these settings than the traditionally hierarchical structure of Caplan's approach.

Four other consultation perspectives (behavioral, process, organizational, and advocacy) also merit the attention of college counseling and mental health center staff. Behavioral consultation (Bergan, 1977) and behavioral-systems consultation (Maher, 1981) were both developed within school settings and provide frameworks within which college counselors can use the significant experience they have with these approaches to assist the work of other staff, administrators, faculty, and students as paraprofessionals. Process consultation (Schein, 1978) uses a facilitator or catalyst who targets the interactions of group members— what they say and do as they set goals, solve problems, or resolve disagreements. As a facilitator, the college counselor has a sense of what the viable solutions are and assists the group at arriving at them. As a catalyst, the college counselor is a codiscoverer of solutions along with the group. Organizational consultation (Aplin, 1985) emphasizes helping people (students, faculty, staff) grow and develop within organizational contexts. The four intervention targets typically involved in organizational consultation are diagnostics, process, structure, and individuals. Advocacy consultation (Daugherty, 1995) has an active, campuswide focus and offers particular promise in working with students with special needs (for example, minority students, GLB students, students with disabilities). College counselors functioning as advocacy consultants deliberately deal with issues of power and political influence and how they can be effected or used. Chapter Nine discusses this idea further.

Prevention and Development: The Goals

Consultation and outreach refer to the method or process of the activity, while prevention and *development* refer to the goals of the activity. *Prevention,* as the name implies, involves stopping a negative activity before it starts. As illustrated by the story at the beginning of the chapter, when negative events such as student suicide or the transmission of HIV are prevented, the extensive negative consequences of these activities can be avoided. *Development* and the related term *student development* refer to efforts to help students develop in healthy and productive ways.

Drum and Lawler (1988) included the concepts of prevention, development, and counseling in a model with seven gradations of assistance for college students, going from preventive to developmental to psychotherapeutic interventions. They see the sense of urgency and level of motivation as being low for strictly preventive interventions (for example, eating wholesome foods) and moderate to low for developmental interventions (for example, developing effective interpersonal skills for romantic relationships). For psychotherapeutic interventions they note that urgency and motivation are high for less severe problems but mixed for more dysfunctional life patterns.

Student motivation is an extremely important factor to consider when implementing prevention and development programs for college populations. As Drum and Lawler (1988) point out, students are more likely to want to participate in counseling than in developmental or preventive programs. They tend to feel the need for a solution to a particular problem more than for development or prevention of that problem. Herein lies a difficult dilemma for college counselors. Should they respond to needs for counseling that are clearly stated by students or to needs for prevention and development that are not as clearly stated or felt by students? Few college counselors have not attempted to present or facilitate a prevention or developmental program with a small or limited audience. Broader community or systems approaches, such as the ecosystems approach discussed later in this chapter or an extension called the initiator-catalyst approach presented in the next chapter, rely much less on student motivation and attendance at programs. They do, however, depend heavily on the motivation and willingness of others in the campus community to become involved and on a sophisticated needs assessment.

Prevention is traditionally categorized as primary, secondary, and tertiary. Conyne (1987) in his book *Primary Prevention Counseling* defined primary prevention as being proactive or reactive, anticipating potential disorder, being aimed at a population at risk, offering before-the-fact interventions, being delivered directly or indirectly, counteracting harmful circumstances that contribute to the problem, promoting emotional robustness in the population at risk, protecting the population at risk, and having the full competence of that population as the goal (p. 15). He differentiated between proactive and reactive primary prevention. Proactive primary prevention is used to eliminate noxious stressors present in the system or society, while reactive primary prevention is an attempt to help individuals cope with existing pathogenic environmental stressors. For example, on a college campus proactive primary prevention might involve organizational activities with a department focusing on how it can decrease the stressors it creates for students. Reactive primary prevention might involve campuswide efforts to help students learn how to manage stress. Secondary prevention is the early detection and treatment of problems before they become serious, and tertiary prevention is the rehabilitation of seriously disturbed people and their return to the community.

Prevention is really a mental health term and suffers some in its application to an educational setting. Education itself, in many respects, is preventive. For example, if we teach students how to manage their lives productively (for example, how to manage their emotions or how to develop effective relationships) we are "preventing" any number of future mental health problems.

One way to define and discuss developmental interventions is to identify the dimensions within which student development takes place. Theoretically, if one knows the typical developmental needs and challenges of students, then both systemic and person-centered programs can be devised to intentionally facilitate growth. Although a number of other developmental theories apply to college students (both traditional-age students and adults returning to school), Chickering's (1969) theory of student development is the most specific to college students because it includes considerable information and research on how the institutional environment (academic and social) affects student development. In an update of this theory, Chickering and Reisser (1993) depend heavily on Pascarella and Terenzini's (1991) book reviewing twenty years of research on college students. The following are the updated Chickering dimensions:

1. Developing competence—intellectual, physical and manual, interpersonal.
2. Managing emotions—awareness and acknowledgment, appropriate channels for release, balance of self-control and release.
3. Moving through autonomy toward interdependence—emotional independence, instrumental independence, healthy forms of interdependence.
4. Developing mature interpersonal relationships—tolerance and appreciation of differences, capacity for intimacy.
5. Establishing identity—comfort with body and appearance; comfort with gender and sexual orientation; sense of self in social, historical, and cultural context; clarification of self-concept through roles and life-style; sense of self in response to feedback from valued others; self-acceptance and self-esteem; personal stability and integration.
6. Developing purpose—vocational plans and aspirations, personal interests, and interpersonal and family commitments.

7. Developing integrity—humanizing values, personalizing values, developing congruence (matching personal values with socially responsible behavior) (Chickering and Reisser, 1993, pp. 45–51).

A number of student affairs and student development offices use this list as a curriculum and target all their activities at one of the developmental goals. They sometimes involve other members of the campus community in this effort.

Because of the increase in the number of returning adult students, it is important to examine Chickering's theory for its relevance to adults. In this regard some of the dimensions make more sense than others. "Developing competence" can apply to adults in the sense that their return to college usually signals a decision on their part to increase their competence intellectually, usually in regard to a new career. "Developing purpose" is also often related to the pursuit of a new career. This pursuit and the accompanying sometimes radical shifts in life-style and focus can indeed signal the development of a new or at least different identity. "Managing emotions," "developing integrity," and "developing mature interpersonal relationships" seem age-related and more applicable to traditional-age students. One could argue, however, that development occurs throughout the life span in all these areas and that the college experience can often profoundly affect adults in these areas even though they are at different developmental stages and have much more life experience than traditional-age students.

A number of developmental theories not specifically related to the college environment can also be useful in understanding typical patterns and issues of adults. Schlossberg, Waters, and Goodman (1995) in *Counseling Adults in Transition* provide an excellent chapter of background information on current theories of adult development. They divide these theories into four categories. The first category, "contextual," includes the theories of Rosenbaum, Kanter, Kohn, Neugarten and Neugarten, and Hareven. For adults in higher education the context includes the campus culture and environment. The second category, "developmental," includes theories that emphasize age and resolution of issues and that are domain-specific. Chickering's theory would fit into this category because of its focus on developmental tasks and domains. Other theories in this second category include those of Levinson, Erikson, Gooden, Josselson, Loevinger, Kohlberg, and Belenky. The authors also include Carol Gilligan's theory, which emphasizes the different paths of men and women, and the theories of Cross and Helms, who cover the development of racial identity. The third category, "life-span perspective," emphasizes individual differences and continuity of individual development over the life span. These theories include those of Neugarten, Vaillant, Pearlin and Lieberman, Brim, and Kagan. Finally, the last category, "transitional," focuses on the impact of transitions on development. Because of the often radical change in life-style that occurs when an adult attends college, these theories have direct applicability to returning adult students. Lowenthal, Chiriboga, Pearlin, Lazarus, Kastenbaum, and Schlossberg are included as theorists in this category. Schlossberg, Waters, and Goodman (1995) find it particularly useful to use transitions as a central point when discussing adult counseling. Certainly, this transition focus also works well when considering development and prevention programs for adult students in higher education.

The idea of using a theory or set of goals to drive outreach and consultation efforts by college counselors has great merit. Counselors might focus on growth in a particular dimension, perhaps even with a preventive aspect (for example, work on stress management to help students learn to manage emotions and to prevent alcohol abuse, or work focused on helping adult students with career and family transitions). The college counselor's role in student development is discussed in Chapter Ten.

Environmental Assessment and Design

In addition to the consultation-outreach and prevention-development distinctions, there is the difference between a direct teaching-skills approach and an indirect approach to general outreach activities. Attempts to modify the campus environment, subsystems, or cultural norms fall into the indirect category. An ecosystems or environmental design approach is a promising example. Conyne and Clack (1981) referred to the ecosystem model as an attempt to apply environmental design to college campuses. According to Aulepp and Delworth (1978), the model is used "to identify environmental-shaping properties in order to eliminate dysfunctional features and to incorporate features that facilitate student academic and personal growth" (p. ix). Huebner (1979, p. 12) summarized the basic elements of an ecosystem intervention process: (1) some effort at gaining institutional or subinstitutional support for the project; (2) a working group ("planning group" or "team") composed of representatives of major constituencies in the setting; (3) a project design, including instrument construction (most teams design their own survey instruments); (4) data collection, typically done using a sampling technique; (5) data analysis; (6) interventions based on the data, often including the dissemination of analyzed data to the original respondents or to subunits responsible for the various areas assessed; (7) a reassessment of the environment after interventions have been made and some time has elapsed.

Barrow, Harsilano, and Bumbalough (1987) reported an application of the ecosystems model to an identified group of January freshmen at Duke University. They formed an assessment and planning team to study what they called the integration difficulties of these students. In Phase I the January freshmen and their environment were studied. The following methods were used: a survey of student reactions, interviews of students, a career-planning-needs survey, interviews with campus student service offices, a survey of team members' perceptions. They identified two trends. First, the differences between regular freshmen and January freshmen were on social and self-esteem dimensions rather than in academic or career development areas. Second, the January freshmen housed together had fewer social integration problems than did those not housed together. Phase II involved interventions such as placing more of the January freshmen together in dorms and instituting a buddy system for them. This is a good illustration of the adaptation of an ecosystems approach for use with a specific campus group and problem.

Many of the task-force approaches that are so popular on contemporary campuses for resolving problems follow this general systems model. The assessment and evaluation components are often not particularly strong, and the "need" is often politically related (for example, the president feels pressure from some constituency to resolve a problem, often because of a particular campus event). However, charging a group of people to examine a problem and come up with solutions is very much in the spirit of this approach. Counselors can and often do play an important role in many of these task forces.

Development of Outreach and Consultation Approaches

Since the late 1960s and early 1970s, college counselors and psychologists have moved in the direction of preventive and developmental activities. Morrill and Hurst (1990) provided a fascinating account of how many of the early theories and applications of preventive and student development approaches were developed at Colorado State University. They described the conditions that led to the now famous "cube" conceptualization of counseling interventions at the individual, group, and systems level and to the development of environmental assessment and ecological mapping. Warnath (1973) in one of the first books about college counseling identified the need for counselors to confront systemic problems in the campus environment and to attempt to intervene in some way. Strange (1994) traced the general growth of a "student development" approach within student affairs, citing the developmental theories of Heath, Perry, Kohlberg, and Chickering, published in the late 1960s and early 1970s, and the beginning of the American College Personnel Association's Tomorrow's Higher Education project as major milestones in the student development movement.

Stone and Archer (1990) argued that the challenges facing outreach and consultation programs will increase. They reported (from a 1990 survey) that counseling-center staff spent about 24 percent of their time in outreach and consultation activities. This is a significant portion of time, particularly if one considers that another sizable portion of time (in addition to individual and group counseling) is spent in training, administration, and other activities. Because of their location in medical settings, student mental health staff probably spent less time in outreach and consultation activities in the past, but many such centers are experiencing considerable pressure to help provide some of the public health prevention activities previously mentioned.

Although almost a quarter of counseling-center staff time is spent in outreach and consultation activities, there are strong demands and needs for more efforts to positively influence the entire campus community. June (1990) in a reaction to the Stone and Archer (1990) article argued for a less conservative, more expansive role for counseling centers. He objected to the emphasis on limits in the article and suggested that counseling centers need to set significant systems-change goals. Crego (1990) offered a similar criticism and called for new paradigms for counseling and mental health services comparable to the "cube" conceptualization, which broadened the scope of service to the entire campus community. Certainly, a major challenge is to develop new paradigms and models for counseling outreach that will provide powerful system interventions.

To update the original "cube" model (Morrill, Oetting, and Hurst, 1974), Pace, Stamler, Yarris, and June (1996) suggested an "interactive cube" with a more global perspective. They proposed several changes from the original cube to their interactive cube (pp. 321–325):

1. From a focus on counseling-center functions to a focus on the institution as a system
2. From the center as isolated, singular, independent to the community as an interdependent system
3. From a fixed structure to a living system
4. From a closed system, unidirectional and nonpermeable, to an open system, multidirectional and permeable
5. From primarily internal decision making to decision making in consultation with the campus community and customer-driven
6. From "all things to all people" resource allocation to a homeostatic balance of resources and services
7. From a noncollaborative style of providing expertise to collaboration with the university community in which all provide expertise

Some of the suggestions for the integrated cube are not clear or well-defined, such as the shift to a "homeostatic balance of resources and services" or the movement from a closed, nonpermeable system to a multidirectional, permeable one. In particular, the major questions relating to resource allocation and how to deal with competing demands are not answered. However, the basic idea presented— that the entire college or university system become the primary target of intervention with the cooperation and agreement of other members of the campus community—does indeed suggest new challenges and types of interventions.

◆ ◆ ◆

For many years college counselors have understood the importance and value of focusing on the college environment and on preventive and developmental activities, and progress has been steady, though modest. As mentioned earlier targeting an entire campus and preventing self-destructive behavior or encouraging development in all students have been at times overwhelming projects for counselors. However, even though technology and resource limitations make this task daunting, the need for college counselors to participate directly in the education process provides a strong argument for continued and even increased campuswide involvement. Schroeder (1996) suggested that the primary role of student affairs should be to promote "seamless" learning, integrating all aspects of learning in the college environment. Although this concept is certainly not new, the emphasis on a direct connection with the primary mission of the institution clearly is a response to downsizing and the elimination of "nonessential" programs. Counseling and mental health centers need to heed this advice and focus on how they might help students grow and develop within an integrated learning environment. Schroeder suggests fewer individual workshops and presentations on relationship skills, stress management, and so forth, and more emphasis on activities like working with an English composition instructor or an English department on units like "anxiety in modern life," which have the potential to help a student learn both to write and to manage anxiety.

In facing the need for more prevention and development activities and increasing demands for counseling, college counselors clearly must develop new ways to approach outreach that allow them to use their time efficiently so that they can have a positive impact on more students. Approaches that focus on the larger campus community and on working with others to improve learning environments and change norms that perpetuate self-destructive behavior are sorely needed.

CHAPTER NINE

COUNSELORS AS INITIATORS AND CATALYSTS FOR CHANGE

One promising approach college counselors can use to meet the increased need for development and prevention outreach involves a further evolution of current proactive approaches. This initiator-catalyst approach is presented in this chapter. The discussion starts with a basic exposition of the approach; subsequent sections describe how to use new technology, harness the power of students, faculty, and staff, make assessments, and take possible political consequences into consideration.

Shifting to an Activist Approach

As mentioned in the previous chapter, Crego (1990) called for a paradigm shift in campus counseling and mental health centers comparable to the shift that began in the 1960s from mainly clinical counseling to a community-based, outreach orientation. The shift suggested here is for counselors to expand their outreach role from being consultants and teachers of skills to being active initiators and catalysts for change. The shift is more practical than conceptual because counselors have written and talked about such proactive approaches for years. Taking on the role of activist is a logical step toward extending current practices, but it is by no means a small or simple one. This kind of action-oriented approach to outreach and consultation is based on two important assumptions.

First, counseling and mental health staffs cannot, by themselves, provide comprehensive student development and prevention programs, nor can they engineer constructive campus change without considerable support. Prevention and development programs that include systems change are complex and therefore require major involvement by many campus groups, including faculty. The counselor's role as catalyst and initiator fits this reality well because it includes a recognition that important components of any community must be involved in systems change. Stone and Archer (1990) recommended that outreach and consultation programs be embedded in the university. This concept is in line with an initiator-catalyst approach, where counselors work toward designing and starting educational and environmental change programs that can be incorporated into the organization and culture of the institution.

The second important assumption underlying an initiator-catalyst role is that objectives must be prioritized. Because all resources are limited, outreach and consultation activities must have goals that hold the most potential for success and that are the most important. To use a term from the business world, counselors need to "leverage" their impact by initiating programs with campus groups that have the most potential for influencing students and the larger community. (A concept related to this idea is the "pyramid" approach (Archer and Kagan, 1973)— training a few student paraprofessionals who in turn train others, thereby maximizing the effect of the training.)

Proposing an initiator-catalyst role for counselors is not to suggest that they should take responsibility for, or have time to be involved in, comprehensive organizational or social-cultural change on campus. An initiator-catalyst is not a "superman" able to single-handedly engineer campus change. Taking on the initiator-catalyst role does mean that counselors should change their focus somewhat and put the time and energy they do have for outreach and consultation into cooperative, campuswide projects that can make a difference for large numbers of students. With the continuing press on resources and the demand for counseling service in all domains, the allocation of resources to initiator-catalyst activities needs to be done with a good deal of circumspection and realism.

The following are guidelines for an initiator-catalyst approach:

1. Adopt a primary role as initiator-catalyst for systems change (environmental, social, and cultural) with a general goal of improving the campus learning and mental health environment. Directors may be in the best position to carry out much of this mission because of their role as the official representative of the counseling or mental health center to the campus community.
2. Maintain an active involvement in the politics of the institution.
3. Seek out and maintain a role in the assessment mechanism of the institution

to ensure that outcomes include the broad-based objectives usually articulated in college catalogues.

4. Become knowledgeable about mass communication techniques in order to develop and maintain a variety of methods for informing the campus community about developmental and mental health issues.

5. Secure a role in faculty development activities that focus on personal and career issues. The extent of this role will depend on resources, the character of the employee-assistance program (EAP), and the type of faculty development programs on a particular campus.

6. Facilitate the development, maintenance, and coordination of paraprofessional peer education and peer counseling programs on campus.

7. Facilitate and coordinate self-help prevention and development programs using the best available technology.

These recommendations parallel a number of suggestions made by Pace, Stamler, Yarris, and June (1996) in their expansion of the cube model (Morrill, Oetting, and Hurst (1974). They emphasize, among other things, a focus on the institution as a system; an interdependent, systemic community orientation; a homeostatic balance of resources and services; and decision making in consultation with the campus community. They argue for counseling services to be advocates for campuswide systems change in a collaborative manner. This is consistent with the notion of counseling and mental health centers employing an initiator-catalyst approach.

Specific developmental and preventive goals for students—such as overcoming abuse and dysfunctional-family experiences, avoiding unsafe sexual behavior, achieving wellness and general health, dealing with stress and depression, achieving academic success, setting career and life goals, developing self-esteem and identity, and developing integrity and morality—can best be met by using this initiator-catalyst approach. In each of these areas, understanding and modifying dysfunctional parts of the campus social and cultural environment, encouraging social and cultural reinforcement of healthy and growth-producing behavior, and educating students directly about how to manage behavior and develop skills remain a priority. These are complex and difficult interventions that require considerable resources and involvement by many campus groups. The counselor must take on the role of initiator and change agent without always trying to take on the task itself.

To initiate positive environmental change in each of these areas, college counselors must pose and answer three seemingly simple questions: How does the campus environment (physical, social, and cultural) encourage negative learning and behavior in this area? How does the campus environment encourage positive learning in this area? How can the campus environment be changed to decrease negative influences and increase positive influences? Answering these questions and developing strategies for intervention require solid judgments about what is positive and what is negative. The need for change and education may be clear to the entire campus community (nearly everyone would agree that substance abuse and unprotected sex can be harmful), or the mandate for change may be clear to only some members of the campus community (not everyone agrees that heterosexual bias or sexism is a negative aspect of the campus environment and in need of change).

In addition to managing the political problems related to differing values and opinions, counselors must find the strategies and technologies to change student attitudes, culture, and behavior. Take, for example, attempts to change behavior with regard to unprotected sexual activity. Research on changing health behavior has demonstrated that exclusive reliance on cognitive interventions to change beliefs and attitudes is not powerful in changing behavior. Findings regarding AIDS education (Rosenstock, Strecher, and Marshall, 1994) indicate that many other factors, such as self-efficacy (self-confidence in the ability to carry out a behavior) and social influences, are important factors in AIDS prevention behaviors such as using a condom or negotiating sexual practices. A more complete discussion of preventive behavior and theory is included in Chapter Eleven, which covers campus public health needs. Thus, it would seem that prevention programs in this area, particularly those that enhance skills, need to help students feel comfortable using condoms. From an environmental perspective, efforts need to be made to evolve a norm in the student culture that encourages discussion about sexual activity and protection prior to sex—a difficult task given our general cultural heritage regarding decisions about sex, and one that is made even more difficult by the widespread use of alcohol as a way to decrease inhibitions.

This example illustrates a number of the complexities involved in changing student behavior and campus norms. Two requirements for this kind of endeavor stand out. First, a team of knowledgeable faculty and staff needs to work with a group of students to devise interventions, and, second, many different student groups must be involved. Many campuses have developed interdisciplinary committees to confront this particular issue (AIDS prevention and safe sex) as well as other health issues. The counselor's major role as initiator and activist is to help such a group get started and maintain its momentum and to find the resources and wherewithal to attempt serious interventions. In this case, the counselor might also serve as an expert consultant, but the role of initiator-catalyst will require considerably more proactive behavior than that of a reactive consultant.

Relationships, personalities, and specific institutional variables are significant factors in these endeavors. Although reason, data, and demonstrated need ought to be the most important variables in the decision to initiate specific preventive and developmental programs and interventions, other, more random factors are often quite significant. A relationship between a counselor and a biology professor who are neighbors might pave the way for a stress-management program for pre-med students, or a long letter to the provost from parents of a student who committed suicide might be the stimulus for a new suicide-prevention program. Effective performance in the role of initiator-catalyst often involves taking advantage of opportunities when they come up. New resources to take on additional prevention and outreach work often are related to a high-profile need. This is not to say, however, that outreach and prevention programs cannot be based on formal or informal assessment of needs, as will be discussed later in the chapter.

New Technologies

An important part of an initiator-catalyst outreach role is active use of modern information technology. College counselors must embrace new technologies and learn to use them as effective tools in prevention and student development. The use of computers, self-help libraries, and other alternatives to counseling has already been discussed in some detail as a way for students to work on their own problems either as an adjunct to counseling or as an alternative. The content is somewhat different when considering technology for outreach and consultation. However, for outreach programs aimed at teaching specific developmental skills (how to relax, how to manage time, how to be assertive, how to improve relationships) computer training programs, self-help libraries, structured manuals, and the like are utilized in a similar fashion. As previously discussed, the distinction between counseling to help with a specific problem (stress) and outreach to help students develop new developmental skills (stress management) is somewhat blurred.

A more pronounced emphasis on growth and development characterizes self-help technology that is intended for personal development rather than for counseling. Instead of using an interactive computer counseling program on shyness or reading a book about it, a student might check out a series of tapes or videos demonstrating various relationship skills. In reality, self-help technological programs offering both specific problem-solving help and general self-improvement are often offered together. For example, a counseling or mental health center's home page probably includes materials on specific problems (dealing with relationship breakups, anxiety, depression) and also general developmental materials (on effective communication, time management, wellness). Gilles-Thomas (1996) lists thirty-two home pages for counseling and mental health centers. A home page is a directory of information from a particular center; it can also include links to information at other sites. If, for example, students are seeking help with interpersonal development, they may access the home page at their university and find links to information on that topic at universities and colleges all over the world. (See the "Internet Site" program example in Chapter Five.) Audiotapes and some videotapes that are developmentally oriented have been available for some time, but newer technologies, like CD-ROMs, open up new vistas for developmental programs. Comprehensive courses on interpersonal skills or ethical decision making, for example, can be made available on CD-ROMs and checked out of a self-help library.

Although incorporation of new technologies is important, continued development of simple and easily available learning aids, such as short brochures, is important. Many of these brochures are problem-oriented, but they can also be developmentally oriented. For example, every new student could receive a flashy and well-constructed brochure outlining the areas of personal development in college and providing ideas and self-help methods for growth in these areas.

The use of technology for modifying and improving the campus environment is somewhat different from its use as an educational or counseling tool. Probably the most significant application of technology comes in the modification of campuswide or campus subgroup beliefs and related behavior norms. Many kinds of communication technologies can be utilized as powerful tools in this area. AIDS education programs utilizing various kinds of information technologies have increased student awareness of the dangers of unprotected sex and in some cases have changed behavior. The fact that a gap remains between knowledge of the dangers and actual behavior (using condoms) illustrates the difficulty of relying only on communication technology to change student behavior.

A hypothetical example of an attempt to change campus norms and behavior with regard to academic dishonesty illustrates some possibilities in this area. Imagine a campus where the general feeling of students is that competition is so stiff and unrelenting and exams are so unreasonable and unfair that cheating, though undesirable, is understandable and acceptable in some circumstances. A task force on academic honesty is formed as a result of the significant increase in cheating cases. After the beliefs about cheating are identified through a survey conducted by the task force, the task force decides that students need to develop a strong norm against all types of academic dishonesty. In other words, the "acceptance norm" for cheating needs to be replaced by a "no tolerance norm." Because an attempt to change the norm can be undertaken only if there is strong support among the faculty and a number of student groups, the task force needs to educate the campus about the problem and its negative consequences. Campus media outlets (computer sign-ons, cable TV, dorm bulletin boards, brochures, the campus newspaper, messages on campus forms and receipts) can be utilized to educate students about the problem and to change opinions about the acceptability of cheating. Because student input is crucial to the success of the project, this communication effort should be made in concert with numerous other efforts such as actions by student government, by faculty and staff, by clubs and student religious organizations, and discussions in classrooms and in focus groups and workshops. Ongoing monitoring of the message, gathering feedback regarding its reception, and collecting data about changing beliefs and behavior are necessary to assess success and to make changes in focus and methods if necessary.

Harnessing Student, Faculty, Staff Power

The involvement of different campus groups having direct involvement or a stake in the issue is at the heart of an initiator-catalyst approach. Student groups have been used extensively as peer educators, and many paraprofessional programs, such as those directed toward substance abuse, AIDS and other sexually transmitted diseases, and eating disorders, have included students in both a counseling and an education role. When programs involving student paraprofessionals have both a counseling and an educational component, the educational role should be clearly identified as having separate goals, methods, procedures, training, and perhaps even personnel. A student who is a talented paraprofessional counselor might or might not be as good at giving a lecture or leading a workshop or managing a campus effort to change attitudes or norms.

Students can be involved as educators and change agents in several different settings including (1) groups with a specific mission—for example, AIDS peer educators, (2) student government and councils, such as a council on women's issues, (3) other organizations taking on specific educational tasks—for example, a Hispanic alliance working on educating the campus about Hispanic culture, and (4) formal or informal faculty and staff groups formed to provide education and systems change, like a faculty-led GLB alliance to promote gay rights and fight homophobia. Many other combinations of student, faculty, and staff groups are working toward various educational objectives on campuses.

The counselor's role here, as discussed previously, should be primarily as an initiator and catalyst. The counselor's overall objective should be to help initiate working groups and facilitate effective group process and action. The counselor must take an active and sometimes political position in this role.

In order to involve students in various outreach activities, counselors might help students gain academic credit for their experience—for example, credit for work in substance abuse education through the health education or psychology department. In keeping with the initiator-catalyst role, counselors would not try to provide credit themselves but would facilitate practicum experiences in the relevant academic departments.

To involve faculty in examining problems in the learning and mental health environment of the institution and in working toward change, counselors must have academic status, be self-assured and confident, be able to demonstrate their expertise, and have faculty connections. The size of the institution is an important variable here. The larger the institution the more difficult it is for faculty, staff, or anyone who is a part of the institution to feel an attachment to the college or university as a whole. Nonetheless, even at large colleges and universities many faculty are concerned about the institution and about the environment for students. Also, on large campuses, faculty with a particular interest or expertise (or both) in the area being considered probably are present and can be drafted. For example, the previously mentioned task force working on academic dishonesty might be of particular interest to faculty in philosophy, law, religion, education, or criminal justice. Graduate students may also have strong interests in various topics related to the campus environment.

One strategy that fits well with the initiator-catalyst model involves organizational development work with faculty departments and administrative offices. When these groups function effectively, students receive a better quality education in a more productive environment. If, for example, the English department faculty are working well together and are providing a reasonably healthy work environment, the faculty will be responsive to students and student needs, or if the financial aid staff feel valued and involved in a healthy developmental process themselves, the service to students will likely be enhanced. The difficulty here in applying an initiator-catalyst approach involves entry by the counselor into the individual offices and departments. Perhaps the most powerful strategy is one of waiting for and seizing an opportune moment. Although it may be fruitful for a counselor to approach a department head or administrator with feedback from students about a departmental problem, impetus for change is much more likely to come from within the organization. A clear understanding that the counseling or mental health center has the expertise and willingness to become involved in this kind of consultation on campus is important. Both the center and the administrative hierarchy must view this as an important role and must provide the necessary resources.

Some counseling centers have developed consultation teams to target the area of organizational development. Working in concert with faculty or graduate students in organizational psychology or management can be effective if a campus is large enough to have faculty with the right kind of expertise.

On small campuses, personal connections with faculty and staff are especially important. Offering workshops for faculty in personal and professional development often provides an entrée into consultation work with faculty groups and departments. These workshops may be particularly effective if given in conjunction with personnel or EAP programs. The initiator-catalyst role in this case would involve developing a faculty and staff consultation service or perhaps initiating an EAP program with a staff-development component as a separate unit. The counselor might begin as initiator-catalyst and then work into a coordinating or governing role as a member on an EAP advisory council.

Another strategy for involving faculty is to include change projects in the curriculum. For example, a campuswide needs survey or data from counseling and other student affairs offices may indicate that it is difficult for transfer students to meet people and become involved in campus life. Projects to improve this situation might be undertaken by a number of different classes. Marketing and communication classes might work on strategies to market campus services to these students. Psychology classes might develop applied projects focusing on the personal growth and development of these students during the first year. Sociology classes might examine the different student groups on campus and how transfer students might be integrated into them. Human-development classes might approach the problem from the perspective of subgroups of transfer students (such as returning adults) and their developmental needs. Finding creative ways to involve faculty and classes in campus problems and attempts at resolving them is central to the initiator-catalyst approach.

Assessing Individual Student Needs and the Campus Environment

An assessment of student needs and environmental influences is at the heart of any attempt to provide preventive developmental education and to modify the campus environment in a positive direction. Counselors and others on campus interested in a student's general growth and development must be able to understand individual needs and the campus environment's effects on individual and student groups before they can attempt to initiate and serve as catalysts for growth and change. Kuh (1982), Friedlander (1978), and others argued persuasively that increasing diversity and rapidly changing social and environmental conditions require periodic assessment of student needs. Student needs might be described as a rapidly moving target. Surveys, interviews, focus groups, and analyses of data (incidence of rape, HIV-positive rate, number of students seeking counseling for a specific problem, drop-out rates) coupled with developmental theory can be used to determine students' individual needs. More difficult than predicting individual needs is assessing the environment to get a picture of how various physical, social, and cultural forces work on campus. Clearly, assessment of student needs and the campus environment is a significant challenge for college counselors. Skibbe (1986) suggested that needs assessments are seldom made because counseling-center staff members do not feel that they have enough expertise. This conclusion is difficult to accept because counseling and mental health staff are generally the most likely of any student affairs staff to have in-depth training in research methods. Chapter Thirteen, which focuses on research, discusses assessment as part of the research mission of college counselors.

A number of published needs assessments have examined campus needs and the needs of specific groups (Gallagher, Golin, and Kelleher, 1992; Bertocci, Hirsh, Sommer, and Williams, 1992; Harris and Anntonen, 1986; Lamb-Porterfield, Jones, and McDaniel, 1987; Deressa and Beavers, 1988; Minatoya and King, 1984; Hurwitz and Kersting, 1993; Gropper, 1991). These assessments used varying methodologies, questions, and samples. In many instances these surveys led to improvement in services and programs and in some cases to increased staff support. However, an ongoing problem is the effective use of assessment data. Sometimes the data are not useful because little time and thought went into the original instrument and its administration; and sometimes little is done with the data because the energy and money run out after the needs assessment is completed. Needs assessments are complex and time-consuming and probably should not be undertaken unless there is some certainty that the information will be used and that resources are available to develop broad-based intervention programs.

Environmental assessment is also a complex task. How does one assess a college or university environment? A comprehensive assessment is theory-driven, uses the best available instruments and technologies, and includes all important aspects of the campus environment (physical, cultural, social) as well as data on the many subcultures and groups on campus. Such an assessment might be a futile exercise on most campuses because resources are not available to respond in a comprehensive way. However, a broad-based assessment would allow counselors and others on campus to target specific groups and specific problems. Carney (1996), in a chapter discussing the dynamics of campus environments, presented several ways of viewing campus environments that could be used as a focus for assessment. He discussed subcultures, typologies, styles, and person-environment interactions under the broad category of "human aggregates" (the collective characteristics of various groups); organizational structures and organizational dynamics under the category of "organized environments" (the structural-organizational aspects of campuses); and environmental press, social climate, and campus culture under the category of "constructed environments" (ways people construct and perceive their environment).

What is the role of counselors in such an assessment? They typically do not have the resources or the mandate to examine the overall environment, yet their students are affected by all aspects of the campus climate, and student growth and mental health are clearly dependent in significant ways on external pressures and cultural forces. Again, the issue is one of opportunities and priorities. There may be opportunities to participate in broad campus environmental assessments. Perhaps a new president sets up a self-evaluation project. Certainly, a part of the effort might be a comprehensive look at the campus climate and student culture. In this kind of situation the counseling or mental health staff should work to play a role in the entire effort.

In reality, however, environmental assessment is much more likely to be done to answer specific questions about specific issues. For example, an increased incidence of suicide may raise the question of what is causing or encouraging this kind of behavior. Or, as has happened on many campuses, evidence of a large-scale problem with eating disorders may surface (for example, reports of vomit in many bathrooms, increased hospital admissions, increased demands for counseling) and raise questions about a campus climate that somehow encourages or produces this behavior. This particular example illustrates the complexity of this kind of assessment because a campus is part of the larger culture and society. Pressures to be thin in order to be a perfect woman come from the larger society and are probably reflected in many different ways on campus.

How are assessment data used in an initiator-catalyst approach? Suppose a noncomprehensive, issue-focused assessment is undertaken because the campus mental health service sees an increasing number of students involved in relationship violence. A survey providing confirmation of the clinical findings can serve as a stimulus for a campuswide consideration of this issue. Using the initiator-catalyst approach, the mental health staff would determine which campus groups might be involved in a prevention program and how prevention efforts might be institutionalized or embedded in ongoing campus programs. Perhaps a student-government committee could be formed to initiate prevention efforts. The department of communication might assume responsibility for a pilot project conducted by a research and training institute using undergraduate communication majors as interns and graduate students as researchers and program organizers.

Program Example: Use of Assessment Data

The president of Grand Valley State Colleges in Michigan initiated a study in 1992 to assess the climate for female students, staff, and faculty. Because of the expertise within the Counseling Center staff, the director of the Counseling Center was part of a small steering committee appointed to carry out the study. The group contacted several possible consultants to assist with the study and chose a consultant who had been a university counseling-center director earlier in her career.

The consultant visited the campus several times to meet with the steering committee and with several employee and student groups to obtain the information needed to design the study. She developed two questionnaires—one for staff and faculty and one for students. In addition, the consultant reviewed various campus policies and publications.

The results of the study indicated that among faculty and staff men and women saw the climate for women differently. Men perceived the climate to be comfortable and friendly and not different from that for men, whereas women perceived the climate to be more friendly for men than for women. There was less of a difference in perceptions between male and female students. The study also revealed a significant amount of homophobia on campus.

As a result of the study, the president chose four initiatives. He recommended that a day-care center be built for children of staff and students, that a task force on GLB staff and student issues be created, that a women's commission be appointed to monitor the climate for women on an ongoing basis, and that a salary-equity study be completed. Although these were not specifically counseling-center initiatives, the director and one staff member were involved in every step of the process. The director initiated the idea for the study, recommended the consultant, worked with her to design the study, and developed a plan for the women's commission.

Source: Pace, Stamler, Yarris, and June, 1996.

Campus Politics and Systems Change

Pace, Stamler, and Yarris (1992), in a response to the Stone and Archer (1990) monograph on counseling centers in the 1990s, suggested that "counseling centers could also influence campus environments by sponsoring speakers, by addressing issues pertinent to women, or by calling attention to overt sexist practices" (p. 187). They acknowledged that taking a stand on issues might affect the way a center is viewed but argued that assuming an activist role would be a worthwhile endeavor. This is an interesting and difficult challenge for counseling and mental health centers. Pace, Stamler, and Yarris (1992) were not specific about how an activist role would work in this particular instance, but, to take their example, calling attention to overt sexist practices might place a center in opposition to the campus administration or to the beliefs of a large minority or perhaps majority of the student body. If, for example, the center supports a group of female students who are trying to force the resignation of a professor who made "sexist" comments in class, how will those on campus who do not believe that the professor should resign respond to the counseling center's involvement? Will these students and faculty see the center as espousing values and views that would preclude them from using the center for counseling or other services?

Any attempt to modify a campus environment in a way that promotes beliefs and values that most members of the campus community do not hold will certainly alienate some groups. A strong argument can be made for activism by counseling and mental health staffs when a particular group of students is suffering because of a systemic problem or because the group is the target of negative social attitudes and behavior. This would clearly be the situation, for example, for GLB or other minority students on most campuses.

The challenge is to understand the political issues related to any particular issue and to accurately estimate the consequences of any strong public statement or action. Several questions should be considered by counseling or mental health centers considering an activist approach to a potentially controversial campus issue. First, what is the best kind of response for the counseling or mental health center? Will a direct statement, such as a press release or letter in the campus paper, be as effective as forceful behind-the-scenes work? For example, would a statement by the center and several student groups condemning the stress-producing treatment of students by several professors in a particular department be as effective as a phone call to the dean or department chair suggesting a meeting or group discussion with the faculty regarding student concerns?

Second, does the center staff agree that the issue under consideration is clearly one that needs strong action? If the staff is split, it will be difficult to present a clear and unified rationale for action. Consider the issue of separate residence facilities for various ethnic groups. Suppose the housing office feels that separatism is not the way to foster race relations. Although most of the staff members in mental health feel that this is a naive position and that minority students need to be together to build their own ethnic identities, two of the staff just do not feel comfortable taking a strong position against the housing office. Should the center take a position in this instance?

Third, how will the activism affect clients and the various constituencies of the center? Will there be negative consequences with one group if the center takes a stand supporting another? For example, on a conservative campus, the counseling staff considers there to be a great deal of homophobia within the student body and the faculty. The center is considering a strong outreach and education program in this area, but some of the center's strongest administrative and faculty supporters have cautioned against such a program, which they feel will be seen as too radical by the campus. They have warned that many conservative students will not feel comfortable coming in for counseling if they believe that the counseling center is promoting GLB issues. In this case should activism be eschewed because of negative consequences? In another example, a counseling-center staff is approached by a coalition of faculty who are trying to reverse a negative tenure decision by the history department regarding a professor who is a popular teacher.

These coalition faculty members are often allied with student interests and are strong allies of the counseling center and student development activities. If the center staff joins the coalition and opposes the history department, what will the long-term effects be on the relationship between the center and other academic departments?

Fourth, how will the proposed activism affect funding and political support for the counseling or mental health center? How will the university administration view the action? For example, a staff member at a mental health center is about to join a campaign launched by a student and faculty AIDS committee to make condoms readily available on campus. The provost was forced to make condoms available at the student health service, but he feels strongly that it is not appropriate for the university to be more involved in this area. He controls the campus budget. Should the staff member join the campaign?

Fifth, can additional departments, agencies, and student groups be persuaded to join in an activist approach to a controversial issue? For example, a counseling center has noted an alarming increase in alcohol and drug problems within the fraternity system. The center is planning a prevention program that includes a long article in the campus newspaper about the problem, with examples from campus fraternities. How can the center recruit other groups to join them in attacking this issue, which is sure to cause a considerable stir within the student and alumni fraternity communities?

Sixth, what media outlets are available to represent the views of the counseling or mental health staff? Are there outlets that will provide enough space and coverage to adequately cover the issue. For example, a mental health center feels that men's problems and concerns have been overlooked on campus and wants to develop awareness of some of these issues. The staff, however, is afraid that the campus paper will misinterpret the center's stance and accuse it of ignoring the ongoing pressing problems of female students. The paper has a long history of poor reporting and simplifying issues. What are the alternative news outlets?

Seventh, how relevant is the issue under consideration to general student well-being and mental health? Taking the previous tenure example, just how relevant is a tenure question to student counseling and mental health needs? Is this an arena in which the center staff should become involved, or should they stick to issues that seem more directly relevant to their mental health and counseling role?

These questions are not intended to discourage counseling and mental health staffs from taking action-oriented and sometimes controversial stands. In fact, the initiator-catalyst approach to outreach requires a proactive approach. Rather, the questions are intended as an aid for developing a planned activism that includes a judicious weighing of the pros and cons, including a consideration of campus politics and the consequences of an activist approach.

In this chapter an evolution of current outreach practices into an active initiator-catalyst approach was suggested. New technologies, using students, faculty, and staff as allies, and assessment—the primary components of an initiator-catalyst approach—were described. Ways of considering the political ramifications of an activist approach were also included.

CHAPTER TEN

SUPPORTING STUDENT AND FACULTY DEVELOPMENT

Student development and faculty development programs should play an important role in college counseling outreach efforts. Programs in these areas are directly connected to student learning, the central mission of colleges and universities. Student development in various domains, such as the interpersonal, ethical, emotional, and career areas, is directly related to academic success. Faculty members have a profound impact on students, and their personal and professional growth plays a significant role in how they teach and interact with students. As with any of the programs and activities discussed in this book, resources and priorities will determine how and whether they can be accomplished. Resources are particularly important with regard to faculty development. Because most counseling and mental health centers are funded in order to provide services to students, any significant efforts in the faculty development require careful consideration and probably extra funding. It may be difficult to make the argument that faculty development is a good investment of resources, particularly for programs that are not obviously related to the teaching and other academic functions of faculty. As is discussed in this chapter, EAPs can be used as a vehicle for faculty development.

Student development has a long history in college student affairs work, and the positive influence of a variety of "out-of-classroom" experiences on student learning and development has been well documented over the years (Pascarella and Terenzini, 1991). An issue of the *Journal of College Student Development* was devoted to the "student learning imperative." The thrust of the lead article (Schroeder, 1996) was that all student affairs functions, including counseling, must focus on student learning and be relevant to the general educational mission of the college or university. An argument, though certainly not a new one, was made that student learning is holistic and that student development activities must be connected to the rest of the educational mission to create what Kuh (1996) calls "seamless learning." The challenge for counseling and mental health counselors is how to connect their outreach and consultation programs, which sometimes seem to be more oriented more toward mental health, to student learning, which is at the heart of the institution.

Less has been written about faculty development than about student development. But there is documentation of a strong need for faculty development in contemporary higher education, and college counselors can make significant contributions in this area. Gooler (1991) discussed the importance of "professorial vitality." He defined vitality for faculty as including continuing intellectual curiosity, understanding of and commitment to institutional purposes, strong satisfaction with work, commitment to professional purposes, and enthusiasm for and anticipation of the future. Many factors influence faculty vitality including reward systems, working environments, potential for career development, opportunities for personal growth, and relationships with colleagues. Heppner and Johnston (1994) suggested broad-based faculty development initiatives that go beyond traditional sabbatical and leave programs and that relate to personal health, career growth, and adult development. Counselors, of course, cannot take on responsibility for the major faculty development programs, which are typically oriented toward improving teaching and research, but they can consult about and help devise programs on environmental and individual issues that bear directly on career success. Sorcinelli (1994) suggested several areas of work stress for new faculty: time constraints; lack of collegial relations; inadequate feedback, recognition, rewards; unrealistic expectations; insufficient resources; and balancing work and life outside work. Each of these are fertile consultation areas for college counselors.

Student Development

How can the initiator-catalyst approach to outreach and consultation be used to make student development a process that is an integral and "seamless" part of the learning environment? What specific kinds of development should be targeted? How are these kinds of development influenced by the college environment? Where do the developmental efforts of counseling or mental health centers fit in the overall goals for student affairs and the university at large? How can the particular talents of counselors and psychologists be utilized to facilitate developmental efforts?

Chickering's seven developmental dimensions, as updated by Chickering and Reisser (1993), were described in Chapter Eight. Although some of the dimensions apply more to traditional-age college students than to returning adults, in general they provide a useful way of looking at college student development. These dimensions fit well with Schroeder's (1996) "learning imperative," which proposes that developmental goals not be separate from intellectual and academic goals. Counselors have the expertise and experience to be particularly helpful in the following general student development areas: achieving academic success and developing career and life goals, developing integrity and morality, acquiring interpersonal competence, developing mature relationships, acquiring self-esteem, and establishing identity. To work as initiator-catalysts in these areas, counselors must target specific skills, activities, and environments that they wish to influence, and they must focus on facilitating productive activities and environments rather than trying to promote student development directly through teaching and intervention programs.

Academic Success and a Sense of Purpose

Most members of the academic community and the general public consider achieving academic success and gaining a sense of purpose as central developmental goals for college students. From one perspective, all the activities of counseling and mental health centers are ultimately aimed at helping a student be successful in college. In a broader sense, however, academic success by itself is only part of this general developmental goal. A sense of purpose, a career, and a satisfying, prosocial life-style do not necessarily come with a high grade-point average, although academic success is certainly a foundation for all of these. Counseling and mental health centers have traditionally provided developmental services in these areas through career counseling and career development activities, personal and academic counseling, study-skills activities and programs, and preventive programs such as stress management, which directly target blocks to academic success.

These activities are often effective with the students involved, but what kinds of creative activities by counselors might widen this impact? As has been mentioned in previous discussions of the initiator-catalyst role, counselors must consider broad possibilities and then prioritize possible interventions according to which will have the maximum effect. Relative to academic success, the broadest intervention would affect the overall campus learning climate. To ascertain what this climate is, counselors might ask these questions: Is there an ethic among students supporting learning and academic endeavors? Do faculty actively examine how they conduct their courses and try to maximize the success for all their students? These questions get to the heart of the entire higher education enterprise, yet counselors cannot single-handedly take on the task of reforming the campus learning climate.

They can, however, take on subtasks. For example, certain undergraduate courses seem to cause many problems for students. Introductory calculus is often one of these. A counselor might want to convene a small group to examine this situation in detail. This group could consist of sympathetic math faculty and graduate students, someone from a learning-resources center, and representatives from minority and women's groups (whose members often do not take calculus because of fears or poor math backgrounds). A staff member from academic advising might also be included to add perspective on how students select and are placed in math courses, and perhaps a math education expert from a teacher-training program could add expertise about teaching methods and process. Ideally, this group would recommend interventions to improve the situation. A number of possibilities might be tried: different teaching methods; preparation strategies to help women, minorities, and other students at risk succeed; math-anxiety programs, study-help sessions; study groups led by students who have taken the course. The counselor's role would be to initiate and facilitate the group's work.

One should not minimize the difficulty of developing this kind of process. There may be no sympathetic math faculty, or other possible group members may feel overworked already and not be willing to participate. Part of the prioritizing process for activities like this must be an analysis of sources of support and of the possibility of success. Too often the activities of counseling and mental health centers are dictated by staff interest rather than by a reasoned examination of priorities and possibilities. Clearly, staff interests are important and must be considered, but they should not be the paramount rationale for a program.

A number of interesting workshops and courses aimed at helping students find meaning and purpose are offered on college campuses. With an initiator-catalyst approach, counselors can work with faculty to design and facilitate programs and courses in this area that are interdisciplinary and have the potential to become a regular part of the curriculum.

Program Example: Workshop on Meaning

This workshop focuses on helping young people confront feelings of hopelessness and despair about the future and on empowering them to exert control over their destinies. The workshop is run by an interdisciplinary group at Humboldt State University

(California) with leadership from the counseling center. Ratings of the workshop have indicated that it has a strong impact and that hope and empowerment increase among the students involved.

A manual outlining eighteen structured exercises is used in a workshop or course format (McMurray, 1993) along with a video and book by Jim Cole, *Facing Our Future: From Denial to Environmental Action* (1992). The program is recommended for groups with from six to thirty participants and for students in junior high school through college; it requires a group facilitator/teacher.

In one of the exercises used to start the discussion, each person answers the question "What have you heard about in the world in the last week that bothers you the most?" A "talking stick" (passed to each student when it is his or her turn to talk) or some other device can be used to provide structure, and students are given the right to pass if they do not wish to answer the question. Several variations of this exercise provide awareness of denied feelings of fear about the future. In another exercise pairs of students respond to opened-ended sentences such as "I think our environment is becoming . . . ," "When I think of the world we are going to leave the next generation, it looks like . . . ," "One of my worst fears for the future is . . . ," "When I try to tell other people about my feelings, what usually happens is . . . " (McMurray, 1993, pp. 13–14). Students share their responses with their partner and then with the whole group. These early exercises are followed by a rich variety of activities designed to move students toward caring about the small group, the community, and the world and to help them develop hope for others and their world.

Source: D. McMurray, Counseling Center, Humboldt State University, Arcata, California, personal communication, 1995.

Integrity and Morality

Many college and university catalogues include some kind of statement about helping students develop integrity and morality. Although ethical development is seemingly not as obvious a developmental goal as achieving academic success or making career and life plans, few would argue against the importance of morality and integrity in contemporary society. Traditional-age college students and older returning adults often view their college years as a time to think about important life issues, clarify values, and develop character. Colleges and universities, particularly secular institutions, seldom have much intentional education related to character and values, yet important developmental growth can and does take place among students.

How can character, integrity, and value acquisition be conceptualized, and what kinds of experiences and environments promote growth and development in these areas? Several approaches have been suggested. As we saw in Chapter Eight, Chickering (Chickering and Reisser, 1993) posits a developmental dimension called "developing integrity," which involves "three sequential but overlapping stages:

(1) humanizing values—shifting away from automatic application of uncompromising beliefs and using principled thinking in balancing ones's own self-interest with the interests of one's fellow human beings, (2) personalizing values—consciously affirming core values and beliefs while respecting other points of view, and (3) developing congruence—matching personal values with socially responsible behavior" (pp. 236–237).

Several related conceptualizations have been developed. Perry (1968) devised a theory of intellectual and moral development specifically for traditional-age college students that was an extension of the work of Jean Piaget. Perry's scheme, similar to that of Chickering and Reisser (1993), hypothesized growth from dualistic thinking through relativism to commitment. Kitchener (1986) discussed a "reflective judgement model," which emphasizes intellectual development and explains how students try to solve "ill structured" problems by focusing on the process of making decisions. Whiteley (1982) examined character development in college students by establishing a residential program and a core curriculum that included training in empathy and social perspective-taking, community building, making sex-role choices, assertiveness, community service, conflict resolution, and race relations. Progress was measured in the following areas: moral reasoning, ego development, locus of control, psychological sense of community, self-esteem, attitude toward people, and sex-role choices.

A number of disciplines and constituencies on campus either study or are concerned with value choice, morality, integrity, and character development. For example, faculty in the departments of philosophy, religion, and psychology directly study these issues, and many other departments, such as English, history, and education, include extensive work related to values, philosophy, and character. In addition, student affairs offices and counselors work with character development and value choice every day. Thus, there is a rich store of interest and expertise related to these topics on any college or university campus.

With this wealth of resources, what can a counselor do to enhance student development in these areas? The most obvious activity is the initiation and facilitation of discussion of value questions by students and faculty in small groups. The counselor can function as catalyst and initiator by bringing various people and resources on campus together to focus attention on these issues. Terenzini, Pascarella, and Blimling's (1996) finding that interpersonal interactions are the most powerful influence on out-of-classroom student learning is relevant here. Counselors and others in the college community need to find a way to get students, faculty, and staff to talk about values, integrity, ethics, and the difficult moral issues facing society. Campuswide conferences, forums, minicourses, residential programs, volunteer opportunities, race-relations retreats, sex-role discussions, and many other programs of this nature are under way at campuses throughout the country. Counselors can work with groups of students and faculty to help initiate and develop these programs, but they also have the unique ability to devise strategies and methods that maximize opportunities for students and others to grapple with these questions personally. These methods require a reasonably nonjudgmental atmosphere and perhaps less critical attitude than is often found in academic discussions. For example, students in a residence hall with a semester theme of values might discuss topics such as euthanasia, biotechnology, and economic fairness. Counselors involved in developing such a program might focus on how to help discussion leaders and presenters set the stage for personal confrontation and discussion of these issues in an open and respectful manner.

Interpersonal Interactions and Relationships

College counselors have always focused attention on helping students develop interpersonal skills and relationships. In fact, most of the personal counseling that occurs on college campuses has an interpersonal focus. Outreach and consultation programs have also traditionally targeted the development of relationships. Clearly, counselors have a high level of expertise in this area and find working directly with students on these development goals rewarding, which may make it difficult to move toward an initiator-catalyst approach. However, counselors should work on leveraging their expertise in this area so that a larger number of students are affected.

This outreach is particularly important in light of Terenzini, Pascarella, and Blimling's (1996) findings about out-of-classroom learning; two of their conclusions are particularly relevant here: (1) "the most powerful source of influence on student learning appears to be students' interpersonal interactions, whether with peers or faculty (and, one suspects, staff members)"; (2) "the learning impacts of students' out-of-class experiences are probably cumulative rather than catalytic" (p. 159). These conclusions, based on a review of years of research, suggest that interpersonal interactions in a variety of settings are crucial to all kinds of learning and that students learn from these interactions gradually, adding knowledge a little at a time.

Given this research, counselors would probably be wise to focus their student development efforts on increasing and improving interpersonal interactions, which can be done in many ways and with many different content foci. For example, to promote the development of integrity and morality, students probably need to interact with faculty and each other in ways that foster thinking about ethics, societal responsibilities, and many other related topics, and these interactions need to take place in many different settings and contexts. Also, if interpersonal interactions are a major source of learning, all students must have the necessary skills. If there are no opportunities for these interactions or if a student is unable to interact effectively, learning in general is retarded. An argument can also be made that interpersonal effectiveness is strongly related to satisfaction in life and the successful negotiation of adulthood.

What are the dimensions of interpersonal learning that are important for counselors to consider and how can these be approached from an initiator-catalyst perspective? Three aspects of relationship effectiveness can be identified. The first is basic interpersonal skills. The ability to talk comfortably in a variety of social settings with friends, colleagues, strangers, intimates is crucial. Interpersonal skills do not develop in isolation. Students cannot be comfortable socially unless they have an adequate level of self-esteem and a reasonably well developed sense of identity. Nor can students be assertive or expressive unless they have the ability to experience and express emotions. Although developmental dimensions are discussed separately here, their interconnectedness cannot be ignored.

The second aspect of relationship effectiveness is tolerance and appreciation of differences (Chickering and Reisser, 1993), an especially important factor in an increasingly multicultural society. The third aspect is the capacity for intimacy (Chickering and Reisser, 1993). Intimate and romantic relationships sustain us all and make growth and change possible, yet students and others in our culture struggle mightily to find, develop, and maintain these relationships. Sexuality and love are profound aspects of students' lives and have an enormous effect on general growth and learning.

Once again the counselor is faced with decisions about resource allocation and effectiveness when considering how to make a difference in student interpersonal learning. Several intervention levels and methods are reasonable alternatives. Direct teaching and experiential training can be effective, and courses, workshops, and retreats are good avenues. Because counselors cannot provide these kinds of experiences to large numbers of students directly, they might best spend their time training leaders, encouraging course development, and initiating and facilitating experiential interpersonal training for students in other ways. On a systems level, counselors can work toward providing an environment that fosters interpersonal learning. For example, counseling or mental health centers might take as a major goal for a year or several years improving campus attitudes toward diversity. This project could include campuswide efforts to fight racism, sexism, homophobia, and other cultural attitudes that mitigate against the appreciation of differences. (A detailed discussion of promoting diversity and associated programs can be found in Chapter Twelve.)

Self-Esteem and Identity

Self-esteem and identity are formed as a result of experiences and learning, largely interpersonal, in a variety of arenas. Having a solid sense of identity means having a reasonably strong sense of self and of who one is in relation to the world. It is, in a sense, a definition of self in relation to others, as we saw when we discussed Chickering and Reisser's (1993) definition of this dimension in Chapter Eight. Growth in all the student development areas previously covered in this chapter would lead to solidification of identity and self-understanding. In addition to these general student development areas, identity development can be facilitated by helping.students take the time to establish a structure for thinking about themselves and their place in the world and for asking and answering questions about how to put sexual, cultural, career, social, and other roles together into a comfortable and acceptable self-definition.

Are there ways to facilitate this integration process, or is integration a by-product of growth in a number of developmental areas? Because other goals, both developmental and preventive, are more specific (AIDS prevention, career development, acquiring interpersonal skills), it is easy to assume that identity formation will occur as a result of general life experiences. In a sense this is true, but there is also a need to help many students move ahead with this process and to overcome obstacles and developmental blocks. Counselors might be involved in several ways. Perhaps an emphasis on how the college or university can provide the time to focus on integration and growth would be most productive. Mentor programs, curricular offerings that require self-definition and expression, writing projects and opportunities to share the results, and outdoor retreats with an inward focus are but a few of the possibilities. Because the goals in this area of student development are the least clear, it is difficult to enlist the support of others, at least initially, in helping students to meet them.

Program Example: Passages Program

The Passages Program at the University of Minnesota, Morris, was developed to encourage students to spend time focusing on their "passage" to adulthood by participating in an exciting, multidimensional program that helps connect them with a compassionate adult member of the community for wise counsel and advice. This relationship is particularly important because many college students do not have mentors and come from families that do not provide the nurturance necessary for them to become generative members of society. The program also recognizes the lack of the rituals and processes that helped adolescents achieve adulthood in most previous cultures.

The basic purpose of the program is to increase students' awareness of how cultures throughout time have recognized the passage to adulthood and to assist students of any age in their passage through life. The program uses various methods—music, poems, dance, lectures, discussions—and covers various topics—Arthurian legend, fairy tales, relationships, archetypes, self-esteem, power, marriage. Students make a commitment to the program; attend weekly lectures; participate in weekly sessions related to ceremony, meditation, and discussion of personal issues; have the option of participating in a group discussion of gender; meet with a mentor throughout the year; and participate in a twenty-four-hour initiation ceremony. Many different faculty members and staff are involved in various aspects of the program.

Source: T. Balistrieri, Counseling Center, University of Minnesota, Morris, personal communication, 1995.

It is not possible to discuss student development programs comprehensively or to provide examples of even a small fraction of the many exciting programs that exist on colleges campuses. This discussion has focused on applying the initiator-catalyst approach to outreach and consultation in areas where college counselors might have particular expertise and that are directly related to the educational mission.

Faculty Development

College counselors can most effectively focus their faculty development efforts in one or more of three general areas: personal and family functioning, career development, and student counseling and advising work. The environmental focus that makes the most sense is the department.

Personal and Family Functioning

Heppner and Johnston (1994) suggested that personal counseling and health counseling need to be available as part of general faculty development efforts. Various kinds of EAP and wellness programs already exist on many campuses, and college counselors have taken different roles in these programs. In some cases EAP counseling has been a part of the counseling or mental health service, although typically these programs are separate. Certainly one way for counselors to affect these programs is to be active either as the EAP provider or in an advisory role. When needs for personal counseling and growth are not being met for faculty, counselors can work to implement such services. Needs assessments and consultation with various faculty groups can lead to the development or improvement of these services.

Even if formal EAP programs are not feasible, counselors can assist in the development of workshops and programs aimed at providing personal development for faculty. Stress management, parenting, couples' and dual-career couples' relationships, and time and priority management are some of the more likely topics. It may be incumbent on counselors to help administrators and faculty understand the direct link between faculty members' job performance and both their personal growth and the satisfaction they find in life. Although there are a number of initiator-catalyst approaches counselors can use to help with the personal development of faculty, workshops directly led by counselors for faculty also make sense. Such workshops have a broad impact because work with faculty has an effect on students. Peer help programs also have some potential. One way to encourage faculty to help each other with personal concerns that is more in the spirit of an initiator-catalyst approach is through mentor programs for junior faculty. Counselors might offer a training program or written material about mentoring that would encourage discussion of personal and adjustment concerns.

Computer personal-growth programs aimed specifically at faculty have considerable potential, as do materials available through other technologies. For example, a college counselor might serve as a consultant or catalyst for a self-help library or lab for faculty; such a library could include personal-growth materials as well as career and teaching/advising materials. Such materials as well as faculty counseling are likely to work best when they are married to traditional faculty development activities or to existing EAP outreach programs.

Program Example: Workshops for Faculty and Staff

The University of Colorado Multicultural Counseling and Consultation Center offers workshops for faculty and staff during the regular year and during the summer. In the summer the workshops are held between 11 A.M. and 1 P.M. The chancellor sends a letter to supervisors telling them to make time available for employees who wish to attend one of the sessions. The workshops are offered by center staff and sometimes by community professionals. Topics vary depending on campus needs. The following are examples of workshops offered during the regular academic year: counseling skills for faculty, leading effective meetings, dealing with change, and stress and stress management. A support group for supervisors is also offered. In the summer workshops have been offered on the following topics: skills for work-group effectiveness, bicultural identity, finding psychological roots (genograms), career fulfillment, creative stress management for women, building relationship skills, procrastination styles, workplace violence and conflict management, and the GLB community.

Source: D. Sease, Multicultural Counseling and Consultation Center, University of Colorado, Boulder, personal communication, 1995.

Career Development

Career development issues are crucial to all faculty. New faculty struggle with promotion, tenure, and finding a niche in the academic world; mid-level faculty must deal with sustaining their careers, career moves, burnout, and changes in direction; and senior faculty must begin to confront the end of their careers and disappointment or flagging interest. All these issues are, of course, directly related to adult development. These issues are made more difficult in contemporary higher education by dwindling resources, demands for increased productivity, and what some faculty perceive as the changing nature of their position in higher education.

Colleges and universities have been inconsistent in their response to the career development needs of faculty. Counselors can probably have their greatest impact by helping administrators and others understand the importance of attending to these needs. If faculty development at a particular institution is narrow in scope and focuses mainly on improving teaching (as important as that focus is), counselors may be able to work on an advisory board to develop new, broad initiatives that would emphasize career and personal development. For example, after participating in a new-faculty orientation program, a counselor might advocate a follow-up session for second-year faculty. Perhaps a luncheon could be arranged with the help of the faculty personnel office; the speaker could focus on transitions for new faculty, and small groups could then discuss the speaker's comments.

Counselors might work with a dean, department, or faculty development office on issues of concern to a particular segment of the faculty. If, for example, a campus, college, or department seems to have a large group of faculty in mid-career who seem disaffected, counselors might work on a team designing a program to enhance career development. This team might also focus on particular environmental issues related to career development. There are many materials available on faculty development that can be used for programs such as this. For example, Simpson (1990) suggests a "regenerative learning model" that would be applicable for mid-career faculty. It includes four stages with target questions in each stage. Following are the stages and some examples of the target questions (p. 35):

1. Dissonance awareness and professional disorientation
   - Can I describe my professional goals? If not, why?
   - What do I want to do and what is expected?
2. Exploration of values, competencies, and options: reconstruction of role
   - What, if anything, do I want to do better?
   - What excites me about my work?

3. Course of action and acquisition of needed knowledge and skills
   - What do I need to be able to do?
   - What skills and/or knowledge bases do I want to acquire to assume a different role?
4. Internalization of new perspective and role integration
   - What am I willing to try to fulfill my needs?
   - How confident am I in the new role?

Counseling and Advising

Training faculty for counseling and advising has traditionally been the most frequent faculty development activity for college counselors because of their expertise in this area. Also, some faculty who are not advisers but who interact on a personal level with their students have appreciated help with basic counseling skills. In addition, effective academic advising involves a discussion with students about their goals and the career development process—areas of professional knowledge for college counselors. Here, as with other aspects of faculty development, direct training and activity by college counselors make sense because of the leverage effect: students benefit when faculty members are effective advisers and counselors. Counselors can certainly work to initiate programs to improve advisement through training of faculty and other advisers.

Program Example: Training for Faculty Advisers

At the University of Missouri at Rolla, a group of faculty and administrators, including the counseling-center director, developed specific guidelines for advisement (paraphrased here):

1. Know the student well enough to be able to write a reference letter.
2. Use good listening and questioning skills to identify academic and personal problems.
3. Discuss career options and interests.
4. Assess the student's ability and offer suggestions regarding a program of study.
5. Be aware of campus services and refer students to them.
6. Know the campus academic rules.

Adviser training focuses on these areas, with counseling staff offering units on interpersonal skills, career development, and referral resources. The counseling-center director also chaired a task force to develop a handbook for advisers and a brochure to help students get the most out of academic advising called "Your Advisor and You."

Source: Robinson and Gaw, 1995, p. 2.

Organizational Development

Organizational development (OD) with academic departments can have a powerful impact on the professional and personal lives of faculty members. Academic departments are often loosely organized, with each professor working fairly autonomously and with leadership sometimes changing fairly frequently. Although faculty rely on each other as a major source of support for their work, departments are often not organized nor do they function as good support systems. Issues of promotion, tenure, merit pay, and resource allocation provide a challenge for any department chair.

Invitations to consult with faculty departments are usually based on the personal reputation of a counselor or on a relationship that a faculty member has with a counselor. If a counseling or mental health center wants to develop an OD program for faculty or is requested to do so, a plan for moving into this area should be developed deliberately. Workshops and other EAP outreach efforts can lay the groundwork for invitations to consult about departmental functioning. Some institutions have formal training sessions for new department chairs. Certainly this would be a good time for counselors to contribute their expertise. Although OD consultation for departments is often problem-centered, developmentally oriented consultations can be extremely helpful. With the general tightening of resources and expectations to do more with less, faculty will need to get as much support and encouragement from their colleagues as possible.

In order to do faculty development work and particularly OD consultation with departments, counselors must have the expertise and status to work with faculty as colleagues. This may be difficult for younger counselors or for those who are not faculty members themselves with teaching and research experience. Also, college counselors are not routinely trained in OD, but efforts in this direction require that there be senior, experienced OD consultants on the staff. It is important for directors to select staff to work in this area who have the requisite expertise, skill, and experience.

◆ ◆ ◆

In summary, college counselors need to develop effective ways to help facilitate both student and faculty development. Student development efforts will be most effective when the goals and objectives are tied directly to the primary mission of the college or university and when an initiator-catalyst approach is used. Several student development areas are particularly appropriate for college counselors to focus on: achieving academic success and developing career and life goals, developing integrity and morality, acquiring interpersonal skills and mature relationships, developing self-esteem and identity. Faculty development efforts can be effectively targeted in the following areas: personal and family development, career development, and counseling and advising students. Also, OD work with academic departments can have a profound impact on faculty development. An initiator-catalyst approach has many applications in faculty and student development; however, traditional workshops are also recommended for faculty development because of the leverage effect on the positive development of students.

CHAPTER ELEVEN

EDUCATIONAL AND PREVENTIVE RESPONSES TO PUBLIC HEALTH ISSUES

The challenge to colleges and universities in managing serious public health concerns such as relationship violence, alcohol and drug abuse, AIDS and other sexually transmitted diseases, stress, and eating disorders is both daunting and exciting. The counseling aspects of these issues were covered in earlier chapters of this book, especially Chapters Six and Seven. College counseling and mental health centers can also play an important and pivotal role in the delivery of prevention and education programs and services in these areas. In Chapter Eight models for consultation and outreach were presented as were definitions of preventive and development interventions. Although the difference between prevention and development is sometimes difficult to discern, it is important for counselors to be clear about the thrust of their outreach efforts. In the case of the public health issues discussed here, a prevention orientation makes the most sense. Clearly, though, some of behavioral change that will prevent these problems involves the development of students.

Prevention can be primary, secondary, or tertiary (Conyne, 1987; Conyne and others, 1994). The initiator-catalyst approach described and advocated in Chapter Nine tends to involve primary or secondary prevention, with intervention on a systems level prior to the beginning of the problem (primary) or targeted prevention programs for high-risk groups (secondary). The initiator-catalyst approach is also more likely to involve consultation, facilitation of program development, or some other indirect catalytic or facilitative approach rather than direct outreach via teaching and training in workshops and lectures. Decisions about the type of prevention and the most effective methods significantly affect the impact and the success of programs in these areas. Conceiving of prevention as primary, secondary, and tertiary is also useful in determining target populations and, to a limited degree, specificity of content.

To further enhance prevention efforts, it is helpful for college counseling-center staff to understand the three models of health promotion most supported by research: the health-beliefs model, the social-cognitive model, and the elaboration-likelihood model. Using these models to explain how change occurs is important regardless of the outreach focus and approach employed. The health-beliefs model emphasizes the influence of perceived susceptibility, perceived severity, perceived benefits, and perceived barriers on health behaviors. A substantial body of research supports the importance of each of these factors (Janz and Becker, 1984), with perceived barriers and perceived benefits being particularly important for life-style behaviors that require long-term change, such as drinking or sexual behavior (Rosenstock, Strecher, and Marshall, 1994). Moreover, the incorporation of belief in self-efficacy (confidence in one's ability to perform a particular behavior or set of behaviors) has enhanced health-beliefs conceptualizations concerning life-style behavioral changes (Marlatt and Gordon, 1985).

The health-beliefs model is supplemented by the social-cognitive model. This model proposes four techniques for altering behavior: acquisition of accurate information, development of social and self-regulatory skills through social modeling, enhancement of skills and self-efficacy through guided practice, and establishment of social supports. Research has demonstrated that people's beliefs in their self-efficacy are more related to engaging in preventive health practices than is fear arousal (Beck and Lund, 1981). Studies have also shown that successful self-regulation typically involves persistence in the face of frequent failures (Bandura, 1994). Use of these techniques both along and together has been documented as effective (Botvin and Dusenbury, 1992; Gilchrist and Schinke, 1983; McKusick and others, 1990).

The elaboration-likelihood model postulates two paths to attitude change: the central route and the peripheral route. Central-route attitude change is based on reflection about persuasive content, such as that delivered in a psychoeducational program. Peripheral-route attitudinal change is based on simple decision rules or cues. A number of studies have documented that central-route change is more influential and more long-lasting than peripheral-route change. There are three conditions for central-route change: motivation to consider the topic, the ability to conceptualize the subject and related information, and the relative favorableness of the resulting thoughts toward change in the desired direction. Much of the research on the elaboration-likelihood model (Heppner,

Humphrey, Hillenbrand-Gunn, and DeBord, 1995), as on the other two models, was conducted on the college population.

This chapter includes a discussion of prevention methods and programs in each of the public health areas mentioned previously, with particular emphasis on the elements of such programs that fit with contemporary health behavior-change models and with an initiator-catalyst approach. These are all important and complex prevention areas, and space does not permit an extensive examination of each. Also, the program examples illustrate only a few of the many creative approaches that are being used on college and university campuses.

Relationship Violence

Previous chapters have documented the increase of relationship violence on campus. Such violence can be physical or emotional and includes a growing number of incidents of "fatal attraction" (Gallagher and Bruner, 1995). Maloney (1995, p. 5) summarized the high price of relationship violence on campus: "In terms of cost, the physical and psychological injury to the college student who is victimized is only the beginning. Batterers may face a marred college disciplinary record, suspension resulting in missed classes, dismissal from college, arrest, a legal record and repeated court dates, and, finally, imprisonment. Liability for a student's safety, hospital bills that may be paid through school insurance, and staff hours that residence life, counseling, and campus police may devote to the problem top the list of other more global consequences of relationship violence on campus."

Counseling-center staff can employ initiator-catalyst approaches to address relationship violence by involving and collaborating with other members of the campus community. Collaboration can include consultation with concerned groups, such as student government, faculty, the judicial-affairs office, campus police. College counselors can also take an initiator role by identifying problems and needs and bringing campus groups together to address the problem. Also, proactive efforts can be made to influence campus policies and to organize special events and media campaigns, among many other possibilities. As discussed with reference to outreach models, the thrust must be to affect the campus culture and collective behavior in as many ways as possible. Promising campus efforts in this area have had a variety of goals, from eliminating sexual harassment to reducing the incidence of date rape.

One of the most serious and damaging categories of campus relationship violence is acquaintance rape. This issue has received considerable national attention. Because of the Higher Education Amendment Act of 1992 and other federal legislation, most campuses have developed written policies and adjudication procedures in this area. A number of universities have already been embroiled in multimillion-dollar lawsuits based on claims of unfair campus judicial-board actions. These lawsuits have been brought by both alleged offenders and victims and are a source of significant anxiety for many campus administrators.

Many of the efforts in this area have been reactive and involve crisis intervention or ongoing counseling. A good crisis-intervention system with immediate counseling follow-up can be considered secondary prevention in that follow-up support can help prevent more serious, ongoing problems. Efforts at primary prevention have also been made (Frazier, Valtinson, and Candell, 1994).

Gray, Lesser, Quinn, and Bounds (1990) developed a successful risk-reduction program aimed at women and based on the health-beliefs model. They evaluated a personalized versus a psychoeducational approach and found that those in the personalized program reported significantly greater perceptions of personal vulnerability as well as intent to reduce risk taking. Gilbert, Heesacker, and Gannon (1991) reported success with an elaboration-likelihood program targeted at men's identification with rape myths, adversarial sexual beliefs, gender-role stereotyping, and acceptance of interpersonal violence.

Program Example: Workshop for Men on Preventing Acquaintance Rape

Alan Berkowitz at Hobart College has allocated significant counseling-center resources to preventing acquaintance rape. He reviewed research on college men as perpetrators of acquaintance rape and sexual assault and identified specific relevant factors, including perpetrator characteristics, situations associated with sexual assault, and men's misperception of women's sexual intent. Berkowitz suggested that these factors combine in a complex interactive manner to produce male sexual violence against women. He designed a widely used workshop for men to prevent acquaintance rape, the components of which are congruent with the social-cognitive model.

The workshop is part of the college's cocurricular program in men's studies, Men and Masculinity. The overall goal of Men and Masculinity, which uses a feminist perspective, is to change attitudes through education and to reduce oppression of women and injury to men. Ideas about the nature of masculinity, male socialization, and gender-role constraints form the philosophical basis of the program in general and of the acquaintance-rape workshop in particular.

The six-step workshop includes an overview, a survey, a videotape, an in-depth discussion followed by a second viewing of the tape, and a summary and brainstorming session. The program goes beyond providing definitions and assigning responsibility to include an emphasis on relationship and sexuality communications, on changing attitudes toward gender, and on empowering men to confront other men.

Source: Berkowitz, 1993.

Another approach to date rape that has been successful on many campuses involves dramatic depictions of date rape by other students. These sessions usually include a series of vignettes about different kinds of date rape and about sexual communication, with time for discussion afterward. Often these programs are initiated by counselors but are put on by theater students or other student groups. Counselors can play a direct role in facilitating discussion, which can be heated and difficult at times, or they can play an indirect, initiator-catalyst role and supervise student or staff facilitators. The intensity of seeing other students just like themselves in these situations tends to involve participants.

Program Example: Date-Rape Drama Performance

In response to reports of sexual violence from a significant number of clients and in recognition of the fact that traditional outreach programs seemed limited in effectiveness, staff of the counseling center at Valparaiso University (Indiana) worked with a theater faculty member and her students to develop and present an intense play depicting an acquaintance rape of a college student. Seeing the play is a mandatory part of new-student orientation as anecdotal evidence suggested that many acquaintance rapes occurred within the first three weeks of school.

The play consists of three acts. Between each act, male and female moderators facilitate audience discussion as well as the questioning of the actors, who stay "in role" in giving their responses. Following the play, the students are divided into small groups for discussion of related issues; the discussions are led by two-person teams consisting of a student and a faculty member or staff member or administrator. All facilitators are volunteers who participate in a day-long training session on content and group-leader skills conducted by counseling-center staff. Staff also coordinate all logistics associated with the play and the subsequent break-out process.

Evaluations of this experience consistently portray it as intense and powerful. Students recall the experience even as upperclassmen. The number of reported sexual assaults on campus has decreased since the program was initiated.

Source: P. Dranger, SAAFE program coordinator, Valparaiso University, Valparaiso, Indiana, personal communication, 1996.

Alcohol and Drug Abuse

Chapter Six included a discussion of the high costs of substance abuse on campuses. One newly developed framework includes a review of these broad impacts

(Bucknam, 1992). A publication from the Harvard School of Public Health entitled *Binge Drinking on American College Campuses: A New Look at an Old Problem* (Wechsler, 1995) emphasized the importance of enhancing awareness of "secondhand binge effects." The concept was first used in the antismoking campaign, where public awareness of secondhand effects led to major legislative initiatives. The basic idea is that students, staff, and faculty who become aware of the negative effects of others' substance abuse on their own lives will begin to exert significant pressure for institutions to respond assertively in this area.

Another promising area of change is related to a growing body of research on misperceptions of peers' use of alcohol and other drugs (Perkins, 1995). Numerous studies have shown large gaps between actual behavior and perceived norms across a wide age range as well as in all cultural groups. The research has also shown that these misperceptions have a significant influence on personal choices (people modify their behavior so that it is congruent with perceived, not actual, reality) as well as on campus culture. Given awareness of the power of perceived social norms, several counseling centers and mental health services have begun to collaborate with campus media to publish weekly or daily behavioral data to counter these false perceptions.

On most campuses, data reveals that one-third of all students preferred to have alcohol-free social events, and seven-eighths preferred no illicit drugs at these functions. This substantial group of students could participate to change the culture on campus to one of reduced use and one where nonuse would be an acceptable stance for an individual to take. More important, the widespread creation of campus substance abuse prevention and counseling programs enabled by the national Fund for the Improvement of Postsecondary Education (FIPSE) program combined with pre-post use of the Core Survey demonstrated that change is possible. Changes typically included decreased binge drinking and drug use as well as increased awareness of campus policies and procedures and campus substance abuse intervention and prevention services. However, the work by Presley and Meilman (1992) and the Harvard Study (Wechsler, 1995) provide plentiful evidence that much more is needed.

Obviously, effective approaches require a systemwide effort among administration, staff, faculty, and students. The following components should be included: awareness and information, support services, enforcement, curriculum, assessment and valuation, peer education, staff and leader training, policies and implementation, and environmental alterations.

The research and practice literature contains a number of examples of outreach and consultation efforts aimed at reducing campus substance abuse. Initiator-catalyst approaches have been quite successful and often include peer education programs that target specific high-risk groups.

Program Example: A Peer Education Program to Prevent Substance Abuse

The Wellness Office with extensive support from the Counseling Center at the University of Cincinnati developed a two-year project to prevent substance abuse that was institutionwide in scope, comprehensive in coverage, and proactive in its approach. The program, which made extensive use of graduate student educators and undergraduate peer educators to give presentations and workshops and to facilitate discussion groups, targeted freshmen, fraternity members, and commuter students. The program emphasized planning and evaluation activities throughout. Structurally, the student educators were supported by a project director, project coordinator, trainer coordinators, and an evaluation coordinator.

The Counseling Center staff served as team members in designing and supporting the project. They also assisted in developing instruments and processes for assessment and program evaluation. Once the framework was established, Counseling Center staff provided some of the training for the student educators in group presentation and facilitation skills as well as ongoing consultation for the program and for individuals.

There were two keys to the effectiveness of the program. One was collaboration. Careful and sustained attention had to be given to the planning group so that it could function effectively as a unit and sustain itself over time. Excellent group-facilitation competencies were necessary in such areas as observation of group process, group teaching and management skills, group problem solving, and conceptualizing the group as an interdependent system.

Of nearly equal importance for the success of the program was the process of planning and formative evaluation. The use of reiterative cycles of careful planning and evaluation was a key way of managing the complexity and uncertainty of the project. Making flexible adaptations based on continuous feedback was central to enhancing effectiveness.

Source: M. Foreman, director, Psychological Services Center, University of Cincinnati, personal communication, 1996.

Systemwide prevention approaches focus on general campus needs and the organization of prevention efforts aimed at the entire community. Counseling and mental health centers have a primary role to play in these efforts. If a campus does not have a comprehensive approach involving all members of the campus community (faculty, students, staff, and administrators), college counselors need to take an initiator role and work toward developing a broad-based approach. This role goes beyond offering outreach programs, workshops, and substance abuse groups. In a sense the initiator role is political, with the counselor developing a strategy to persuade various members of the community to participate. Once a comprehensive effort is undertaken by a campuswide group, a catalyst consultation approach can be utilized by the counseling or mental health staff. In this role the counselor operates as expert and collaborator, offering both feedback and empirically supported intervention options, while the consultees (perhaps a campuswide task force or student affairs office) are responsible for decision making and implementation.

Program Example: Substance Abuse Advisory Council

The Substance Abuse Advisory Council at Valparaiso University (Indiana) was formed in the fall of 1990 to coordinate and plan policies and services in the areas of alcohol and drug education and substance abuse prevention. The committee was also charged with providing the major impetus for expanding awareness of these issues within the university community. Members of the committee represented a broad cross-section of students, staff, faculty, and administrators with an interest in or responsibility for resolving alcohol and other drug-abuse problems. Counseling staff coordinated the Substance Abuse Advisory Council, established priorities, and led all meetings.

By the spring of 1992, the Substance Abuse Advisory Council had developed a plan for an institutionwide approach. This plan incorporated desirable general outcomes, desirable specific outcomes, the Council's own goals for self-education and organization as well as program goals for students, faculty, and staff. Educational resources, academic departments, student affairs offices, and student organizations were identified to assist with achieving all these goals.

In 1994, the institution received a FIPSE grant to establish a separate Office of Alcohol and Other Drug Education. The Substance Abuse Advisory Council played a pivotal role in obtaining the funds to expand prevention efforts. Under the grant the Substance Abuse Advisory Council was charged with developing a long-range program to address substance abuse issues; coordinating and unifying existing policies and services being provided by many diverse groups within and outside the university; increasing awareness of alcohol and drug issues among students, faculty, and staff; receiving comprehensive training in substance abuse prevention and intervention; and advocating for additional institutional resources. By 1996, many of these goals were accomplished, and the Office of Alcohol and Other Drug Education had received hard funding as one of three core counseling programs at the university.

Source: J. Nagel, coordinator, Office of Alcohol and Drug Education, Valparaiso University, Valparaiso, Indiana, personal communication, 1996.

AIDS and Sexually Transmitted Diseases

The need for significant prevention through outreach and consultation in the area of sexuality on campus is obvious (Levenson, 1986; Manuel and others, 1990). One in every six young Americans has a sexually transmitted disease (STD);

HIV/AIDS, a lethal viral disease for which the long-term benefits of protease inhibitors are still unknown, continues to increase among this population (Corey and Corey, 1997); and approximately 10 to 15 percent of all couples with STDs will face significant fertility problems later in life, mostly because the diseases are undiagnosed or untreated (Herer and Holzapfel, 1993).

House and Walker (1993), in a seminal paper on preventing AIDS through education, pointed out the historical pattern: fear of lethal diseases that differentially affect disenfranchised groups leads to social and political decisions that diminish responsiveness. Thus far, AIDS has been more prevalent in marginalized groups (for example, gay men, substance abusers, Hispanics, African Americans), and the prevailing view among many heterosexual nonminority students on colleges campuses is that AIDS is not yet a mainstream problem. It is important for counseling and mental health staff who are working in this prevention area to understand this perception and the implications. Any hesitancy to move into full-fledged prevention efforts on campus needs to be confronted in a politically energetic and sophisticated way.

Because a definitive cure for AIDS is not yet in sight, education is the most powerful tool available to prevent the deadly consequences of the disease. Many obstacles to AIDS education exist, including beliefs in invulnerability, low self-efficacy regarding safe sexual behavior, discomfort with open discussions of sexuality, resistance to sex education in schools, and religious values that oppose the use of condoms. These obstacles occur on college campuses. Traditional-age college students do not think frequently about their vulnerability and mortality, and frank discussion of sexual activity is difficult from both a self-efficacy perspective and because of cultural norms, so consultation and outreach efforts on campus must be as powerful and theoretically sound as possible. Fortunately, opposition to educational programs or to making condoms easily available is usually not strong except in conservative or religiously affiliated schools. Exposure to extensive education about AIDS and HIV in professional training programs, however, is not always as strong as it should be (House, Eicken, and Gray, 1995).

Guidance on how to organize AIDS prevention programs comes from Ostrow (1989), presented in House and Walker (1993, p. 285), who argue that the following seven components are necessary for community-based change:

> (1) A major long-term commitment to inform and motivate the public to change behavior is needed, (2) programs must be designed to reach all at-risk populations with their specific needs, (3) it is both appropriate and necessary to design education programs that slant messages toward members of specific high risk cohort groups, (4) it is essential that all AIDS education programs be culturally and community sensitive, (5) education programs that merely provide

information will be extremely limited in effectiveness, (6) programs that provide specific tools and techniques for implementing behavior change will be most effective, and (7) peers teaching peers will have positive results in both attainment of knowledge and behavior change.

These components include elements from the three prevention models previously discussed.

House and Walker (1993) recommend use of the following sequential steps when planning and organizing an HIV education program: (1) obtain commitment from members of the campus community, (2) establish an education task force, (3) review existing information and materials, (4) identify the high-risk groups, (5) develop, implement, and evaluate a short-term plan of action, (6) develop and implement a long-term plan of action, and (7) evaluate the program results.

Preventing or at least reducing the spread of AIDS and STDs requires solid collaboration among the counseling center, health services, wellness programs, and other student affairs offices as well as connections to relevant academic departments. Because prevention is so important and the task is so enormous, the initiator-catalyst approach makes sense as a way to maximize counseling-center resources. In this situation one of the goals might be the expansion of resources for prevention. Although counseling and mental health personnel have the skills to provide direct educational services that focus on behavior change, resources should not be used only in this domain. It may be more important and useful for a counselor to spend time working with campus organizations and groups to create a comprehensive AIDS prevention program than to offer workshops on sexual communication or STD prevention. This work may have a political component if opposition to AIDS education and condom use has to be overcome.

In general, counselors can be particularly helpful in the following areas:

1. Assessment—identifying the attitudes and sexual behavior of potential target groups and the norms that must be changed in order to teach HIV-prevention behavior.
2. Task forces—initiating, organizing, and facilitating campuswide task forces to deal with AIDS prevention and education.
3. Peer education—initiating, consulting with, and advising peer education programs, including assisting with training and evaluation.
4. HIV testing and follow-up—initiating and facilitating easy and anonymous testing for HIV, counseling students who are HIV-positive, and providing preventive counseling and programs for those who test negative but who are involved in high-risk behavior.

5. Campus and subgroup communication about sexual practices—initiating and facilitating efforts to change norms that inhibit open communication about sexual practices among students of all sexual orientations.
6. Classroom discussion of AIDS prevention—encouraging the discussion of AIDS-related topics in appropriate classes.
7. Research—facilitating and supporting campus research projects on HIV prevention.

Program Example: AIDS Education Program

"Occidental College [California] has designed and implemented a Safer Sex and Awareness Program that is ongoing, interdepartmental, multidisciplinary, and campus wide. Several offices of the Dean of student's staff, including the associate dean, the director of residence life, the director of the health center, and the counseling center staff, coordinate efforts to assure the greatest possible effectiveness of our AIDS education program. Aspects of the program include: (1) An AIDS policy covering hiring, housing, admissions, classroom attendance and attendance at campus events, as well as benefits information that would be true in the case of any disability or life-threatening illness. (2) Condom machines with safer sex information cards laminated on them in both men's and women's bathrooms in residence halls, the student union, the library, and the athletic buildings. (3) Articles in the student newspaper every other issue (bi-monthly) covering such issues as how to put on a condom so that it doesn't break and how to enjoy intimate experiences without exposing yourself to sexually transmitted diseases, as well as specific signs and symptoms of various sexually transmitted diseases, and other related issues such as masturbation, virginity, and responsible choice making in intimate relationships. (4) Educational presentations in residence halls, to fraternities and sororities, sports teams, staff and faculty, and to other interested groups. The presentations involve all aspects of sex and sexuality education including: sex and relationships, sexually transmitted diseases and AIDS, sexual enjoyment and dysfunction, acquaintance rape and violence toward women. These presentations are followed by question and answer sessions that provide a chance for audience members to ask just about anything they have ever wanted to know about sex, and the groups are often relaxed enough that many difficult questions do get asked. Some people wait to ask the questions after the audience has begun to leave; others write confidentially to the counseling center; still others make use of individual or couples counseling to work on their sexual concerns."

Source: McCollum and Devore, 1988, p. 72.

Stress

Numerous studies have presented evidence of the high levels of stress and anxiety reported by college students (Bruch, 1997; Smith, 1993; Weidner, Kohlmann, Dotzauer, and Burns, 1996). Demands for performance, stiff competition, irregular deadlines, and lack of self-management skills are key factors contributing to college student stress. College and university students respond to stress in the same way as people in the general population. Although most students do develop stress symptoms, they are typically mild or moderate and do not significantly interfere with academics or functioning. Some people, however, are sensitive to stress (most likely because of biological susceptibility plus a lack of helpful attitudes and good behavioral coping skills). In fact, one subgroup responds to high levels of demand with hyperarousal (manifested in symptoms like obsessive thinking, abdominal discomfort, and inability to concentrate), while another subgroup responds with hypoarousal (manifested in depression and sometimes suicidality). As with many other mental and emotional problems, an inability to cope with stress has significant effects on a student's academic performance, on others, and on the institution. Reduced immunological functioning leads to a greatly increased likelihood of illnesses and accompanying missed classes and deadlines. The need for relief requires countless hours of support from friends, faculty, and staff. The most serious cases can end in academic failure or in withdrawal from college or in actions to end one's life.

Outreach and consultation efforts in this area by college counseling and mental health centers receive somewhat less attention than they have in the past as energy is shifted to other, more dangerous or volatile campus health issues. However, most university counseling and mental health centers still offer both proactive and responsive programs and services to assist students in dealing with stress and anxiety. Counseling programs for stress were discussed in Chapter Six. In this chapter the focus is on outreach efforts that target students who do not seek out counseling but who may be experiencing significant stress and who can profit from improving their coping mechanisms and skills. This goal can be approached from two general directions: environmental assessment and intervention, and broad-based educational and skill-building programs. Environmental assessment and intervention might include attempts to change the overall culture or targeted OD approaches to help various organizations provide less stressful work and learning environments. Academic departments or service areas known for producing stress (for example, architecture and law schools, financial aid and registration offices) might be targeted. Direct education, such as stress-management workshops, self-help brochures, a peer education program, or a campuswide effort to improve stress management, can often be facilitated using an initiator-catalyst approach.

Program Example: A Health Promotion Course

A course at the University of North Carolina at Asheville effectively infused student development needs into the academic curriculum. The three-credit, semester-long course focused on stress management, aerobic conditioning, interpersonal skills, health, and nutrition. A number of traditional and nontraditional learning methods were used, including lectures, an interpersonal lab group, aerobic exercise, a visit with a family physician in training, and the development of short- and long-term personal health contracts.

Many qualitative indications, like student enthusiasm, attendance, and involvement, along with findings from an end-of-course quantitative survey suggested that participation in the class was linked to large and sustained changes for many students. Stress reduction and improved relationships were frequently mentioned as positive outcomes.

Source: McClary, Pyeritz, Bruce, and Henshaw, 1992.

Students, particularly those who are stress hyporesponders, may attempt suicide as a way to deal with stress. The stress is typically a result of interpersonal problems or academic difficulties or both. Westefeld and Furr (1987) documented that 32 percent of college students contemplate suicide, with 1 percent making attempts. The response needed to manage such attempts is considerable but is dwarfed by the resources needed when the suicide is lethal or near-lethal.

Demands are greatest for an immediate response from the counseling center to students in trouble. Although it is important for campus counselors to make quick responses to students who are suicidal and to provide training and consultation for other members of the campus community to help them deal with suicidal threats and gestures, resources should also be allocated for primary prevention programs. Once again, it is necessary for the counselor and the institution to understand the range of responses along the prevention continuum. Both primary prevention programs—efforts to develop a campus environment that encourages personal growth and creates a caring community—and secondary prevention programs—efforts to have everyone on campus recognize the signs of potential suicide and intervene in some way—are important, as is therapy for students who are already suicidal.

Program Example: Suicide-Prevention Project

"A Suicide Prevention Project was initiated [by the Counseling Center] at the University of Florida in November 1986. The project was designed to educate the university community about stress, self-destructive behaviors, and suicide. Administrators decided on an early intervention emphasis rather than on one focusing primarily on providing help for students who were already suicidal. . . . This was accomplished by several different outreach programs and media campaigns with the theme 'This Campus Cares.' [Examples of these included a self-help booklet for students, public service announcements, and use of the theme in all ads for counseling center outreach programs.]

"[Additional aids were developed, including] a brochure for parents of new students and a campus-wide self-help book collection. The brochure uses several case vignettes to depict common student problems such as academic struggles and career indecision, potential substance abuse and eating disorders, sexual decision making, depression and loneliness, and identity confusion. Each vignette is followed by suggestions of effective and ineffective intervention strategies available to parents. The focus was on increasing parents' awareness of normal developmental changes as well as possible problems in a nonthreatening way, and advocating assertive communication and support by parents. Campus helping resources were also provided and parent consultation encouraged.

"The second project had the purpose of promotion of positive mental health through the collection of self-help psychology books for the campus main libraries and residence hall reading rooms. Topics included combating depression, building self-esteem, making peace with food, coping with stress, recovering as adult children of alcoholics and adults abused as children, building intimate relationships, engaging in safe sex, and surviving a loss."

Source: Funderburk and Archer, 1989, p. 278.

Eating Disorders

National attention to the problem of eating disorders began in the early 1980s. Since that time, identification of affected students (the vast majority of whom are women) has increased dramatically. The typical college student's knowledge of the disorder has also increased considerably. Most students seeking information or services for themselves or for a friend can recognize the disorder by the accompanying behaviors and symptoms. Yet such knowledge by itself has been insufficient to stop some students from continuing to have pathological and potentially lethal feelings, thoughts, and behavior patterns related to eating disorders.

Given the embeddedness of eating disorders in North American youth culture, peer education is one of the most powerful means for effecting change. In an initiator-catalyst approach college counselors can establish and support such a program. D'Andrea (1987) suggested several factors that contribute to the effectiveness of peer programs, including operation of the program as a student organization, training in empathy skills, clear definitions of the role of peer educators and of the populations served, diversity in the peer education group, campuswide networking, and good working relationships with counseling staff as trainers and consultants. To achieve excellence, such peer education programs must provide high-quality recruitment and selection, training, and ongoing supervision (Salovey and D'Andrea, 1984). As previously discussed with regard to peer counseling programs, the organization and operation of a successful peer education program require considerable expertise on the part of the professional adviser or consultant.

Program Example: Peer Education Program for Eating Disorders

The Wellspring program at the University of Delaware makes extensive use of peer educators to promote health in a variety of areas. A subgroup of five to six peer educators work specifically with students with eating disorders. Once these peer educators receive extensive content and skills training, they provide informational and personal counseling, present workshops on many related topics, support a computerized dialogue network on the topic, and maintain a resource library. Both the individual counseling and the outreach are closely supervised and monitored to minimize over-involvement by peer educators, boundary problems, and burnout.

Individual counseling is offered through walk-in and scheduled appointments. Presenting problems range from mild issues related to physical self-esteem to full-blown anorexia and bulimia. Most counselees are referred to other campus resources for auxiliary information. Difficult cases are transferred to the counseling center after three to six sessions.

The presentations and workshops cover a wide range of topics and are offered in residence halls, Greek houses, and academic classes. The objectives are to raise awareness, to support healthy choices, and to inform students of available assistance.

The interactive computer-based dialogue network is popular with students who are not yet ready for a face-to-face encounter. The peer educators provide timely answers to questions posed anonymously by students. Both the questions and the answers can be read by anyone who logs onto the network, and readers are free to add their responses. The peer educators also maintain a special topical library to help individuals who need information for themselves, a friend, or a course paper.

Source: Sesan, 1989.

A number of other initiator-catalyst approaches to preventing eating disorders are currently being used on a variety of campuses. College counselors can play an important role in these efforts. Some institutions have formed campuswide task forces to address the issue. Other schools have supported efforts to change cultural norms in targeted groups such as sororities. Still others have attempted to infuse discussion of female sex roles and their influence into the academic curriculum. Other possibilities include combined counseling and educational programs, identification and early-intervention systems, telephone information lines, and campuswide media programs. The more counselors can be initiator-catalysts for these efforts, the more prevention activities they can facilitate and the more systemwide change they can effect.

◆ ◆ ◆

All the campus public health concerns discussed in this chapter are serious and, in the extreme, life-threatening. Counseling students in trouble provides some immediate help to those students, but the real challenge is to work toward early intervention and prevention. These public health problems are not unique to the college campus; however, the organization of the campus as a community with subcommunities allows for the kind of initiator-catalyst interventions advocated here.

CHAPTER TWELVE

PROMOTING CAMPUS DIVERSITY AND MULTICULTURALISM

M ost campuses are a diverse mix of people—different races, ethnic groups, genders, ages, sexual orientations, and levels of ability and disability. Racism, sexism, prejudice, discrimination, fear, anger, and in some cases violence are not uncommon reactions to differences among various groups (Ehrlich, 1995). College and university campuses usually proclaim the diversity of their student bodies as a great opportunity for learning and student growth, and indeed they can be. Harnessing diversity as a stimulus for such growth involves helping different groups overcome bias and prejudice and helping the general community to appreciate and learn from differences (Berg-Cross, Starr, and Sloan, 1993).

College counselors have often been called on to work with individual students who are victims of various kinds of prejudice and discrimination, and they have worked hard to make their counseling services available to these students. Many of these efforts were described in Part One of this book, with a particular emphasis on clinically relevant topics in Chapter Seven. Atkinson, Morten, and Sue's (1993) model of multicultural counseling was highlighted. This model encourages the counselor to move beyond the therapist role to an activist stance. This view clearly fits well with an initiator-catalyst approach.

In this chapter the focus will be on the counselor's role in working with groups and with the institution in a preventive and developmental fashion. Preventive, in that two of the goals are to prevent prejudice and stereotyping from interfering with individual student learning and growth and to prevent the formation of campuswide cultures that foster conflict and violence among groups. Developmental, in that a major goal is helping all members of the campus community to use their differences to enrich their college experience (Adams, 1992). Several questions immediately emerge. What determines a population of diversity? What needs might individuals in these groups have for outreach and consultation services from counseling and mental health centers? How similar and dissimilar are the various minority groups in their issues and needs? How many counseling-center resources should be invested in special services targeted toward these groups? How much emphasis should be placed on facilitating the multicultural growth of all students?

Only a limited number of diverse populations will be discussed in this chapter: women, minorities, GLB students, students with disabilities, and adult learners. These populations are important constituencies within most colleges and universities. Moreover, members of these groups commonly experience both prejudice ("negative attitudes . . . that are irrationally based") and discrimination (limitations on "the group's life chances and life choices . . . in comparison to the majority group") (Pettigrew, 1994, pp. 2–3). Although levels of direct discrimination are being reduced on many campuses, levels of indirect discrimination, which are subtle and are typically embedded within the common traditions, structures, and practices of higher education, have resisted identification and change. Many times, in fact, policies and practices created with the intention of having positive effects on the institution end up causing indirect discrimination. For example, assessing performance and assigning grades on the basis of competition among students runs counter to norms in many cultures that are collectivistic in nature. Obviously, simply dropping such policies is untenable, yet developing suitable, nondiscriminatory alternatives requires creativity because of the absence of models.

Two of the most divisive factors on campuses are competition for scarce resources and voluntary separation based on ethnic and racial allegiances. Discrimination, prejudice, and stereotyping can be exacerbated by intergroup conflict and limited intergroup personal relationships. Group norms sometimes develop that limit institutional and personal growth relative to awareness of discrimination and appreciation of diversity. Fortunately, studies in social psychology have demonstrated that altering group norms can have a profound impact on changing individual behavior. Changing group norms begins with overcoming the lack of awareness and discussion of these issues that is typical on most campuses. Pettigrew (1994) discussed four social-psychological processes that can then be employed to foster positive norm change: urging acceptance of the inevitability of institutional change, using behavioral change to produce attitudinal change, promoting intergroup contact under optimal conditions, and dispelling intergroup fears. Collectively, these processes can lead to reductions in both prejudice and discrimination. Staff of college counseling centers and mental health services can play important roles in promoting these processes. Counselors have the knowledge and skills to facilitate productive intergroup contact, and they have expertise in helping individuals and groups work through resistances. They can also help to develop an institutional culture that embraces rather than fears change and one that emphasizes actions more than words. In addition, Pettigrew emphasizes the importance of open access for all students to all campus organizations and of noticing and reinforcing all existing cross-cultural bonds. College counselors can operate as advocates and change agents for such openness and as support persons for students attempting such entry.

Women

Though 51 to 56 percent of students in higher education are women (Touchton and Davis, 1991), sex equity has still not yet been achieved in colleges and universities (Lonnquist and Reesor, 1987). Inequity is evidenced both inside and outside the classroom (Hall and Sandler, 1982; Sandler and Hall, 1986; Crawford and MacLeod, 1990; Cooper and Passafume, 1996).

Differences in the classroom environment for men and women students are believed to be one of the principal causes of the paucity of women in the physical sciences (Flam, 1991) as well as in computer science (Kolata, 1984). Other factors affecting students' choice to enter these disciplines include differences in play experiences and in experiences that promote interest (Cooper and Robinson, 1989) and culturally based career socialization pressures (Gottfriedson, 1981). Teachers' opinions have also been shown to create a chilly climate for female children and adolescents (Albertson and Kagan, 1988).

Investigators have studied specific processes that affect gender climate in the classroom. For example, Crawford and MacLeod (1990) tested the hypothesis that professors' discriminatory behavior was partially responsible for female college students' participating less often and less assertively in class than male students. They found that participation was related to the quality of the teacher-student interaction and that women faculty generally provide more support for questions and discussion than did men faculty. Constantinople, Cornelius, and Gray (1988) similarly reported that male college students were more active in the classroom than female students, but that behavioral factors rather than gender of the instructor influenced this phenomenon. The most direct research evidence on the "chilly climate" has emerged from the Project on the Status and Education of Women (Hall and Sandler, 1982, 1984). This broad-based project concluded that faculty's "differentially critical evaluations," "inequitable treatment," "negative use of language," and "mismanagement of discussion" are central contributors to a negative climate for women. Further, the project data indicated that this chilly gender climate is experienced more intensely by female graduate students, women in traditionally masculine fields, female minority students, and older women.

How might counselors use their outreach and consultation expertise to assist their campuses in improving this climate? In a study on how a number of universities meet the unique needs of women, Kunkel (1994) identified five categories of need: community, equity, safety, education and awareness, and support and advocacy. The need for community is the desire for connection and networking. The need for equity takes many forms such as the need for equal treatment, equal expectations, and equitable pay and advancement. Safety needs are associated with the significant level of personal violence on campus, most of which victimizes women. Fulfilling the need for education and awareness as well as for support and advocacy requires recognizing both blatant and subtle prejudice and discrimination and then challenging and changing them. Staff in college counseling centers or mental health services can utilize the initiator-catalyst approach to foster progress in each of these areas. The following are some ideas for these campuswide programs, each of which involves initiation, facilitation, or support by counselors:

Community. Women's studies, topics selected specifically for women's programs and groups, special events and programs, infusion of women's issues into courses, informal and formal structured women's networks, and expositions of women's art, music, writing can promote community. Counselors can perhaps be most helpful in providing consultation for the groups that organize these events and in advocating for groups and norms that support formal and informal networks for female students and staff.

Equity. Periodic studies of campus climate, reconsideration of campus policies, prevention of subtle discrimination, awareness of gender stereotypes that lead to inequities, and attention to classroom climate, salaries, and treatment of women by campus agencies can help achieve equity. One of the most helpful roles for counselors here is assessing the campus climate and providing data on student experiences as a stimulus for change.

Safety. Programs on the prevention of sexual and domestic violence, date rape, and sexual harassment, as well as attention to campuswide safety issues such as lights, escort services are important here. Counselors have often taken the lead with regard to violence prevention. Considerable attention must be aimed at changing campus norms regarding sexual communication and male attitudes toward women and sexuality.

Education and awareness. A variety of campuswide programs can challenge the values and belief systems of some groups. Learning about discrimination and coming to grips with one's own prejudices and stereotypes are difficult developmental processes. Counselors can add a perspective on developmental and learning theory to these programs. Ongoing campuswide education efforts are important and need to be separate from political and advocacy efforts, at least as much as possible. For example, a campuswide group to promote education and awareness of gender issues will increase its effectiveness if it includes a broad range of campus constituencies. Highly political and visible advocacy groups probably have limited potential for providing education, although they may be important in the political change process.

Support and advocacy. Campus programs and groups promoting all of the above needs of women will by definition have a support and advocacy function. Counselors can enhance this support by working with advocacy and other groups to facilitate communication and conversation. When working with these groups is not possible, counselors can often have an important mediating role in helping oppositional groups communicate on these issues.

Clearly college counselors can use their expertise in a variety of ways to develop and facilitate campus programs that help women students overcome the various effects of sexist attitudes and discrimination. Because of the divergent opinions on the role of women and the sensitivity of many men to criticism, almost all these programs require delicacy. Although the male gender role has not been selected as a focus in this chapter, any work on gender issues by necessity involves a discussion of both gender roles, and often programs have better results if they include both men and women. One effective type of program that has developed on some campuses involves student groups of men and women who are dedicated to working for fair and equitable sex roles. Sometimes these groups focus on sexual violence, but groups that emphasize male-female communications in general also exist.

Sexual harassment also needs to be addressed on campus. Riggs (1993) summarized a set of studies that found that 20 to 30 percent of undergraduate female students are subjected to some form of sexual harassment by at least one of their professors during their undergraduate years, with even greater proportions of women graduate students reporting such experiences. According to these studies, administrators at approximately 60 percent of the large research institutions believe that sexual harassment is a problem on their campus. While definitions of sexual harassment vary, most are based on experience of behaviors such as demands for sexual favors under threat, physical touching out of context, and sexually directed remarks, rather than subjective judgment of being sexually harassed. Payne (1991) found that harassers select as their victims those who perceive themselves as relatively powerless. She adds that a number of myths (for example, the consenting-adult myth) emerge when harassment episodes become public or are adjudicated. More important, she identifies a number of typical responses by institutions that block systemic progress: ignoring the behavior, impugning those trying to change the system, protecting the perpetrators, and ignoring the issue. Counselors can work through various offices (student affairs, faculty and staff personnel, classroom teaching) to initiate and facilitate awareness programs that focus on the problem and help raise the consciousness of many in the campus community. These kinds of efforts will not work unless a "we are in this together" approach that avoids assigning blame is adopted, along with firm communication of appropriate laws and institutional policy. Support from high-ranking administrators is crucial, although gaining such support is perhaps the most difficult step in developing such a program. Administrators need to see this kind of a program as a positive public relations activity rather than as an admission that the institution has serious problems with sexual harassment.

Program Example: Miniconferences for Employees on Awareness and Prevention of Sexual Harassment

The University of Florida embarked on a large-scale effort to provide sexual-harassment education to all employees. The project was a collaborative effort by the provost, the affirmative-action office, and personnel services and included changes in campus policies. The Counseling Center was involved throughout the process, and a faculty member provided psychological expertise to the multidisciplinary task force that designed the program. The Counseling Center provided input in various areas including development and revisions of policies and procedures as well as program development and implementation. The task force sought broad-based support and reactions from a large number of diverse campus groups. This inclusiveness was central to the acceptance of the changes.

The program, a half-day miniconference, is offered ten times a year. It includes the provision of general information, small-group discussion, and follow-up large-group sharing, questions, and answers. The small-group discussions use case studies as stimulus material; the case studies are set in various universities and often involve some ambiguity. Participation in the small discussion groups is by random assignment, and only first names are used. Thus, workers from many levels within the university come together as equals without the normal hierarchical distinctions.

The program is based on the social-cognitive model of change; the inclusion of the entire work force as participants makes a strong statement about institutional commitment to the issue, which is reinforced by direct support from upper-level administrators at the beginning of the miniconferences. In addition, peer support is a key to individual attitudinal and behavioral change.

Source: J. Resnick, director, Counseling Center, University of Florida, personal communication, 1996.

Minority Groups and Multicultural Issues

As discussed in Chapter Seven, considerable attention has been focused on multicultural counseling (Pederson, 1994). Although limited in amount, impressive research has been done on the general topic of counseling minority students (for example, Trippi and Cheatham, 1989, 1991) and on minority-student identity development (Helms, 1990). In contrast to this research focus on clinical issues, the research agenda on multicultural outreach and consultation has received little attention in the counseling literature. This paucity of research perhaps reflects the difficulty counselors and others face in trying to devise methods to make campuses hospitable to diverse groups of students.

How can counselors help campuses make progress in the fight against discrimination and prejudice? Productive multicultural outreach and consultation would have staff of university counseling and mental health centers moving into Atkinson, Morten, and Sue's (1993) roles of advocate, consultant, and facilitator of indigenous support and healing systems. Creativity in outreach programming is necessary as well. The initiator-catalyst approach creates secondary change by first changing those who work with others. Once this primary group is altered, the changes they have made will be passed on to those with whom they interact.

Two general areas seem to be the focus of many campus efforts: increasing the positive valuation and appreciation of diversity and decreasing discrimination and prejudice through awareness and education. Counselors can play an important role in both areas. Much of this kind of education comes from interaction among various campus groups and from engaging students in discourse and thought about their own attitudes and behavior in their classes, workshops, retreats, and social and interest groups. Counselors can contribute a great deal to the planning and supervision of these activities.

Program Example: Workshop on Valuing Ethnic Diversity

The Counseling and Mental Health Center at the University of Texas, in conjunction with the Office of Personnel Services and Employee Relations, targeted managerial and supervisory staff as an influential group for promoting diversity awareness and sensitivity. The day-long workshop that was created was led by three people and utilized lectures, small-group discussions, structured exercises, a videotape, and large-group processes. The intervention had several goals: to establish a climate of safety, respect, and support in which participants could explore their ethnic and racial stereotyping; to have participants develop empathy for persons who are discriminated against so that they would be motivated to modify their own discriminatory attitudes and actions; to provide opportunities to explore both individual and institutional forms of racism; to encourage participants to make a commitment to change one small aspect of a prejudicial attitude or behavior as part of a personal action plan; and to have participants make attitude and behavioral changes on an ongoing basis after the conclusion of the workshop.

Two follow-up activities reinforced the workshop. The first was a brown-bag lunch series open to all "graduates" of the seminar. The second was a subsequent program in which participants viewed and discussed the parts of the video not used during the initial workshop.

Source: Baron, 1992.

Alexander Astin's (1993a) seminal research on diversity and multiculturalism on campus collected data on eighty-two outcome measures for twenty-five thousand students attending 217 four-year colleges and universities. His analysis showed that exposure to "cultural awareness" workshops is positively associated with six different measures of academic development (critical thinking, general knowledge, public-speaking ability, listening ability, writing ability, and preparation for graduate school) and six different measures of student satisfaction. Such workshops are also positively correlated with retention of undergraduates. More important, Astin's work pinpoints high-impact areas within the institution, the faculty, and the student body. Those institutions that enhance diversity in these areas have better academic outcomes than those that do not.

Staff in college counseling and mental health services can target one or more of the diversity-enhancement areas with initiator-catalyst outreach and consultation efforts. For example, counselors can initiate and help design campus retreats with key administrators, faculty, staff, and students to identify diversity-enhancing objectives along with concomitant supports and barriers. Such retreats can include sufficient time for break-out groups to focus on all high-impact areas. Alternatively, carefully constructed assessment instruments, such as those used by Astin, can be employed. A well-constructed survey might yield interesting data on the level of racial harassment on campus as well as specifics about the relationships and situations in which this harassment occurs.

In addition to focusing on the general campus issues of discrimination and diversity awareness, counselors have a role in working with programs and systems to help promote the academic and personal success of students in minority groups. Clearly, work with the entire campus can help improve the climate for minorities, but targeted programs to help these students achieve in an environment that is sometimes perceived as hostile are also important. College counselors should be involved in minority peer counseling, mentoring, and assistance programs and in the development of special services for minority students. They can help with training, supervision, consultation, needs assessment, and program design and evaluation. As was mentioned in Chapter Seven, counselors need to take a visible role in working with minority groups and organizations. Outreach and consultation work can help provide the visibility needed to ensure that students feel welcome to use campus counseling facilities.

Program Example: Peer Mentoring for African Americans

In the fall semester 1986, the Counseling Service at the University of Missouri at St. Louis implemented the Helping Hand Project, a peer-mentoring program for entering African American students. The recruitment form is mailed to all newly enrolled African American students at the beginning of each fall semester. A mentoring team consisting of upperclass students with different majors is assembled during the preceding summer. When the applications are received, each protégé is matched with a mentor who has a similar major and background. Mentors then design experiences that match their protégés' needs throughout the year. The protégés meet weekly with their mentors to discuss key issues such as stress management, academic performance, dating, class difficulties, work issues. Protégés and mentors also interact regularly with faculty and staff to familiarize protégés with campus resources. The goal of the project is to foster protégés' autonomy, thereby increasing their chances of being successful in attaining their goals.

Upperclass mentors benefit considerably from participating in the Helping Hand Project. Mentors gain substantial leadership and counseling experience from facilitating discussions and working individually with their protégés. Mentors also learn from each other and the program coordinator in their weekly supervision sessions, where they discuss their protégés' progress and plan project activities. Mentors also use supervision sessions to share personal information that relates indirectly to their role as mentors. Because of these personal disclosures, a camaraderie develops among the mentors and between the mentors and the coordinator. Thus supervision sessions serve as a "therapeutic" setting in which mentors applaud their successes and assist each other during difficult times. With guidance and encouragement the mentors have assumed increasing levels of responsibility in the project.

Source: B. Jenkins, staff psychologist, University of Missouri at St. Louis, personal communication, 1996.

Students with Different Sexual Orientations

Currently no group experiences more overt discrimination or prejudice on campus than GLB students. This discrimination results from pervasive homophobia. A study by D'Augelli and Rose (1990) found that most students are strongly biased against lesbians and gay men. More than half of the students surveyed believed that homosexuality was wrong. Negative sentiments were greater toward gay men than lesbians, with men being more homophobic than women. Another investigation reported that homophobia among heterosexual males may be targeted more toward gay men than lesbians and that gender roles are more highly connected to homophobia than is gender (Kerns and Fine, 1994). Given the political polarization related to homosexuality, as is evidenced in the controversy surrounding gay marriage, it seems safe to predict that discrimination and strong homophobic attitudes will be with us on college campuses for some time.

Counselors and psychologists have begun to recognize the need to provide special services and programs for GLB students (Berne, 1992; Morgan and Nerison, 1993). The counseling field appears to be moving toward an inclusive definition of multiculturalism, with the general view being that homosexuals constitute a "normal" and oppressed minority. For example, Pope (1995), in his article "The 'Salad Bowl' is Big Enough for Us All: An Argument for the Inclusion of Lesbians and Gay Men in Any Definition of Multiculturalism," makes such a case. Similarly, general books on counseling, such as Hackney and Cormier (1996) and Gelso and Fretz (1992), also propose this broadened definition of multiculturalism. And GLB concerns have been included in considerations of minority issues and discrimination.

Although the GLB minority is not necessarily visible, the effects of discrimination and homophobia are extremely negative and far-reaching. It is important for counselors to represent this minority group because so many members of the group are afraid to represent themselves. A number of successful programs to provide visible support for gay students have emerged. These programs typically involve recruiting faculty and staff as "allies" or "friends" of GLB students; these allies display some sign of their support in their offices (Wells, 1995). Special outreach developmental services for GLB students have also been instituted on some campuses. GLB studies programs and events are becoming another popular avenue for increasing awareness of homosexuality as a positive force, and counselors have provided support and help in organizing these programs. Counselors have also been instrumental in the development and maintenance of GLB student organizations. These organizations are critical for the development of GLB students' positive sense of identity. One of the most difficult tasks for GLB students is coming out to their parents. Counselors can provide materials and group meetings for parents of GLB students and can help GLB parent organizations develop programs for parents of students who have recently come out to them.

Program Example: GLB Supportive Programs and Services

The Pennsylvania State University has developed a model GLB program using an initiator-catalyst approach. It covers the spiritual, emotional, intellectual, and social aspects of being gay. It also emphasizes the developmental tasks of coming out, developing a positive self-concept, obtaining and maintaining primary relationships, handling homophobia and harassment, and dealing with discrimination. The program

stresses the importance of maintaining primary relationships and of overcoming si-
lence, lies, isolation, rejection, intimidation and physical violence, and denial of basic
civil rights. Cass's (1979) six-stage model of homosexual identity formation is given
considerable attention.

Counseling and Psychological Services makes its own contribution along with supporting, both directly and indirectly, the contributions of a number of other student
affairs offices. Staff specifically focus on the emotional and spiritual components by offering closed and private support groups, individual counseling, a weekly discussion
group for lesbians and bisexual women and one for gays and bisexual men, and workshops on same-sex attraction. The other offices involved include career development
and placement, health services, performing arts, human-resource development, GLB
organizations, residence life, and the vice provost for educational equity. These offices
focus on emotional, physical, intellectual, social, and spiritual dimensions as appropriate, with programs and services embedded within each unit.

Beyond this collaboration of numerous offices and organizations, the GLB support
program fostered the evolution of relevant campus policies as well as discussion of the
importance of personal commitment carried into action.

Source: Carter, Feldbaum, and Puzycki, 1996.

Programs focusing on homophobia and on helping GLB students overcome
the effects of negative developmental and environmental influences are becoming increasingly common. There is still a considerable amount of risk for advocates of these students on some campuses, but counseling and mental health
services have often been in the forefront in providing programs to improve the
campus environment. In addition to the "ally" programs previously described,
counseling centers have taken on campus homophobia by developing special services and by attempting assessment and intervention. Work in this area demonstrates some of the difficulties in using an initiator-catalyst model. If a campus
counseling or mental health service takes a strong stand as an advocate for GLB
students, it risks considerable criticism from those on campus who espouse the notion that homosexuality is pathological or sinful (or both). As mentioned in Chapter Nine, which elaborated the initiator-catalyst model, an agency should take
on advocacy roles only after an analysis of the impact on all the different campus
constituencies. Making such an analysis will avoid surprises and will help the
agency devise a strong and meaningful advocacy position.

Program Example: GLB Ally Program

The University of Illinois, Urbana-Champaign, has a longstanding GLB ALLY program.
The ALLY consultation and outreach activities are coordinated by the Sexual Orientation Diversity Allies Committee of the Counseling Center. Becoming an ALLY appears
to be a developmental process with the following stages: becoming aware, gaining

knowledge, gaining skills, and taking action. The materials utilized by the program are incorporated into a training booklet; it contains a heterosexual questionnaire, a list of definitions, an explanation of developmental issues of GLB students, a coming-out handout, a homophobia and heterosexual handout, a homophobia scale, a list of commonly held incorrect beliefs, action ideas for interrupting heterosexism, suggestions for combating heterosexism, a list of GLB inclusive language techniques, suggestions for working with GLB students, a list of the qualities of an ALLY, and a list of "things you should know" as an ALLY.

The list of qualities of an ALLY underscores the contents of the booklet. According to the list, ALLYs have an understanding of sexual orientation and are comfortable with their own. An ALLY recognizes that the coming-out process is unique to GLB students and is a long-term event. An ALLY is aware that GLB students internalize the same messages about sexual orientation (for example, homophobia) and sexuality as most other people. An ALLY honors the diversity of humanity as expressed within the GLB community.

Source: Sexual Orientation Diversity Allies Committee, 1995.

Failure to address homophobia in the student body at large will result in limited systems change. Schreier (1995) called for a paradigmatic shift in college psychoeducational programming from models emphasizing tolerance to models emphasizing nurturance. "Tolerance-oriented programming focuses on agents, rather than victims of discrimination; states limits of acceptable behavior; and anticipates students' resistance to new ideas. The nurturance approach aims to involve all students in the creation of an empowering campus environment" (p. 19).

Students with Disabilities

As discussed in Chapter Seven, considerable attention has been given to counseling and direct support services for students with disabilities. Approximately 10 percent of the students attending postsecondary institutions report at least one disability (National Clearinghouse on Postsecondary Education for Individuals with Disabilities, 1992). Federal laws governing postsecondary education and disability rights have created significant changes within higher education. A publication from JKL Communications Law Reviews summarizes some of the areas of change. "Post-secondary institutions are affected . . . in three principal areas: testing (for admissions, evaluation of academic performance and graduation); the delivery of course materials; and access to the non-academic benefits (social & athletic) of the educational experience" (Latham and Latham, 1995, p. 1). University and college campuses respond in the three areas in different ways and with vastly differing levels of organizational commitment. The degree of involvement of counselors in providing related services varies considerably from institution to institution.

In regard to outreach and consultation services, the important questions are how the campus environment affects disabled students and what types of changes and improvements are needed to prevent failure and to help disabled students thrive. In a sense, these are the same questions that have been asked about other minority and "different" groups, but the answers are somewhat more complicated because of federal law and the need for expensive special support services.

Counselors can help the institution examine the general climate for disabled students as well as faculty and staff attitudes that are helpful or discouraging to these students. It may be difficult to garner much support for this kind of preventive approach because so much energy has been expended by institutions in deciding what services and physical modifications are required by law and in finding the funds to complete the necessary physical changes.

An initiator-catalyst approach can be utilized to focus on broad campus-climate issues. For example, counselors can assess the academic and social climate for disabled students and provide this information to the campus at large. This assessment might provide the impetus for a campuswide effort to consider the needs of these students, similar to the efforts on behalf of women and other minority groups. As with all such undertakings, considerable political analysis and strategizing about how to garner support in a particular institution are necessary. Counselors might also focus on specific campus groups. For example, in conjunction with the academic affairs office and the office for students with disabilities, counselors might design or facilitate an education program for faculty on dealing with disabled students, perhaps as part of faculty orientation or a seminar series on teaching methods. Counselors can also work with appropriate disciplines to encourage inclusion of topics related to disability in course curricula. Counselors might also be involved in the development of peer education programs set up to foster campus awareness about disabilities. Counselors can also provide consultation and training for prevention and education programs aimed at specific groups of disabled students. Rather than directly providing support groups, counselors should take an initiator-catalyst approach and set up ongoing support groups led by students or staff.

Program Example: Providing Assistance to Students with Learning Disabilities

College students with learning disabilities often have mental health problems that can significantly impair their academic performance and their lives. Psychologists and counselors at the University of Minnesota's Counseling Services Office of Students with Disabilities served as team members to assist students with learning disabilities. In this role, they often provided consultation and recommendations to involved faculty and administrators concerning students' emotional and psychological issues and their impacts.

Staff also supported the program through other actions: (1) They developed institutional guidelines and policies related to the mental health concerns of individuals with learning disabilities. (2) They provided assistance for service providers in creating personal and institutional codes of ethics applicable to their work with students with learning disabilities. (3) They created a local referral system and update it periodically. (4) They make it a priority to provide both preservice and in-service training for service providers about the mental health difficulties and psychosocial issues of students with learning disabilities. (5) They conduct qualitative and quantitative research on the specific mental health problems of individuals with learning disabilities. (6) They obtain feedback from students with learning disabilities about which techniques, materials, and resources are most helpful to them in working through their psychosocial issues.

Source: Price, Johnson, and Evelo, 1994.

HEATH, a program of the American Council on Education, is a particularly rich source of assistance for outreach and consultation projects in this area. HEATH operates as the National Clearinghouse on Postsecondary Education for Individuals with Disabilities. A useful newsletter is published three times annually and is available from the HEATH Resource Center, One Dupont Circle, Suite 800, Washington, D.C. 20036-1193, (800) 544-3284. Requests can also be made by Internet: heath@ace.nche.edu or fax: (202) 833-4760.

Adult Learners

Students over the age of twenty-five are the fastest-growing group of those attending college today (Chartrand, 1992). In some ways, these adult learners are similar to most other students, particularly the serious ones, in their investment of considerable time and energy along with economic resources in their education and in their hopes that immersing themselves in curricular and, to a limited extent, cocurricular experiences will directly benefit them. In other ways, however, they are distinct from other students. For example, they face different developmental tasks related to their age, stage of life, and individual circumstances. Moreover, they are much more likely to commute rather than to live on campus, and they are not likely to have many same-age classmates. Consequently, they often feel isolated and alone, and it is not uncommon for them to report a fair amount of shame about "being behind where they should be" as they compare themselves with their own models and projections of adult development. These feelings are especially prevalent among those at colleges and universities that primarily serve traditional and residential students, while they are somewhat less prevalent at institutions catering to the nontraditional, commuter student. Thus, the mostly subtle prejudice and discrimination that these students experience result from the policies, procedures, and customs that define each particular college environment; these policies differ greatly because of differences in institutional goals and priorities. Still another significant factor for adult learners is that they are often first-generation college students; many come from families of blue-collar workers and nonprofessional laborers.

Those planning outreach and consultation activities for the adult learner must consider the above factors when making decisions about the type of content that should be offered and also about the method of content delivery. For example, appropriate topics for this group of students include using university resources, balancing career and family, marketing strengths and assets in the job-search process, managing money effectively, while modes of information delivery might be a special newsletter for adult learners on campus, an e-mail listserv system, a designated space where nontraditional students can gather and study, and a network of peer educators who support the early success of newly matriculating nontraditional students. Supplemental services, such as on-campus day care or an on-campus locker, can also make the lives of adult learners easier.

Program Example: Support Activities for First-Generation Adult Learners

The counseling center is among a host of other offices at Palo Alto College (San Antonio, Texas) that has put together a comprehensive series of workshops for adult learners including blood-pressure screenings, tax-preparation sessions, discussions of the middle-class nature of the university, and cultural festivals. These workshops are buttressed by supportive services that welcome and involve family members. Discussion sessions that help this group of students integrate their educational choices with their postgraduation objectives are also offered on a regular basis.

Source: P. Parma, program coordinator and counselor, Palo Alto College, personal communication, 1996.

◆ ◆ ◆

The challenge for college campuses in reaching out to diverse groups in order to help them take advantage of the full range of opportunities for growth is enormous. Part of meeting this challenge involves focusing on the campus environment and confronting discrimination, racism, prejudice, and fear. College is an appropriate and useful place for students to reexamine their beliefs and values regarding minority groups, and counselors can play an important role in designing and facilitating the development of truly diverse learning environments where differences are appreciated and celebrated.

PART THREE

ADMINISTRATIVE AND PROFESSIONAL ISSUES

In this final part of the book, which is devoted to administrative and professional issues, a number of important topics are addressed. Program assessment, evaluation, and research are covered in Chapter Thirteen, and Chapters Fourteen and Fifteen discuss contemporary ethical, legal, training, and accreditation issues in college counseling. Administrative and organizational issues within the institution are examined in Chapter Sixteen, and internal management, leadership, and quality control are covered in Chapter Seventeen.

CHAPTER THIRTEEN

RESEARCH AND EVALUATION FOR PROMOTING SERVICE EXCELLENCE

The International Association of Counseling Services (IACS) standards (Kiracofe and others, 1994) include "research" as a core function of university counseling services. These standards state than "an integral responsibility of the counseling services is to conduct ongoing evaluation and accountability research, to determine the effectiveness of its services, and to improve the quality of services" (p. 39). Research in the IACS context is a combination of evaluation of clinical services, program assessment, and scholarly study. Because of resource limits, changes in health care, and the need to prioritize functions, the importance of such research activities needs to be examined (Steenbarger, 1995a). Is research a reasonable and legitimate goal for student counseling and mental health services? Of what value is a research program to a counseling or mental health service and to the institution? This chapter consists of four sections. In the first, general issues surrounding these broad research activities in the college counseling center are discussed. The second section covers the research process and describes tools and methods that can be employed along with recommendations for matching the approaches used with specific situations. The third section presents illustrations and program examples of counseling-center research. The fourth section describes how to set a research agenda.

The extent to which counseling and mental health centers engage in program assessment and research is probably a function of many factors, including the individual interests and abilities of their staffs and directors and their philosophy of what a counseling or mental health center should provide. Centers using an outreach model, with the entire campus community as the focus of service, will view services and program evaluation as well as both applied and basic research as an essential part of their role as a consultant to the entire campus. For example, assessment often serves as a foundation for initiator-catalyst approaches to outreach. In addition, documenting outcomes of services and program effectiveness is a crucial part of demonstrating accountability (Steenbarger and Smith, 1996).

Goals and Challenges

Stone and Archer (1990) reported that one major obstacle counseling centers face when deciding whether to engage in research is the narrow definition of what such research entails. They suggested that practitioners too often equate research with the carefully controlled experimental studies that are published in many journals. The much broader definition of research described in the IACS standards allows counseling-center staff to make other kinds of evaluations part of research. Boyd, Roberts, and Cook (1994) presented a comprehensive set of goals for a counseling-center research program: provide an understanding of student characteristics, assess changing student characteristics, identify potential demands for services, document personal outcomes of counseling, serve as a data resource for the campus.

These goals are congruent with the way IACS defines research. Moreover, although all these goals appear to be quantitative, it is clearly possible and often desirable to include qualitative and anecdotal data in these kinds of studies. A well-written and concise narrative reporting observations of students can have a significant impact on faculty and administrators.

A number of challenges must be overcome to create and implement a successful assessment and research program. First and foremost, the counseling or mental health center must find the time and resources, which means giving such activities staff time and financial support. Second, the almost total lack of interest by many practitioners in research endeavors must be overcome. Steenbarger and Manchester (1990) labeled this lack of interest "research phobia" in their discussion of research on college health. Further evidence of practitioner antithesis to research activities was presented by Stone and Archer (1990), who summarized studies showing that younger counseling-center psychologists are practice-oriented. They also presented data indicating that the amount of time counseling staffs spend on research is small; 2 percent was reported in one Big Ten survey. On a more positive note, Stone and Lucas (1991) in a survey of several prominent counseling and counseling-psychology journals found that authors of about 8 percent of the empirical studies published were from counseling centers, with the figure rising to 9 and 10 percent in the applied journals.

Third, ways must be found to use research to demonstrate the value of counseling and mental health services. In one sense, this challenge is embedded in all the others. If a center provides timely and useful data to the institution about the importance of counseling and related programs and services, its value to the institution and to students will be better understood. For example, a carefully conducted study by Wilson, Mason, and Ewing (1997) documented that when students who obtained personal counseling were compared with a group of students with matching academic records and potential who did not receive counseling, those who were counseled were 14 percent more likely to remain in college. Such data speak loudly to those who care about degree completion and to those focused on the bottom line. In addition, college counselors can clearly make strong contributions to the overall mission of a college or university by researching questions such as how to prevent sexual violence. Their understanding of students and their practical experience can also be particularly useful to academic faculty conducting applied psychological research. Collaborations with academic faculty encourage a team approach and may be particularly appropriate because of the time and resource limitations most college counseling-center staff face.

Program Example: Data Collection as a Core Counseling-Center Activity

The Counseling Center at the University of Maryland serves as a model for incorporating program assessment and research as core activities. The Center is large and diverse. It has six special administrative units that engage in research activities: Counseling Services, the Testing, Research and Data Processing Unit, the Disability Support Service, the Learning Assistance Service, the Retention Study Group, and the Parent Consultation and Child Evaluation Service.

Boyd, Roberts, and Cook (1994) reported the large variety of data that the Counseling Center gathers in its research program. These ranged from studies of student behavior, of first-year students' attitudes and expectations, and of senior students' views of college through empirical studies of at-risk groups to research on psychotherapy processes and outcomes. These data may be gathered and analyzed by more than one unit. For example, lists of client problems are compiled by the Disability Support Service, the Learning Assistance Service, and the Parent Consultation and Child Evaluation Service. Follow-up evaluations are performed by Counseling Services and also by the three services just mentioned. Sometimes only one unit is engaged in a specific type of research. For example, only Counseling Services does needs and perceptions assessments.

Source: Boyd, Roberts, and Cook, 1994.

Although most counseling and mental health centers are not as large and do not have such an extensive history of research, some meaningful focus on research is usually possible and, indeed, is becoming essential. Small centers face particular challenges in freeing resources to conduct indirect and scholastically rigorous research activities such as the environmental-impact studies and studies of student behavior carried out by the Testing, Research and Data Processing Unit at the University of Maryland.

Conducting Research in Counseling and Mental Health Settings

Steenbarger and Manchester (1990, 1993a, 1993b) and Steenbarger, Schwartz, and Manchester (1993) wrote a four-part series of articles on doing research in college health that is a useful resource for staff of college counseling centers and mental health services. The goal of these articles was to demystify the scholarly process and to reduce the fears and anxieties that keep many practitioners from engaging in this work. Concepts from these four articles as well as additional clinically oriented research techniques are covered here in some detail as they are essential to conducting evaluations of clinical services, program assessment, and research.

The first piece, subtitled "An Introduction to the Research Process," suggests typical reasons why staff members conduct research; these reasons include career enhancement, personal gratification, social enhancement, and professional enhancement, while the major opposing forces are time constraints and lack of interest.

Research is defined in this article as "the organized search for new knowledge" (Steenbarger and Manchester, 1990, p. 120). Typically, research studies have one of five objectives: extending a published finding to a new population or setting, testing a commonly held assumption, providing valuable information to practitioners, opening a new field of inquiry, or testing the effectiveness of a treatment. Without research, the college counseling field would stagnate, and counseling centers could not adequately provide services in newly emerging problem areas. Moreover, both basic and applied studies are necessary. For example, basic research on relationship violence in college students may yield important findings that have implications for treatment or prevention. Observations of and research on healthy relationships led to psychoeducational efforts to impart the skills that were uncovered. Or applied research evaluating a catalyst-initiator model for reducing sexual assaults might be useful in identifying potent change processes. The alternation of observation and theory provides a means of improving the quality of services and programs. The two outcomes of research—identification of patterns among events and an understanding of their causes—can lead to enhanced prevention and intervention efforts. Often the connection between observation and research leads to reciprocal changes—for example, research designed to investigate certain observations is, in turn, likely to lead to the selection of different aspects to observe.

The introductory piece by Steenbarger and Manchester gives extensive coverage to the research hypothesis, "a tentative statement that suggests a relationship between two or more phenomena" (1990, p. 121). For example, some research hypothesizes a relationship between improved interpersonal relationships and relief from depression. Other studies hypothesize a connection between aerobic exercise and depression relief. Staff working in counseling and mental health centers might obtain inspiration for hypotheses from a number of sources, such as clinical observations, published research, or dialogues with colleagues. Research hypotheses, whether exploratory or confirmatory, refer to observable events that are both falsifiable and tentative.

Once a hypothesis is selected, it is important to review the literature. Reviews are much easier and less time-consuming than they once were because of the availability of on-line searches on CD-ROM like Psych-Lit or ERIC. In fact, many staff can access these resources through their office computers if they are networked with the main campus computer system. As an example, a counseling center might want to offer and evaluate an eating disorders therapy group. A literature review could indicate what is already known about such groups, could identify the dominant conceptual or theoretical frameworks, and could describe methods of inquiry used by others investigating this area. Reading recent books and talking to knowledgeable peers about the topic can also assist in the review process. At this point the hypothesis often has to be revised. For example, a counseling center may want to study the best way to provide therapy to students experiencing test anxiety. The initial hypothesis may have been that poor study habits cause test anxiety. However, the literature review may suggest that maladaptive cognition is a more likely cause.

Steenbarger and Manchester's second article focused on how to design a study. The initial concern is adequacy of sampling. Far too often, samples of "convenience" rather than representative samples are selected. For example, a survey of the drinking behavior of all men attending an introductory meeting on Greek life would not adequately represent all college males. Even if a well-developed sample of men from one university is selected, generalizability to all college males is still questionable, and the need for multicampus investigations is great.

Random assignment ensures representative samples. Generally, if staff wish to evaluate the differential effectiveness of two treatments—individual versus group counseling for clients with eating disorders, for example—it is important to assign clients to each treatment randomly. Otherwise bias in assignment is likely to lead to bias in findings. The number of subjects necessary for reaching reasonable conclusions connects the issues of sample and assignment. For example, case studies require few subjects. Initial research on highly specific and relatively small populations, such as college students with dissociation identity disorder, might best be conducted using such a case-study approach. In contrast, tightly controlled experimental research, such as a study of cognitive-behavioral therapy versus interpersonal counseling, typically requires a minimum of ten subjects per group, with subjects in each group matched on all important variables that could confound the results (for example, introversion-extroversion). Survey-based research—for example, measures of self-esteem—necessitate even larger samples.

Operationalization is the translation of the concepts into observable, measurable indices. In quantitative studies, these measures must be both reliable and valid. For example, a measure of anxiety should accurately assess that construct and should do so with consistency. In qualitative investigations, trustworthiness and replication are the parallel processes. A study on intimate relationships could use semistructured interviews with a number of students. Results of such semistructured interviews would be replicable and trustworthy if there were considerable theme consistency across interviewees and interviewers as well as across independent sources categorizing the verbal responses. Whether quantitative or qualitative, studies conducted by college counseling-center staff should protect confidentiality and provide anonymity, should include the voluntary, informed consent of subjects, and should emphasize safety.

The third article by Steenbarger and Manchester discusses "representative designs and their challenges." Survey, epidemiological, and experimental studies are described. Survey research, which is mostly correlational in nature, can be used to address many questions in college counseling and mental health. Needs surveys can be employed to determine priorities for outreach programming, and satisfaction surveys can be used to evaluate reactions to treatment. Knowledge of and attitudes toward sex roles and relationship violence, for example, can be assessed. Prevalence data, including aggregate information on presenting concerns, provide estimates of the extent of the problem in the population. A growing number of psychometrically sound surveys can be examined for possible application in this or other studies. Use of well-substantiated indices avoids the "fatal flaw" of using unproved instruments. Having a reasonable balance between convenience and representativeness of the sample is usually the best approach when using such instruments.

Epidemiological designs are excellent for the measurement of longitudinal change—changes over a period of time. These designs can be retrospective. For example, use of the Time Line Feedback Sheet (Sobell and others, 1980) yields fairly accurate data on drinking for the past six to twelve months. Prospective studies follow a selected group of students over time. For example, freshmen and sophomores who complete a survey of their interests and extracurricular activities retake the survey two years later. Increases and decreases in levels of campus involvement can then be determined.

Experimental designs result from intentional human intervention. They are often used to determine treatment efficacy. Comparing therapy A and therapy B —for example, cognitive versus interpersonal treatment of depression—gets at the effectiveness question. Data are now being collected on actual client response versus expected client response using eclectic therapy (Howard and others, 1996). This type of experimental research offers high promise for bridging the gap between scientists and practitioners that has plagued the field.

The final article by Steenbarger and Manchester covered analyzing and communicating results. Descriptive statistics, including measures of central tendency (mean, medium, and mode) and measures of dispersion (range, standard deviation, and distribution characteristics), are important data in most research. As an illustration, a counseling or mental health center might want to assess frequency and intensity of client presenting problems by class level. Or staff might want to determine caloric intake of women with an eating disorder.

Inferential statistics are employed to test hypotheses based on samples. These statistics can assume normalcy of the distribution (parametric) or nonnormalcy (nonparametric). For example, levels of student stress are likely to be normally distributed, whereas levels of psychotic thinking among mild, moderate, and severe depressives is not. Correlational analyses are employed to test the hypothesis of a positive or negative relationship between two or more variables. Academic performance could be hypothesized to decrease as level of mental distress increases among college students. Significance levels indicate the degree of risk researchers are willing to take in the accuracy of their correlations. Tables for determining the significance of correlations can be found in most statistical texts and computerized statistical packages (SPSS, SAS, BMDP).

Analysis of Variance (ANOVA) finds its niche in testing a hypothesis involving two or more groups. Staff at a counseling and mental health center, for example, might want to investigate levels of perceived stress among students in the various colleges within a university. If they want to also measure levels of ·

perceived need for stress-reduction programs and to evaluate how both perceived stress and perceived need for programs change consequent to a series of stress-management seminars, then use of Multiple Analysis of Variance (MANOVA) methods would be appropriate.

Nonparametric rather than parametric statistics are required for many research projects at counseling and mental health centers. Specifically, when the data are categorical (race, class level, academic major, presenting problem) or ordinal (mild versus moderate versus severe symptoms) or rankings (for example, class rankings), then nonparametric statistics, such as the chi-square or Mann-Whitney U test, should be employed.

Counseling-center staff often communicate the results of their findings through conference presentations in an increasing variety of formats, such as poster sessions, papers, symposiums, roundtables, and conversation hours. Staff also contribute to growth in the field by authoring articles in professional journals. For college counseling and mental health centers, popular outlets include the *Journal of College Student Development*, the *Journal of College Counseling*, the *Journal of College Student Psychotherapy*, the *Journal of Counseling and Development*, the *Journal of Counseling Psychology*, and *The Counseling Psychologist*.

The series of articles by Steenbarger and Manchester is excellent because it uses straightforward language to simplify the research process and its illustrations include a number dealing with college mental health issues. The absence of the presentation of alternative research methodologies, however, might limit the attractiveness of conducting such studies for practitioners who work with one client at a time or in small groups.

One of the most underutilized sets of research strategies is single-subject designs developed under the behavioral and, later, cognitive paradigms. Such designs include careful assessment of the client with ongoing evaluation of change. Typically, these designs enable determination of the degree of change causally connected to the intervention. Further, there is great variety and accompanying flexibility with single-subject designs.

Reversal designs involve providing an intervention, withdrawing it, and then reintroducing it. For example, a therapist could introduce the technique of thought stopping to a client with a great amount of irrational self-talk. Diminishment of such inner dialogue could be assessed. Then, continuing to monitor these irrational self-statements while stopping and then restarting the intervention could determine its causal effectiveness. Multiple baseline designs involve sequentially applying across persons, settings, times, or behaviors. Staff could provide mandatory alcohol- and drug-use assessments and psychoeducation for students caught in violation of residence hall use policies. If reductions in such violations varied with the introduction of this intervention to halls in a sequential manner, then efficacy and causality would be supported. Changing-criterion designs involve tying an intervention to a "shaping" procedure. A counselor working with a client wanting to lose weight could set progressively lower daily caloric-intake levels and higher daily exercise expectations. If the client loses weight in relation to the changing criteria, then it is likely that the intervention is working. Alternating-treatment designs assess the differential effects of introducing more than one intervention strategy at the same time. A client with severe test anxiety may be helped through a comprehensive stress-inoculation training. Discussion with the therapist might reveal that the physical-relaxation component was far and away the most helpful and thus is likely to be the main strategy for the future.

To be meaningful, change in single-subject research should be reliable (distinctly noticeable) and clinically significant (able to make a decided difference in the client's life). Kazdin's book (1993) on behavior modification in applied settings presents these designs along with numerous intervention strategies and case illustrations. Hill and others' (1996) work on analyzing counseling sessions in great detail presents a qualitative approach to single-subject research.

Another greatly underutilized set of research strategies is sometimes labeled "nonexperimental research." McBurney (1994) included observational research, archival research, and case study as three such methods. Observational research is a "study method in which the researcher observes and records ongoing behavior but does not attempt to change it" (p. 169). Archival research is a "study method that examines existing records to obtain data on test hypotheses" (p. 169). A case study is an "exploratory study of an existing situation as a means of creating and testing a hypothesis" (p. 169).

Qualitative rather than quantitative methods are often appropriate for nonexperimental research designs. Qualitative methods include standardized interviews, in-depth interviews, participant observations, and naturalistic observations. Analysis is often conducted and conclusions reached by a content analysis of information contained in the field notes. The primary goal of such research is to determine meanings rather than causes.

The skills that college mental health providers utilize in their clinical work with clients are essentially identical to the skills needed to conduct nonexperimental, qualitative research. Moreover, a number of leading counseling journals, including the *Journal of Counseling Psychology* and the *Journal of College Student Development*, have advocated for increased use of such research methodologies and have devoted specific issues to them. Research of this type offers the possibility of bridging the scientist-practitioner schism noted by so many (Stone and Lucas, 1991).

Research Standards: Illustrations and Examples

Program examples of various types of college counseling-center program assessments and research are provided in this section. In each case, the topic, type of research, and methodology employed are described. As a conceptual base, the IACS standards are useful.

The first standard concerns ethical practice, which should be the basis for any type of research undertaken. Section 6 of the American Psychological Association's (1995a) *Ethical Principles of Psychologists and Code of Conduct* circumscribes the specific areas of concern: the researcher must be responsible, protect subjects from harm, obtain informed consent, not use deception, assure privacy and freedom from coercion, and debrief subjects (summarized by McBurney, 1994). A number of these issues are of particular concern when the study involves counseling clients. How truly voluntary is participation? What is the tension between gains for science versus benefits to the person? How might participation increase the client's problems? What feedback is given to the clients regarding results? How much opportunity does the participant have to withdraw from the study?

College counseling and mental health centers need to incorporate specific policies and procedures regarding evaluation of clinical services, program assessment, and research into their handbooks in order to increase the likelihood that appropriate ethical concerns will be systematically addressed and to add a layer of protection beyond approval by an institutional review board. These policies and procedures should especially cover the conduct of research on counseling processes and outcomes and other client-based research.

Program Example: Guidelines for Research on Counseling Processes and Outcomes

The Student Counseling and Development Center at Valparaiso University (Indiana) uses the following guidelines:

1. Counselors shall abide by the *Ethical Principles in the Conduct of Research with Human Participants* (American Psychological Association, 1982). Responsibility for the establishment and maintenance of accepted ethical practices remains, at all times, with the individual researcher.
2. Careful review procedures for formal research efforts shall be established in order to assure that research does not unduly interfere with direct service delivery responsibilities of the Student Counseling and Development Center.
3. Student Counseling and Development Center research efforts dependent on client/student involvement shall be consistent with the following guidelines:

a. Prior to participation in planned research, the researcher shall inform all participants of each aspect of the research and shall respond to all questions about the research which are of concern to participants.

b. Staff researchers shall respect a client's individual freedom to decline to participate in and/or withdraw from research at any time. In those cases where clients elect to be part of a planned research effort, a signed agreement should be established between the researcher and participants which clearly states the responsibilities of each in undertaking research.

c. After research data are collected, the researcher shall provide participants with relevant information about the nature of the study and shall make a concerted effort to eliminate any misconceptions that may have arisen during the course of the research.

d. Individual information obtained during the course of research shall remain confidential unless otherwise agreed upon in advance, in writing.

e. Research participants shall have access to copies of the research results, if so requested.

f. Every precaution must be taken to preserve client anonymity in designing outcome studies. If the confidentiality of counseling relationships cannot be maintained to the satisfaction of the individual researcher, such effort shall be terminated.

Source: Cooper, Passafume, Satkamp, and Gaebel-Morgan, 1996.

The second IACS standard emphasizes a regular review of counseling services based on intrainstitution evaluation and interinstitution comparison. These reviews are the most common and perhaps the most important area of college counseling-center research. Such studies provide important data to staff, both as feedback and as quality control, and to administrators, as justification for the allocation of resources. The information generated by such investigations is typically the cornerstone of periodic reports of center activities.

Program Example: Research on Counseling Outcomes

The Metropolitan State College of Denver Counseling Center had a long tradition of justifying its resource allocation by documenting its contribution to the mission of the institution, its assistance in retaining students, its support for troubled students and those in crisis, and its provision of indirect services such as consultation, teaching, training, research, and prevention. Pressures to compete with managed care led to the addition of an assessment of counseling outcomes as proof that the Counseling Center was serving students as well as or better than external competitors. Such assessment is supported by a number of groups including the Joint Committee of the Accreditation of Health Care Organizations, the American Psychological Association

Committee for the Advancement of Professional Practice, and the Practice Research Network.

The Counseling Center obtained information from one group of clients through the combination of an index of personal hopefulness, a measure of psychological symptoms, and scales assessing life-role functioning and problems. These respectively assessed the factors of remoralization, remediation, and rehabilitation outlined by Howard, Lueger, Maling, and Martinovich (1993). Another group of clients completed a set of more medically oriented questionnaires. Selection of the instruments was made by a research committee composed of interested staff and graduate student interns with assistance from academic faculty supervising one intern's dissertation. Results were collected in both a process and summative manner.

The Counseling Center gained a number of benefits from engaging in this outcome research, including improved treatment of individual clients, enhanced services, more complex supervision of trainees, improved accountability, and encouragement to conduct research. The experience also highlighted the importance of direct staff involvement in selecting and using the specific measures and of counseling centers working collaboratively with academic programs within the institution.

Source: Vollmer, 1996.

Investigations of student characteristics or evaluations of program effects constitute the third area of research suggested in the IACS standards. Numerous examples of such work are published in the professional journals mentioned previously. Professional conferences of organizations such as the American Psychological Association, the American Counseling Association, the American College Personnel Association, the American College Health Association, and the National Association of Social Workers are also distribution points for these study results.

Program Example: Investigation of Student Characteristics

After reviewing the documentation demonstrating positive payoffs for direct assessment of the counseling needs of college students, the staff of the University of Delaware Counseling Center decided to survey a sample of students at their institution. They were particularly interested in gender differences in responses as several previous investigations had reported such differences. The center used a highly reliable measure of student needs that had been employed in several other studies. The questionnaire included a number of items describing personal, career development, and learning skills concerns, plus the staff added new items to query about fears for the future. Female students reported greater needs for assistance with several concerns, including test anxiety, depression, assertiveness, and speech anxiety. In addition, female students reported significantly greater fears for the future on most of these items.

Source: Bishop, Bauer, and Becker, 1998.

Staff at college counseling and mental health centers also have the expertise to conduct program evaluations. Program assessment consists of many types of indices, such as client-satisfaction surveys and student-needs questionnaires, as well as many techniques, such as comparison with the IACS standards and benchmarking. Such studies are important for accountability and for determining whether the continued allocation of resources for specific programs is warranted.

Program Example: Investigation of Program Effectiveness for Different Kinds of Students

An investigation at the University of Missouri–Columbia Counseling Center hypothesized that clients who had more stable goals and aspirations and low defensiveness would benefit more from computerized career-guidance systems, an intervention that is relatively nondirective and nonsupportive. The hypotheses were based on adaptive counseling and therapy principles. Instruments used had established psychometric properties and included a survey of goal stability and defensiveness and a measure of career decision making. The study used the SIGI-PLUS interactive career guidance system (Katz, 1975).

Regression analysis of this quasi-experimental situation was employed to test the hypotheses, which were supported by the findings. The implications of the results of this study are that counseling clients who have low defensiveness and high goal stability will be more satisfied and will show more gains with computerized career interventions, while clients who have high defensiveness and low goal stability will probably gain more from intensive, personal interventions.

Source: Kivlighan, Johnston, Hogan, and Mauer, 1994.

A fourth area of research is collaborative projects with students and faculty who want to evaluate program effectiveness or investigate student characteristics. Such collaborative efforts offer several advantages to college counseling and mental health staff. First, such research usually takes less time than other types of research. Second, collaborative scholarship often benefits all involved as it provides research expertise to the practitioner and applied expertise to the academic. Third, joint scholarship efforts build bridges between counseling services and academic affairs. These connections are increasingly necessary because the integration of student affairs and academic affairs is becoming important for the survival of counseling services.

Program Example: Collaborative Research on Student Characteristics

A study at Haskell Indian Junior College (Kansas) was an exploratory investigation of the relationship between American Indian cultural commitment and precounseling attitudes. The quasi-experimental study, which was a collaboration between the academic side and the counseling center, categorized four levels of commitment to culture. Since the data were interval level (meaning that differences between levels were consistent) and normally distributed, the researchers employed MANOVA and ANOVA procedures, as well as post-hoc comparisons. Results supported the research hypothesis. Specifically, American Indian college students strongly committed to their tribal culture had significantly lower scores on personal need for counseling, confidence in mental health professionals, and interpersonal openness compared with similar students with higher commitments to Anglo or both cultures. These findings led the counseling staff to develop nonclinical alternative services for the culturally committed group and to adjust expectations of time needed for the therapeutic relationship and openness to develop in those who did seek counseling.

Source: Price and McNeill, 1992.

The active collaboration of staff, faculty, and students in the research process often facilitates the development of rigorous yet applied studies. Such investigations hold promise as one means of bridging the scientist-practitioner divide that has impeded progress in the counseling field.

Program Example: Collaborative Research on Program Effectiveness

A study of the differential effects of rape prevention programs on attitudes, behavior, and knowledge at the University of Missouri at Columbia used a rape myth acceptance scale, a consent/coercion measure, and a therapist rating scale in a survey-based investigation of the topic. Academic faculty and counseling center staff collaborated to design the study and to support and develop the interventions used. Specifically, using the elaboration-likelihood model helped the researchers formulate dependent variables to assess program effectiveness. Time was used as an independent measure, with five separate assessments spread over five months. An interactive drama appeared to be more effective than a didactic-video approach, and both interventions created change not seen in controls.

Source: Heppner, Humphrey, Hillenbrand-Gunn, and DeBord, 1995.

The fifth and final area of research suggested in the IACS standards is foundational contributions to the fields of counseling, psychology, or student personnel services by means of scholarly endeavors. Examples of works of significance authored by college counseling-center professionals abound in the literature.

Program Example: Research Summary Leading to Large-Scale Changes in Practice

The lead article in the July 1992 *Counseling Psychologist* by Brett Steenbarger (counseling director at SUNY-Syracuse Medical School) presented a cogent conceptualization and summary of the research on brief therapy. The piece was written at a time of significant downsizing of both university and community counseling and mental health centers. The impact of managed care was increasing. The ideas in the article about methods useful in brief therapy and about using the timing of sessions as a strategy assisted in significantly transforming the perspectives of college counselors. Today, most college counseling and mental health centers as well as community agencies have embraced some type of brief-therapy model.

Source: Steenbarger, 1992.

Program Example: National Research Consortium Project on Impacts of Counseling Services

The AUCCCD Research Consortium consists of a group of college and university counseling centers across the country that are dedicated to establishing a database on the impacts of college counseling and mental health services. Two studies have already been completed. The first study, "Nature and Severity of College Students' Counseling Concerns" (Baron, 1993), sought to establish a baseline on severity of clinical issues being presented to college mental health professionals. The second study compared these data to a matched nonclinical student sample (Alexander and Baron, 1995). The Research Consortium is presently engaged in a large-sample multicampus study of processes and outcomes (Drum and Baron, 1996). A number of well-supported instruments are being used for the investigation, including a measure of client counseling concerns, an index of readiness for change, and an outcomes assessment questionnaire as independent variables, and therapist ratings of client functioning and client ratings of satisfaction with services as dependent variables. The goal of this project is to answer the question "How much therapy provided within what therapeutic relationship by what types of therapists for what types of clients with which problem(s) is sufficient to achieve what level of improvement?" (p. 3).

Source: Baron, 1993; Drum and Baron, 1996.

Developing a Research Agenda

Barring a change in their organizational culture or activities, it is unlikely that most counseling and mental health centers will be able to enlarge their program-assessment and research agenda. Therefore, centers that wish or need to change will have to undertake projects that have an impact on the larger student-affairs and university environments within which they operate. Large and middle-size centers may be able to broaden their agendas in this way more easily than small centers in that large centers can create a committee or coordinated subgroup of the most interested staff, who would have some investment in the development and implementation of these projects. Inclusion of interested faculty in relevant disciplines and of other student affairs staff could also be helpful.

Staff of small centers are likely to have more difficulty building a comprehensive research program because they have fewer personnel and less time. Their reliance on external support, especially for investigations not based on sensitive clinical data, is probably essential. Forming a small-college counseling-center research consortium might be another alternative.

Counseling and mental health centers wishing to develop or expand their research activities can follow these steps. First, a committee or subgroup should be established to discuss the issues and initiate studies in most or all of the five areas designated by the IACS standards.

Second, partial release time should be provided to staff so that research activities are not an added responsibility. Establishing a release-time policy for scholarship clearly communicates how important research is for the center.

Third, staff should be given the opportunity to discuss priorities for possible types of research. The concepts and tools presented in this chapter or the information supplied by Steenbarger and Manchester and many other applied researchers might be valuable stimuli for such a discussion. Once priorities are established for types of research, further suggestions as to specific studies of each type should be solicited.

Fourth, efforts made to disseminate and discuss results should match efforts made to design the project and collect and analyze the data and information. Failure to disseminate results widely is likely to have an adverse effect on continued internal and external support for the research agenda. Some staff and some administrators will probably continue to have negative attitudes toward research until they see obvious positive outcomes of its use.

Fifth, on a regular basis, the research committee or subgroup should obtain feedback from various constituencies, both within and outside the counseling or mental health center, in order to evaluate the progress of the program-assessment and research efforts, make plans for altering and ending studies, and initiate new projects.

◆ ◆ ◆

Research by college counselors can and must be seen as a vital part of the basic mission of the counseling or mental health center. Efforts in this area should be founded on a broad and applied definition of research activity that emphasizes the assessment of services and programs, the investigation of student behavior and characteristics, the discovery of data relevant to issues of significance on campus, and the contribution to knowledge and techniques that advance the science and practice of college mental health.

CHAPTER FOURTEEN

ETHICAL AND LEGAL REQUIREMENTS OF PRACTICE

The ethical and legal issues related to counseling and mental health services on college and university campuses have become increasingly complex. Lawsuits are being filed by students and their parents; professional practice standards are becoming increasingly precise and demanding; and ethical dilemmas, particularly regarding relationships among faculty, trainees, and students, abound.

Although psychologists, counselors, and other mental health practitioners may not always view it as a good thing, the public is scrutinizing their work more than ever before, and consumers expect results, sometimes unrealistically. College counseling and mental health workers are caught in many binds, but two in particular create a number of ethical and legal (malpractice) problems. The first concerns the fundamental conflict between the need to provide and manage counseling and other services for a very large number of students and the need to provide high-quality and comprehensive care with assessment, diagnosis, and treatment carefully documented. The second is the conflict between a client's right to confidentiality and the obligations of the counselor to the campus community. This chapter will define and examine these and many other legal and ethical dilemmas facing college counselors and will explore ways to manage them consistent with legal, ethical, and common-sense guidelines.

Two studies of ethical problems in university counseling centers and ethical beliefs of counseling-center staff highlight some of the confusing ethical issues. Malley, Gallagher, and Brown (1992) conducted a Delphi study of fifty-four counseling-center directors. They identified a number of ethical situations that the participants found "very difficult to resolve" or "extremely difficult to resolve." Five of these concerned confidentiality and sharing information with parents and members of the academic community. Four situations had to do with the therapists' relationships with clients (encouraging dependence, becoming emotionally involved, meeting personal needs, and sexual intimacy). One situation concerned therapists' failing to take appropriate steps with suicidal or homicidal clients. Sherry, Teschendorf, Anderson, and Guzman (1991) surveyed 137 counseling-center staff members, asking them to rate forty-nine aspects of professional behavior according to frequency and degree of ethicality. In general, staff reported that they are practicing in an ethical fashion; however, the researchers did identify some areas of concern, including testing conditions and use of test results, and failure to seek supervision from minority professionals regarding cross-cultural issues with clients.

The ethical dilemmas reported in the *National Survey of Counseling Center Directors* (Gallagher, 1993, p. 32; Gallagher and Bruner, 1994, pp. 18–19) illustrate specific concerns:

- How do we handle the HIV-positive client who refuses to inform his sexual partner?
- What can be discussed with parents of a client who commits suicide?
- What do you do if two different clients report being raped in a residence hall by the same person but neither wants to file a report?
- A client reports that a minor sibling is being sexually abused but requests that this remain confidential. Is there a mandate to report?
- A client reported to a trainee in our center past sexual involvement with a teacher but does not want it reported. The trainee's faculty supervisor is insisting that he needs to report it. Any suggestions?
- We have received release requests for deceased clients' records; what should be done?
- How do we provide feedback to staff physicians who refer students to us? On the one hand, they need to know how successful we have been in helping their patient. On the other, we have confidentiality requirements to observe.
- We're getting pressure from dean of students and residence staff to disclose identity of and/or information about clients who might be disruptive or otherwise be sources of concern to those departments.
- Should we break confidentiality and inform the court that a student would likely commit suicide if sentenced to jail?.
- How should we deal with requests for mandatory discipline counseling?
- Client reported violent home life where there are three children under eigh-

teen. Tight call as to whether there was enough to evoke action to report the situation to department of social services.

The ethical and legal challenges and the constraints to be discussed fall under several broad headings: confidentiality, suicide and duty to warn, practice limits, involuntary assessment and counseling, dual and multiple relationships, records and recordkeeping, counseling and supervision of minorities, the use of medication as part of treatment, and the extension and integration of ethical codes.

Confidentiality

Before discussing the complexities of this issue, we need to differentiate the ethical and legal dimensions of confidentiality. Certainly the importance of confidentiality as a cornerstone of the client-counselor relationship and as an important basis for trust between client and counselor is recognized by all mental health professions. However, confidentiality may or may not be supported by state law. Privileged communication, the legal right and obligation of the therapist not to disclose information gained during counseling, is granted to various professions by state law. The specific professions covered (social worker, psychologist, counselor) vary from state to state. Even this privilege is subject to exceptions, such as the mandatory reporting of child and elder abuse.

As Stone and Lucas (1990) suggested, the principle of confidentiality is unassailable; however, in practice the obligations of counseling and mental health services to the institution, the necessity to obey state law, and the obligation to follow appropriate standards of practice do not allow absolute confidentiality. Other considerations also impinge on confidentiality. The conflict between maintaining confidentiality in student counseling and working with staff and faculty on referrals and matters of student behavior and discipline has always raised thorny questions. Rockett (1989), in responding to an article by Grayson (1986) regarding confidentiality on small campuses, discussed the likelihood of interacting with clients in other contexts (for example, having them in class, seeing them at various activities, or having close relationships with faculty and staff who refer) and the difficulties these interactions and relationships present. He took exception to some of Grayson's recommendations for keeping a low profile, arguing that this is not possible if one wants to offer a developmental, outreach-oriented counseling service.

The following guidelines are suggested to help counseling and mental health centers manage confidentiality issues:

1. Maintain copies of applicable state laws and ethical codes as part of the center's operating procedures. Hold regular training sessions with staff and reception personnel and discuss cases and problems that have arisen.
2. Include a clear and honest statement about the limits of confidentiality in the informed-consent form all clients sign.
3. Inform members of the university community about confidentiality and maintain a unified approach when asked for information.
4. Develop a standard consultation process with the director or a senior clinician for questionable cases.
5. Maintain a close liaison with the college or university attorney and ensure that he or she understands the applicable law and ethics codes.
6. Help clients understand the importance of feedback to referral resources, and unless inappropriate encourage them to sign a release allowing appropriate feedback.

A number of difficult issues related to confidentiality and release of records have been reported. When counseling and mental health units are part of general health services, there often seems to be a problem regarding the inclusion or non-inclusion of counseling and mental health notes in the general medical record. Counselors usually do not want to include the records or any notation in the medical records, and medical personnel argue that they cannot treat students unless they know something about their psychological condition. Release of records and information about students to deans, committees, and faculty for use in making decisions about a student's academic standing and progress can also be difficult. Even when students give their permission, the counselor must decide how much information to give and how to balance being a reporter and an advocate. Reports to outside agencies, like the FBI, Treasury Department, and state professional licensing boards are also complicated ethically. Do students really have a choice about giving consent? Also problematical is the release of records of deceased students to next-of-kin. Often, parents of suicidal students want to understand how their child became so desperate, and they request records. Subsequent legal action by the parents may be related to how they assess the treatment provided by the counseling service and the college or university.

Release of records is usually covered by the same state law that covers general confidentiality; however, counseling records are also covered under federal law in the Family Rights and Privacy Act (Buckley Amendment.) As a general rule, the less information released the better. Counselors should attempt to satisfy legitimate requests with a summary of the case and not release the raw record, even when the entire record is requested. A treatment summary often provides enough information. If release of the entire record is required, the counselor should attempt to release it to another licensed mental health professional so that it can be interpreted. In states that require that records be released directly to the client, counselors should attempt to meet with and interpret the record to the individual involved. If state law requires release of the entire record, counseling and mental health staff need to be aware of this provision as they write up their case notes.

Use of some of the newer technologies, such as voice mail and e-mail, raises interesting confidentiality questions. How secure is a message left by a student for a counselor on a voice-mail or computer system? On many campuses these systems are shared with other offices. As a general rule, counselors should not transmit confidential information via voice mail, answering machines, or e-mail, and every effort should be made to protect the confidentiality of messages left on center computers and voice mail.

Counseling and mental health centers are also faced with many mundane and perennial confidentiality problems: inadequate soundproofing, training staff and trainees not to discuss cases in public areas, use of student receptionists and secretarial help (often required because career clerical personnel are not available), carelessness by staff in handling confidential documents, and storage and destruction of old files. For example, is it reasonable to use an outside agency to destroy records? Although many suggestions and guidelines might be offered here, perhaps the most important factors in all confidentiality matters are awareness and vigilance. It is an absolute ethical and moral responsibility of all professional personnel to constantly monitor the confidentiality in their work settings. One idea that has merit is to designate a staff member every several weeks to do a security confidentiality audit and report back to the entire staff.

Suicide and Duty to Warn

In suicide and duty-to-warn situations, issues of confidentiality are complex. How do counselors handle suicidal clients and clients who are potentially dangerous to others? How do they handle information about other students who are dangerous to themselves and others? How do they decide whether the student is really suicidal? In reviewing surveys of college students, Dixon, Rumford, Heppner, and Lips (1992) reported that around 50 percent of the student respondents reported some level of suicidal ideation during the previous year, and 8 to 15 percent had taken some action as a result of those thoughts. Any college counselor will confirm the fact that many students think about and talk about suicide. The counselor must decide when this talk is serious enough to warrant intervention. Such intervention is a deliberate breaking of confidentiality and must be justified. The counselor must protect the student and at the same time must learn to tolerate a considerable degree of ambiguity regarding suicidal threats. Intervention is a serious step and may involve hospitalization, notification of parents, and the student's leaving school. The situation is further complicated when the parents are a significant part of the student's problem and the option of seeking support from home is not viable.

Duty-to-warn situations are also often ambiguous and difficult. Fulero (1988) in a review of Tarasoff legal cases up to 1988 pointed out some of the difficulties involved in duty to warn. (Tarasoff was the case that established the precedent that therapists have a legal duty to warn intended victims of their clients.) These difficulties included the problems counselors and other mental health professionals have in predicting violence, the fact that they risk the therapeutic relationship and might be sued by the client if they warn a potential victim inappropriately, and the possibility of being sued by the victim if they fail to warn. College counselors face these dilemmas frequently. In 1993, 90 (25.4 percent) of the 355 counseling centers reporting in the *National Survey of Counseling Center Directors* indicated that they had warned a third party about a student who posed a danger to another person, and, in 1994, 69 (22.3 percent) of the 310 centers reported a warning (Gallagher, 1993; Gallagher and Bruner, 1994).

The appropriateness of warning potential victims of clients with AIDS has also been debated by college counselors and mental health workers. If typical duty-to-warn situations are ambiguous, AIDS-related situations are even more unclear. The nature of the threat from HIV infection is somewhat different from the possibility of a direct violent action, but the resulting danger appears to be similar. Harding, Gray, and Neal (1993) report, "To date, no courts have addressed the therapists duty to warn sexual partners in a case involving HIV" (p. 303). Some states have passed laws absolving doctors, and sometimes all therapists, of liability regarding duty to warn partners of AIDS clients, but the ethical dilemma still exists. Harding, Gray, and Neal (1993) list thirteen problems with regard to this issue. Some of the most perplexing for the counselor are: "What evidence of infection is required to determine if a client is infected with HIV?" "If the client 'promises' to notify a partner or partners, has the therapist fulfilled her or his ethical or legal responsibility, or is subsequent confirmation necessary?" "How does the counselor respond to a client's 'questionably safe' behavior (for example, sexual behaviors such as oral sex), which are still being debated?" (p. 302).

Each center should have a clear policy on dealing with suicidal clients and on duty to warn. In all cases this policy should require a consultation with another professional. For suicidal clients, it is helpful to have explicit guidelines and training for staff on assessment of lethality and on involuntary commitment procedures. The center and the college administration also need to decide how to respond to attempts and threats reported by the campus community. In general it is better to err on the side of intervention and to confront a student about whom there has been a suicide report. Counselors should have a group of student affairs personnel selected and trained to make these interventions, with close consultation available for referral and back-up.

Liability issues inevitably bring up questions regarding insurance coverage. Although counselors on many campuses are included in the omnibus coverage for faculty or as part of a self-insurance program, specific liability insurance should be provided for counselors as it usually is for physicians who work on campus or who are connected to medical schools. Increasing litigation involving nonphysician mental health providers makes this coverage important.

Limits of Practice

Gilbert (1992) in an article on limiting treatment of students with severe psychopathology argued strongly that college counseling and mental health services must not attempt to offer treatment beyond their resource limits. As he put it, "It is misguided kindness, as well as being ethically unwise and legally risky, to attempt to carry out a treatment mission with inadequate resources out of compassion for the client" (p. 698). Because there is little evidence that brief therapy, which is the kind of therapy offered by most student counseling and mental health services, can help people with severe personality disorders, psychosis, and other disabling psychological disorders, he argued against such treatment and in fact suggested that it might "enable" the psychopathology. Gilbert also pointed out the core dilemma regarding treatment limits: given the increasing pathology of student clients (or at least the increasing presentation of pathology), which students will be served and which will not? Counseling and mental health centers do have the right to limit counseling, and Gilbert's treatise on the dangers of attempting to provide limited services to severely disturbed student clients deserves serious consideration.

But what is the college or university to do with students who have personality disorders or other serious emotional problems that are not amenable to brief intervention? Should they be expelled from school if their difficulties are disruptive to the institution? What will happen if the counseling or mental health center refuses to treat them? Can the institution deny services to some and not others? Will the counseling service be forced to respond to overtly disturbed students? What are the center's and the institution's responsibilities under ADA? In Chapter Six clinical responses to severely disturbed students were discussed in some detail, however the ethical and professional issues identified here remain troublesome.

May (1992) in a commentary on Gilbert's paper adds fuel to the fire by questioning the current treatment of students with disorders that are "popular" with counselors. "It seems to me that many students who might be called borderline or narcissistic present themselves at counseling centers these days under the labels of 'Adult Children of Alcoholics' or 'sexually abused.' These labels sometimes allow the counselor an illusion of a discrete piece of work that might be done, a therapeutic approach in which one can have faith. It is interesting to note that each of these labels also tends to set up an energetic and externalizing alliance between counselor and student: The problem, the trauma, resides in bad parents and cruel events" (pp. 702–703).

The resolution of the dilemma of whom to serve is not easy, but a reasonable approach is to set clear limits and priorities. The brief-therapy model suggested previously provides a structure for setting limits and priorities, and many of the important issues—assessment, referral, and crisis management—have already been discussed. Perhaps the most important ethical and legal issue involves making the limits set clear to clients, the campus community, and staff counselors. It may make sense to include an explicit statement of limits in the informed-consent form once the agency develops a policy. As has also been suggested, group counseling is a way to extend services to some students who might require more counseling than can be offered on an individual level.

Involuntary Assessment and Counseling

What is the ethical and legally justifiable role for a student mental health or counseling service to play in university administrative and judicial activities? Should psychologists or psychiatrists who work in counseling and mental health centers provide assessments of students that will be used in deciding whether they are removed from school or readmitted? Should counseling services provide assessments or counseling (or both) for students as part of a sanction from the judicial system? One major danger of participation in this activity is that the counseling or mental health service will be seen as an arm of the administration and will lose its reputation as a safe and independent agency with service to students as its major objective. However, the counseling service has an obligation to help the institution and to try to engage students who have behavioral problems.

There is certainly nothing illegal in performing mandatory assessments and providing involuntary counseling; however, as discussed in Chapter Seven many college counselors find them to be questionable professional practices. Gilbert and Sheiman (1995) argued that mandatory counseling on college campuses is legally and ethically questionable, does not work, does not address behavior, and damages the counseling center's integrity and effectiveness (p. 3).

Special considerations need to be taken into account regarding involuntary assessment and counseling related to psychiatric withdrawal from and readmission to the institution:

1. Establish a clear policy on assessment for psychiatric withdrawal and readmission. The content of this policy will depend on the size of the school and decisions about the role of the counseling or mental health center. If the center is involved in these assessments, they should be done thoroughly, with the best available assessment techniques, and by a qualified professional.

2. Involuntary psychiatric withdrawals require due process. In general, antisocial and disruptive behavior should be handled through judicial proceedings. The staff of the counseling or mental health service should insist on being only consultants to those who make the decisions.

3. If psychiatric assessment is required for readmission, a report by a psychiatrist or other mental health professional should be required. College counseling personnel have little basis for making a judgment about readmission without an evaluation by the treating mental health professional.

For most issues, involuntary counseling of students referred by a judicial system should involve a one-session involuntary assessment only, as recommended in Chapter Seven. At that time the student and the counselor can negotiate further counseling if the student so chooses, but a specific number of sessions should not be prescribed. Considerable potential for effective ongoing counseling exists with these mandatory assessments, although outside judicial systems (in cases of driving under the influence, for example) may specify more than one session, which complicates assessment of the client's motivation for counseling.

Dual and Multiple Relationships

Just what are the limits on relationships between professionals and clients, former clients, and trainees? What kind, if any, of these dual and multiple relationships are ethical? Can a counselor have coffee with a former client? Can a supervisor date a student, a former student? Can a counselor socialize with a faculty member she has seen for crisis counseling? The ethical implications of dual relationships are much discussed by counseling and mental health professionals. A continuum of these relationships runs from those that are obviously unethical, such as sexual intimacy with a client, to less clear social relationships, such as having coffee or a beer with a trainee. Most college counselors agree on the obvious situations. For example, 85.3 percent of respondents in a survey of counseling-center professionals agreed that it was unquestionably not ethical to date a client; 4.6 percent said it was ethical only in rare circumstances; 3.7 percent said they did not know; and 6.4 percent reported that it was unquestionably ethical (Sherry, Teschendorf, Anderson, and Guzman, 1991). (Note that this survey was done prior to the 1992 revision of the American Psychological Association ethical code.) Even this situation was not totally clear-cut given the somewhat surprising percentage of professionals who indicated a belief that this behavior is ethical. In a less clear-cut situation, initiating informal social contact with a former client, 38.5 percent reported this behavior as unquestionably not ethical; 44.0 percent said it was ethical in rare circumstances; 4.6 percent said they did not know; 8.3 percent indicated that in rare circumstances it was not ethical; and 4.6 percent said that it was unquestionably ethical. One can begin to see the variation in opinions depending on the circumstances. As previously reported, counseling-center directors listed issues related to dual and multiple relationships as among the most troublesome (Malley, Gallagher, and Brown, 1992).

Difficult issues regarding diversity emerge when these relationships are considered. Does the increasing movement toward avoidance of dual relationships make it difficult for minority staff to socialize within their cultural group? Doesn't effective outreach to African American and other minority groups involve considerable contact with these groups of students and faculty? In other words, it would appear that there is a direct conflict between avoidance of dual relationships and effective multicultural counseling.

The general conflict seems to be between the need to stop the highly publicized dual relationships in which professionals clearly take advantage of their clients or trainees and the need for effective multicultural counseling as well for genuine interpersonal relationships with students and supervisees.

The best approach to this issue appears to be regular discussion with colleagues and honest self-analysis. A mechanism or structure that encourages staff to grapple with the issues and to bring up questions about potential dual relationships can be extremely helpful. If, for example, a staff member is going to lunch fairly often with an intern and becoming friendly or a staff member is spending a great deal of out-of-session time with a client helping her pursue a judicial complaint against another student for sexual assault, questions might be raised, and given the proper atmosphere and forum they can be discussed and examined by staff members who can provide advice and recommendations. More difficult, but still important, is the creation of a work atmosphere that allows colleagues to question each other if they see possibly inappropriate dual relationships developing.

Dual relationships that result in a conflict of interest can occur when college counselors also engage in private practice. This is a fairly common phenomenon because of the relatively low salaries college counselors receive. Most colleges and universities have some form of outside-employment review process to ensure that employees do not engage in activities that conflict with their primary jobs. Faculty often consult outside the university, and private consulting and therapy are sometimes considered to be similar activities. The most serious conflicts occur when counselors charge students who are eligible for free agency services. In general this practice is avoided as a serious conflict of interest. Some college and universities also allow counselors to use their offices for a limited number of private clients after regular office hours. The director's role in ensuring that these activities do not interfere with the mission of the agency is crucial. The director can also advocate for counselors to have private practices, particularly if the private work provides them with opportunities to expand their skills by seeing different kinds of clients with a wide range of problems.

Records and Recordkeeping

Many college counselors are uncertain about what to put in a student's record, realizing that somewhere down the line the student may have to sign a disclosure release in order to get a government job, practice law, or for some other reason (see previous discussion of release of records and confidentiality). Some counselors have even kept dual records, one set of official records and one set of personal therapeutic notes, although these secondary records can also be subpoenaed. New professional practice standards and the need to maintain a record of adequate treatment as liability protection have increased recordkeeping requirements for college mental health professionals. Generally, a signed informed-consent form (covering confidentiality limits, center policies, risks and limits of counseling), identifying and demographic information, an initial assessment, a treatment plan, a note for each session, and a closing summary are required. Notes documenting consultation about difficult issues, such as suicide, abuse, repressed memories, are particularly important to demonstrate adequate professional practice.

The administrator of the center is the official custodian of the records and has the basic responsibility to ensure that legal and professional standards are being followed. This responsibility includes adequately protecting the records and maintaining them for a specified period of time. After a clear policy on records is established, the administrator should establish a procedure for checking records and providing feedback to staff regarding their adequacy. This need not be a time-consuming activity, but it is crucial for ensuring record integrity. Computer records require the same level of security and maintenance as hard copy. Outside consultation and periodic checks may be helpful in assuring adequate security.

Woody (1991, pp. 145–162), in an excellent book on quality care, provided guidelines for recordkeeping. They are summarized here:

- Use records for quality care.
- Use relevance and materiality as criteria for records.
- Use record entries to protect the rights of client and counselor.
- Remember that complaints are almost always based on what the therapist said or did.
- Err on the side of too much rather than too little in records.
- Follow state laws about records.
- Follow professional guidelines about records.
- Develop standardized record policies.
- Use standardized data-collection forms.
- Be sure entries are organized, legible, and consistent.
- Divide the file into sections.
- Use a face sheet to record provision of written or oral instructions to the client.
- Keep closed files in a systematic way.
- Preserve records for longer than the prescribed time depending on the nature of the case.
- Record all client contacts.
- Ensure that all entries are honorable, learned, professional, and factual.
- Collect information about clients that will help planning, marketing, and operations.
- Be sure records reflect professional and reasonable and prudent treatment decisions.

Counseling and Supervision of Minorities

Is it ethical for a white, middle-class college counselor who has had no formal training or experience in African American culture to counsel an African American student who grew up in an African American community? Is it ethical for a heterosexual counselor who has little experience with gay culture or knowledge of gay development to supervise a student counselor who is working with a gay student? Can a strongly identified African American psychologist with little experience in Native American culture effectively supervise a Native American intern? One could argue that all these therapists are operating beyond their area of expertise because they lack information and experience about the cultural background of their clients or supervisees and because without multicultural training they are unlikely to be aware of their own biases against minority groups.

One of the ethical problems facing college counseling and mental health services in providing truly multicultural counseling is staffing. Many college counseling operations are small or medium-sized and cannot provide a staff that truly reflects the diverse population of their campus. The basic answer to this problem is providing effective multicultural training for staff and trainees as well as being creative about hiring a diverse and outreach-oriented staff. Suggestions for achieving these goals have been discussed in previous chapters.

Use of Medication

In addition to the service-delivery issues previously discussed, a number of ethical and professional questions are raised by the increasing use of psychotropic drugs, especially some of the newer drugs like Prozac, as an adjunct to therapy. It is not unusual to have a student walk into a college counseling or mental health center and ask for Prozac, reporting that his mother, father, aunt, minister, doctor suggested that he needs it for depression. Kramer (1993), in his best-selling book *Listening to Prozac*, explores the "miracles" of Prozac and the notion that Prozac can improve functioning and make one better than well. College counseling personnel, if they have easy access to psychiatric support, are certainly not immune to the pressure from students and from their waiting lists to try antidepressants and antianxiety drugs to provide symptom relief (or perhaps personality change, as reported by some Prozac and other antidepressant users). Does it make sense to start students, particularly those in their late teens or early twenties, on a path of using medication to handle psychological problems such as depression and stress? Are these problems really biological problems, a result of malfunctioning brain chemistry? Should counseling always be provided to students who are on medication or is a short med check by a psychiatrist sufficient?

Making clear-cut recommendations is difficult. College counseling and mental health centers are probably unlikely to overuse medications. Most counselors and the students they serve have a healthy respect for, if not suspicion of, medication. Clearly, though, each center needs to grapple with these medication issues and make some decisions. It probably does not make sense for a counseling and mental health center to provide counseling for complicated medication cases unless the center is located in a medical setting where blood work and other medical tests are easily available or where in-house psychiatric coverage is provided with medical and psychiatric inpatient back-up. In some instances, particularly in rural areas, it may be necessary to rely on general medical practitioners. As mentioned previously, it is incumbent on counseling staff to become knowledgeable about medications. Even if college counselors do not believe in the use of antidepressants and tranquilizers, they are likely to encounter students who are using them or who want that option.

Extension and Integration of Ethical Codes

Two additional questions regarding legal and professional issues need to be examined. First, what professional and ethical standards apply to paraprofessional programs? For example, is a paraprofessional counselor held to the same standards with regard to confidentiality or dual relationships? Most paraprofessional training programs cover some basic ethical issues. One useful task for peer counselors is to assume the responsibility for developing a code of ethical behavior for their program. Usually students in these programs are extremely bright and sincere and can do an excellent job of translating a professional ethics code, such as those published by the American Psychological Association or the American Counseling Association, into a workable code for their organization. Certainly this kind of exercise, with consultation from a faculty adviser or trainer, will go a long way toward ensuring that peer counselors pay attention to ethics. Legal issues are more the purview of sponsoring organizations and professional advisers than of paraprofessionals. These issues generally relate to boundary issues and supervision and monitoring.

The second question relates to the multidisciplinary nature of college and university counseling and mental health services. How do these agencies integrate the ethical codes of psychiatrists, psychologists, social workers, mental health counselors, and other professionals? Corey, Corey, and Callanan (1997) included as an appendix to their book on ethics in the counseling professions the ethical codes of several professional counseling groups, and they discussed the general issues such as confidentiality, competence limits, and dual relationships that apply to all helping professions. The question is one of detail rather than of basic issues. It may make sense to focus on the general issues with a multidisciplinary staff and to deal on an agency level with specific differences.

◆ ◆ ◆

In some respects more questions have been raised in this chapter than have been answered. Ethical and legal questions and issues often do not have simple or precise answers. The field of ethics as a topic for study and research has been growing. An issue of *The Counseling Psychologist* was devoted to this topic, with a lead article by Meara, Schmidt, and Day (1996) arguing for a move from "quandary ethics" to "virtue ethics." "Virtue ethics focuses on character traits and nonobligatory ideas that facilitate the development of ethical individuals" (p. 4). Clearly the staffs of college counseling and mental health centers need to devote time and energy to ethical and legal issues and strive to maintain high ethical and professional standards. They also must follow professional practice standards that ensure high-quality services and protection from liability actions.

CHAPTER FIFTEEN

PROFESSIONAL TRAINING AND ACCREDITATION

College counselors find the training of graduate students and even para-professionals to be one of the most enjoyable and exciting parts of their jobs. The challenges are enormous and the rewards high. Trainees stimulate thought and creativity, and they help counselors stay alive professionally and avoid burnout. Accreditation and licensing are not nearly so stimulating or interesting as topics and activities for college counselors, but they are clearly a part of the contemporary college counseling scene and promise to become increasingly complex.

Training Programs

Although there are many challenges regarding training, perhaps the most salient is the cost. The issue for most college counseling and mental health centers is how to develop high-quality training programs that are cost-efficient. In addition to cost-benefit questions, a number of other issues are important. An ongoing challenge in training professionals involves student selection and the use of effective models. For practicum and internship programs, articulation between graduate programs and training sites is crucial and often problematical. Supervision and evaluation of trainees are made difficult by the increased accountability and monitoring required because of potential litigation and liability and by the need to respond to impaired trainees. A major need also is to provide trainees with multicultural understanding and skills. Another interesting dilemma for training agencies is how to respond simultaneously to demands for specialization and demands for general training.

Involvement in paraprofessional training and programs brings a whole set of somewhat different challenges for counselors. Issues of competence, limits, supervision, monitoring, and organization are all important and must be dealt with effectively to maximize the "pyramid" effect (that is, working with a small number of students who will in turn affect a much larger number).

Cost-Benefit Considerations

College counseling and mental health centers usually have a number of reasons for providing training. Foremost is the fact that training programs provide an exciting and stimulating environment that helps staff members examine their own practices while contributing new thinking. Also, most training programs are a part of on-campus graduate education. Although college and university administrators understand the value of training to staff and the need for professional training programs, bottom-line considerations often require that training programs pay their own way or even add services. There is a delicate balance here. Too much emphasis on "using" trainees as "cheap help" can create a poor training experience and poor service. Yet overly ambitious programs that focus on the trainees' needs without consideration of the agency's primary service mission can be expensive and can use resources that are intended to benefit the general student body.

Analyzing and evaluating the actual costs of training are technical challenges, but college counseling and mental health agencies need to know what their training programs cost. Few studies, however, have been published that examine the costs of various training programs. Schauble, Murphy, Cover-Paterson, and Archer (1989) provided a model for a fairly comprehensive analysis of the costs of full-time internship programs in psychology. They concluded that internships are cost-effective compared with hiring additional regular staff.

Studies of the costs and benefits of training programs can greatly aid in the planning, development, and preservation of these programs. Centers with training programs should periodically evaluate costs, especially if they are planning to expand staff time devoted to training. A cost-benefit analysis could be a useful assignment for a trainee or graduate student. In addition to tracking costs (money and time spent), counselors must forcefully remind administrators and others in the academic community that counselor training is an academic function and an integral part of the teaching mission of the institution.

Selection of Students

Practicum and internship sites are often the place where students who have poor or marginal abilities to work effectively with clients are identified. All students who are admitted to or do well academically in training programs do not necessarily have strong potential as therapists. The needs of the agency must be considered, and the staff members involved in the selection process must devise means to assess clinical potential and to decide when this potential is not present. This issue is also difficult in paraprofessional programs. Students with many positive attributes may apply for training, and a decision has to be made as to just how much time and energy can be spent in training them. Selection procedures that include several interviews, videotape work samples, and simulated counseling are useful ways to gain information to be used in this process.

Training Models

Effective training models must be designed that match the objectives of the program. A model for training and supervision of paraprofessionals is different from a model for practicum students and interns. For example, a behavioral model may be appropriate for teaching paraprofessionals how to give study-skills workshops, while a more flexible, self-directed approach may work better for advanced trainees like interns. In addition, an agency usually must struggle to balance the need for general training and the specialized interests of the staff.

The following are basic elements to consider in constructing a training model and program:

- General philosophy and goals
- Specific competency and behavioral goals for trainees
- The developmental process for trainees and how the program allows for this progression
- The content of seminars, including basics and special options
- Administration and coordination of the program
- Selection, training, and evaluation of supervisors
- Personal growth of trainees and, if necessary, therapy for them
- Evaluative process for trainees, including provision for remediation and termination
- Costs of the program
- Adequate selection for and accurate marketing of the program
- Ongoing communication and articulation with academic departments, including the development of policies and procedures to deal with impaired trainees

- Periodic self-evaluation, outside evaluation, and accreditation of the training program
- Serious consideration of trainees' feedback about the program and their experiences in it
- Inclusion of a variety of therapeutic approaches (unless it is a specialized program featuring a particular approach)

Articulation Between Academic Programs and Training Sites

One of the greatest challenges for academic departments and on-campus training sites is to provide an integrated and coordinated program that successfully meshes academic preparation with practical work. Practicum and internship sites often complain that interns and practicum students do not have adequate preparation. This is usually a sign that there is not enough communication between academic programs and campus counseling and mental health centers. There is a need for both academic programs and training sites to agree on a sequential training approach and to understand how each of them contributes to student learning with this approach. This kind of articulation takes time and is usually achieved in a series of meetings, workshops, or retreats for faculty and site staff. If the academic programs are off-campus, the training director or coordinator must maintain regular communication with them.

Supervision of Trainees

Providing quality supervision is perhaps the most important challenge for a training site. Until fairly recently, practitioners had little research or theory on which to base their clinical supervision. Stoltenberg and Delworth (1987) and Stoltenberg, McNeill, and Delworth (1997) provided one of the first comprehensive models of counseling supervision, and Dye and Borders (1990) developed standards for supervision. Research on supervision has increased since the mid-1980s, and publications have begun to describe supervision techniques that have some empirical support (see Holloway, 1995). One textbook for practicums and internships includes a number of forms and checklists to help training sites with organization and quality control of supervision (Boylan, Malley, and Scott, 1995). Because many practicing college counselors and psychologists were not trained in supervision skills, centers should create continuing-education programs to enhance skills and knowledge in this area.

Understanding the developmental nature of supervision is crucial. New trainees with no experience require a different kind of supervision than advanced interns or postdoctoral students. Grater (1985) discussed the stages of supervision.

The mix of small-group, large-group (case-conference), and individual supervision is important here, as is the balance of general counseling supervision with specific skill supervision (for example, consultation skills and skills in counseling clients with specific problems such as eating disorders). Moreover, Cooper (1984) recommended that supervision should focus on client factors, therapeutic relationship issues, and persona as professional issues, with the relative balance of these depending on the developmental stage of the trainee as well as the specifics of the case.

The need for a supervisor to keep a developmental record or overview of trainee progress is apparent. Training sites and academic departments must devise ways to assess and follow individual trainees' progress so that their learning can be sequential and intentional and their training needs can be met. Although the supervisor is the primary monitor and facilitator of learning, the entire professional staff (except in large centers) should meet periodically to evaluate and discuss training programs.

One aspect of supervision that is significant, and that is as much a matter of client welfare and ethics as it is a supervisory issue, is monitoring the clinical work of supervisees. It is imperative that clients not be put at a disadvantage because they are being counseled by a trainee. It is generally a good idea to keep a record of every supervisory session, to document discussions with supervisors about each client, and to have a supervisor sign all trainees' client records. Although some of these recommendations would add considerable time to the supervision process, they deserve serious consideration and will probably ultimately be included in standards of practice. It is easy for supervisors to become involved in the excitement of learning and to focus on trainees' growth and development; yet not doing an adequate job of monitoring cases may compromise quality. Sufficient time needs to be allocated for such monitoring. One effective strategy is for the supervisor to spend a brief time each week reviewing cases prior to selecting particular cases or issues to discuss. With a brief-therapy model the volume of cases can be significant, so devising a check-off form or other mechanism for monitoring cases is helpful.

College counselors involved in training programs also serve as socializing agents for their respective professions. Student trainees must learn to assume a professional identity and to take professional responsibility for their actions. Although an internship, which is seen as the capstone of professional training, is perhaps the time when the most significant socialization occurs, the process begins at the practicum level. In a practicum or internship setting the development of professional identity is enhanced by mentor relationships with staff. Students have typically had courses in ethics and professional issues, so the role of the training agency is more personal. Students must get a sense of what it is like to be a professional counselor, psychologist, or social worker, and they can do so only by getting to know professionals in those areas. The problem in mentoring programs is how to avoid unhealthy dual relationships. Slimp and Burian (1994) discussed relationships between staff and interns. They identified four kinds of dual relationships that are potentially harmful: sexual, social, therapeutic, and business. Sexual, therapeutic, and business relationships between trainees and staff seem to be clearly inappropriate, but social relationships are problematical. Certainly, some social relationship is necessary in mentoring. The issues involved were discussed in some detail in Chapter Fourteen.

Evaluation and Remediation of Trainees

Evaluation is one of the most difficult parts of supervision. Tough decisions sometimes have to be made about trainees, and it is not easy to decide when students need remediation or when they must be dropped from the program. Clear performance criteria can help, but the supervisor's judgment is critical. Structured periodic evaluations involving several staff members can help identify problems early and provide consultation about the learning process. Training programs need to clarify their policies about how to handle students who cannot satisfactorily complete a practicum or internship. Options might be to take time off, to seek personal therapy, or to take remedial coursework or skill training. Ongoing feedback to students is essential; failure should not come as a shock to the student.

Personal deficiencies and needs for growth and development in particular areas present a challenge, especially if the student needs therapy. Training sites should develop resources for personal therapy and also consider providing personal growth and support groups for trainees. To avoid multiple relationships and to enhance openness, such therapy should not take place at the training site nor should center personnel be involved. If possible, free or low-cost therapy opportunities should be negotiated with local private practitioners, and support groups should be led by professionals who are not involved in the training program. If personal therapy is required as part of the program, either implicitly or explicitly, this requirement should be made clear to perspective trainees before they apply.

Multicultural Understanding and Skills

Each training program is faced with the challenge of helping teach effective multicultural counseling skills to trainees. This is clearly a developmental process, with different students having different needs. The process should start at the beginning of the student's graduate program, and the training site's role should be to focus on how multicultural awareness, attitudes, and skills affect the counseling process. But because of the complexity of the issues and the developmental nature of growth in this area, it is not unusual for trainees to need work on basic self-awareness as well as on applications to counseling.

Sue, Arrendondo, and McDavis (1992), in a strongly argued "call to the profession" for multicultural training standards, suggested three dimensions characteristic of the culturally competent counselor (p. 481). First, a culturally skilled counselor is actively in the process of becoming aware of his or her own assumptions about human behavior, values, biases, preconceived notions, personal limitations, and so forth. Second, a culturally skilled counselor actively attempts to understand the worldviews of culturally different clients without making negative judgments. Third, a culturally skilled counselor is in the process of actively developing and practicing appropriate, relevant, and sensitive intervention strategies and skills in working with culturally different clients.

Training students in each of these dimensions raises interesting challenges. Trainers need to be patient, to be both gentle and confrontational, and to be persistent in order to help trainees undertake the difficult task of examining personal assumptions and biases. Having a diverse staff and training group can facilitate this process considerably because trainees are exposed to people of diverse races, ethnic backgrounds, sexual orientations, and degrees of able-bodiedness. The second dimension, understanding a client's worldview, requires some success at self-examination and identification of one's own worldview and how it might bias understanding of other worldviews. One problem is trying to teach the predominant worldview of each minority group. Although minority groups share many common cultural experiences, including oppression, they also have a rich diversity of experience and perspective. Trainers are faced with the quandary of teaching general worldviews for different groups without stereotyping each one. Weinrach and Thomas (1996) called for a critical reassessment of multicultural theory and approaches and listed as one of their three pertinent questions the issue of within and between-group differences. Teaching appropriate intervention strategies and skills requires at least some progress in the first two dimensions, personal awareness and active understanding of worldviews. Perhaps most important for teaching sensitive, culturally competent intervention skills is the opportunity to counsel a diverse population. If the agency does not have a strong outreach program and a reputation as a user-friendly facility for different minority groups, then this and the other multicultural training components will suffer.

Specialization Versus General Training

Although this topic has been covered to some degree in the section on training models, its importance requires further attention here. Most training at the practicum level is general and basic. Students must learn basic skills and confront their fears and anxieties about talking with clients. Yet many additional specific skills and areas of knowledge are crucial for success in college counseling. An understanding of gender, cultural, and other differences, as discussed above, is certainly basic and important. An understanding of widespread problems of college students, such as sexual abuse, eating disorders, substance abuse, and problems associated with a dysfunctional family history, is also a necessity. Each of these areas is a specialty in itself, and many other special populations and problems exist. How does one provide basic training without getting too involved in specialty training?

Trainers must define what is basic for their site and limit the special-population and problem issues included in their training program. The strong values and interests of particular staff members may make setting such limits difficult. The talents of each staff member should be plumbed in training, but should a center offer extensive training in one area simply because several staff members have a strong interest in it? The key recommendation is for staff members to articulate the goals of their training programs and to define the basic levels of training they wish to offer. A site that has particular strength in one area may want to offer a specialized training program, but it should be separate and not a major focus of a general practicum or internship.

Paraprofessional Training

Many of the issues in professional training also apply to paraprofessionals; however, because most of these programs are fairly specialized and student trainees have different levels of commitment and experience, there are some unique challenges. The cost-benefit issue is even more salient with paraprofessionals because of the high turnover in most of these programs. Centers can partially justify professional training as a contribution to the education of graduate students, but paraprofessional training must be justified primarily by the services provided to the campus.

Training models, distinctions between peer counseling and peer education, and the type of training focus (specialized or general), as well as many other issues related to paraprofessionals, were discussed in some detail in this and previous chapters. Specifically, the choice of training models and the focus and process of training require considerable attention in paraprofessional programs.

Training of paraprofessionals also implies responsibility for their activities. When the college counseling or mental health center is charged with the administration of the program, this obligation is clear. When training is done for other campus groups and agencies, the counselors doing the training are challenged to ensure that what they train students to do is commensurate with the supervision and support available. Trainers are also often required to provide consultation for paraprofessional programs as part of their training activities.

Accreditation and Licensing

The accreditation and licensing movement in human service fields has mush-roomed since the mid-1970s, and counseling and mental health staffs have not been immune to the many implications for their services and their own profes-sional lives. College and university counseling and mental health centers are most directly affected by two kinds of credentialing: accreditation of services and train-ing programs and licensing of staff.

Accreditation of Counseling Centers and Programs

The primary accreditation agency for college counseling services is the Interna-tional Association of Counseling Services (IACS). Guidelines were published in the *Journal of Counseling and Development* (Kiracofe and others, 1994). The guidelines of the Council for the Advancement of Standards for Student Services/Development Programs (Miller, Thomas, Looney, and Yerain, 1988) also includes a section on counseling services, although these are far less rigorous than the IACS standards. The Accreditation Association for Ambulatory Health Care accredits student health centers and includes counseling and mental health services offered under their aus-pices. Other professional standards and state laws also govern the operation of counseling and mental health services.

The American Psychological Association accredits psychology internships. Seventy-four internship sites in university counseling or mental health centers were listed in 1996 by the Association of Psychology Predoctoral and Postdoctoral In-ternships as being approved by the American Psychological Association, and an additional seventeen satisfied the requirements to be listed in the directory even though they were not approved by the American Psychological Association.

The myriad of laws, standards, and accreditation criteria that apply to college counseling and mental health work can be complex and confusing. For example, specialty guidelines for counseling and clinical psychologists specify different peri-ods for keeping psychological records; state law may designate yet a different pe-riod; and if the center is located in student health services, medical standards for records may also apply. In some states, staff members in college counseling and mental health services (psychologists, social workers, mental health counselors, psy-chiatrists) have to be licensed. In many states, however, licensure is not required for positions in colleges or universities.

Accreditation processes create several kinds of challenges for college coun-seling and mental health operations. The most obvious is once again the cost-benefit question. Accreditation of centers is becoming increasingly expensive. For example, the cost of American Psychological Association accreditation of an internship was $1,650 per year in 1996, with an accreditation site-visit cost of $2,400 (W. Beard, American Psychological Association accreditation office, personal communication, 1996). Are the expense and time required to satisfy accreditation standards worth the benefit? This becomes an especially germane question in lean budget times. Related to the cost-benefit issue are concerns about restrictiveness and reasonableness; these concerns are sometimes expressed when a center must hire a certain kind of staff in order to meet accreditation guidelines or when guidelines set by a national organization appear not to make sense for a particular agency.

The accreditation movement has generally been seen as a positive force in the development of counseling and psychology services and professions. Groups of professionals have labored long and hard to develop standards that have in large part improved services offered. Part of the value for the center is in use accreditation to improve services and to gain the resources necessary to conform to the highest professional standards. Certainly being accredited can help a center maintain a strong "immunity" to liability actions.

But college counseling services must at times deal with the unreasonable and restrictive aspects of accreditation. For example, a counseling center may want to have a combined internship program for psychologists, counselors, and social workers, but an accreditation agency may require that its interns have a separate program. Or there may be restrictions on who can supervise students doing a practicum in a counseling center in a particular specialty (psychology, social work, marriage and family counseling, mental health counseling), which reduces flexibility for the center. Or demands by accreditation site visitors to add yet another training seminar or procedure can seem excessive and prove to be problematical. Because of such problems, college counselors need to lobby professional organizations and accreditation agencies to maintain "reasonableness" in the accreditation process.

Sometimes administrators and other campus members see accreditation and licensing as a rather large hole into which they are asked to deposit money regularly. Although accreditation can often be helpful in evaluating resources and creating high-quality programs, counseling and mental health centers must continually educate administrators and others on campus about the value of accreditation. There is a need to involve the different campus constituencies in the accreditation and evaluation process. Consumer involvement in the general administration and governance of counseling and mental health services, including the accreditation process, is important and requires careful and strategic thought.

For many small colleges accreditation is not feasible because resources are not available. Colleges with small counseling or mental health services also usually do not have the personnel or resources to seek formal accreditation of training activities even though they may have practicum trainees or interns. How can these centers maintain high-quality professional standards and keep up with important professional guidelines without the assistance of periodic accreditation visits and structured guidelines? The responsibility is clearly on the individual staff members. They can still familiarize themselves with accreditation guidelines and with current training and ethical issues, and they can work toward satisfying as many of the requirements as possible given resource and staff limitations. Periodic self-studies, followed by a consultation visit from an outside observer, will provide many of the benefits of outside accreditation. Consortiums of small-college counseling and mental health centers can exchange consultants and offer each other guidance. Organizations such as the AUCCCD and the American College Health Association could facilitate this kind of exchange by establishing guidelines for small centers and helping establish a consultation and visitation process. Regional meetings open to directors and staff of small counseling and mental health services also foster excellence.

Licensing of Professional Staff

Although in many instances licenses are not required for counselors, psychologists, and social workers in colleges and universities, administrators of counseling and mental health services should encourage their staffs to be licensed. Because of liability questions and the desirability of providing professional standards of treatment, it is important for college counselors to be licensed in their appropriate specialty. Licensing can also be justified as a way of providing licensed supervision so that trainees can themselves be licensed.

Time and expense are stumbling blocks. Considerable time is involved in the application process, and clinical supervision time must also be provided. Directors need to develop ways to provide the necessary time to both applicants and supervisors. In addition, licensing fees for counselors, psychologists, and other mental health workers have increased as the cost of administration, licensing boards, and hearings has grown. Because most college counselors are moderately paid, finding several hundred dollars to obtain and maintain a license and additional money to pay dues to several different professional associations can be difficult. College counseling and mental health administrators should, whenever possible, find creative ways to generate money for professional licensing and dues.

In addition to licensing, there are advanced professional certifications, such as the Diplomate in Professional Psychology. Preparation for obtaining these certifications provides important opportunities for professional development and growth. Directors should encourage staff to continue their professional growth in this way and through other professional development activities.

◆ ◆ ◆

Staff members in college counseling and mental health centers are in an excellent position to offer high-quality training programs. Professional training programs help centers play an important role in the academic mission of the college or university, and they help keep professional staff stimulated and excited about their work. Accreditation and licensing, although time-consuming and expensive, contribute to providing high-quality services and programs in college student mental health. They also help centers demonstrate that they are operating according to professional standards, probably the single best shield against liability and malpractice claims.

CHAPTER SIXTEEN

ORGANIZING AND DELIVERING COUNSELING SERVICES

Counseling and mental health services on college campuses are organized and administered in different ways. Although great variation exists, a number of general organizational and administrative issues must be considered and confronted by all college counseling and mental health services. These can be divided into two categories: general issues regarding basic functions, funding, and relationships to the college or university as well as to the national health-care system; and internal concerns that can more accurately be called management and leadership issues. In this chapter the general organizational and administrative issues will be discussed: in the next chapter the internal leadership, management, and operational questions will be addressed.

The external issues include the ongoing debate and discussion about the role and functions of counseling and mental health services, funding questions (including privatization possibilities), campus organizational structures (the relationship of counseling centers, mental health services, career counseling units, and learning-skills centers), the impact of managed care, and organizational models and funding options for the future. Some of these topics have been discussed or alluded to in previous chapters—for example, recommendations for a brief-therapy and group-therapy model of service delivery and for an initiator-catalyst approach to outreach and consultation were presented, as were a variety of suggestions for increasing funding and expanding counseling services.

Role and Functions

The IACS accreditation standards (Kiracofe and others, 1994) list three essential roles for counseling services serving the university and college community: a counseling and therapy role, a preventive role, and a role in creating a campus environment that facilitates the healthy growth and development of students. These roles are carried out, according to the accreditation standards, in six functional areas: individual and group counseling, crisis-intervention and emergency services, outreach programming, consultation services, research, and training. On the surface, these roles and functions appear to be rather straightforward and noncontroversial; however, current developments, particularly the advent of managed care and exploration of outsourcing and privatization by some colleges, have led to questions about definitions, about how these roles and functions are assigned to units within and outside the institution, and about how realistic it is for various types of institutions to attempt to provide all these services. Few counselors or even administrators would argue about the desirability of these functions; however, the questions of what is affordable and to what degree each should be provided generate a considerable variety of opinions and beliefs.

The overarching question, which will be addressed in several ways in this chapter and which has already been discussed in many different contexts throughout the book, is which functions should be emphasized within a limited-resources framework. From a broad perspective, two strong opinions are usually voiced. The first is an admonition for counseling centers to stick to functions and roles that are clearly educational in nature. For example, Stone and McMichael (1996) ask why, since programming (teaching), training (teaching), and research (research) have a "clear and unambiguous" connection to the mission of a university, most of the resources in college counseling are devoted to counseling. Bishop (1995) emphasized the importance of keeping the educational mission in mind. "It is legitimate for any educational institution to ask how the activities of a college or university counseling center relate to the educational mission of the school. Institutions of higher education are not mental health organizations" (p. 37). Crego (1995) argued strongly for a "broad developmental approach" designed to promote student life; this approach would include counseling-center functions like psychoeducational programming, development of prevention programs, and consultation (p. 9).

Those voicing the other opinion urge college counselors to join in a managed-care, medically oriented approach to campus mental health. Steenbarger (1995b) advises that "counseling settings that do not incorporate managed care principles and medical linkages into their repertoires will not survive" (p. 4). This seeming

polarity of approaches is not really new, considering the fact that campuses have
had counseling and mental health units for many years. The mental health units,
usually contained in medical settings, naturally see their function in medical terms,
while the counseling centers, usually part of the student-life division, tend to be
educationally oriented. As has been mentioned, however, increasing seriousness
of problems and demands for counseling combined with increasingly limited resources have made this basic question about appropriate roles and functions considerably hotter and more relevant to both counseling and mental health services
than it was in the past.

Broad organizational structures and various counseling and mental health
models will be covered later. The focus here will be on an analysis and summary
of the roles and functional areas that are outlined above and that have, in large
part, been suggested in previous chapters of this book. Although an emphasis
on prevention and systemic change has developed in the last several decades, individual and group counseling are still vital aspects of any campus counseling or
mental health effort. The recommendations put forth earlier in this book were for
extensive use of group counseling and other adjunctive approaches along with
well-defined brief therapy. The importance of presenting clients and the campus community with a clear definition of the counseling services that can and will
be offered cannot be overemphasized. The offerings may vary from campus to
campus, depending on resources and campus philosophy, but limited resources
and the need to provide a variety of other, more community-oriented services
necessitates limits. It may be unfortunate and in some ways unfair, but campus
counseling and mental health services typically cannot provide extensive psychological services for students. The ADA does require reasonable accommodation,
yet there is no case law to suggest that colleges and universities are responsible for
providing extensive counseling to accommodate students who cannot function
as students without ongoing psychotherapy.

There are many valid reasons why counseling (personal, academic, and
career) should be made available to students. Certainly, counseling as a kind of individualized and integrative learning process fits into an educational framework.
In addition, counseling as a process that enables students to learn and achieve
by helping them overcome personal problems and developmental blocks is a
reasonable and cost-effective part of the educational process. The term *medical offset* has been used to demonstrate the value of counseling and psychotherapy as a
method of reducing the need for more expensive medical treatments. A similar
term, *educational-failure offset,* might be coined to describe the value of providing
college counseling as a way to avoid the high economic cost of educational failure. These costs are incurred by the institution, the student, and society at large.
For example, the institution may spend hundreds or even thousands of dollars

recruiting a student. If the student leaves school because of personal problems, the considerable funds expended to recruit that student are lost. Or if a sophomore engineering or architecture student, in whom considerable educational resources have already been invested, drops out, these funds have not been productively spent in that they have not produced an engineer or an architect. If any student leaves school and does not return, the loss of income over the course of a lifetime is quite significant. In addition to the economic losses, there are intangible losses to the student and to society.

Crisis-intervention and emergency services are also a part of the educational-failure offset process. Most colleges and universities, particularly residential ones, are faced with students in emotional crises on a regular basis. Although the extent to which the institution can or will provide ongoing counseling in such cases may vary, such situations must be handled when they occur. A suicidal student in a college residence hall, a young woman who has been raped and is decompensated, or the murder of several students on a campus requires immediate action on the part of the college or university. It is true that campuses in urban areas can simply send students to psychiatric emergency rooms, but the treatment is often not satisfactory nor is it geared toward the specific developmental needs of college students. Also, not all significant crises are psychiatric emergencies. A sudden parental death or divorce, failure on a test, or a broken relationship can trigger an intense crisis, yet one that is not appropriate for an emergency room.

The role of counseling or mental health personnel can vary considerably in these crisis situations, depending on the resources available in the community. As with all services, some limits have to be established. It is not possible for professional counselors to come to a residence hall or a classroom whenever there is a crisis. Part of their job in this regard is to provide consultation and training for the campus community and to help faculty, staff, and students handle crises with which they are confronted. It is clear, however, that counselors and mental health staff must play a central role in helping campuses deal with severe individual crises and emergencies and with events that disturb the entire campus community.

The functions of outreach programming and consultation were discussed previously in some detail. These functions are a central part of the mission of a counseling or mental health center because they are the primary mechanisms for providing both preventive and developmental educational activities. Developmental activities, which may include outreach workshops, classroom lectures, and environmental assessment and intervention projects, have the goal of helping students learn important skills that will foster their development in a variety of dimensions. This growth, in turn, will allow students to use the institution effectively to obtain a high-quality education. Similarly, prevention programs help students learn skills and gain information and positive attitudes that prevent them from engaging in activities that interfere with positive mental health and with the educational process. Both types of programs are profoundly important parts of college counseling and mental health. The emphasis in this book has been on an initiator-catalyst model of outreach and prevention. Outreach and consultation services should go beyond the reactive phase and emphasize campuswide prevention programs. College counselors must also take on an activist role in response to important campuswide issues. This is not to say that they can or should always be the primary intervenors or educators. They can be catalysts as well. Ideally, the college counselor will be able to stimulate interest in and development of needed programs and services and involve many members of the campus community in their delivery and, ultimately, in their coordination.

The training function as presented previously includes practicum and internship training for graduate students as well as paraprofessional training for undergraduates. The size of the center will probably determine the size and extent of graduate training, while the outreach and consultation objectives will influence the amount of paraprofessional training. Paraprofessional training can involve teaching both counseling skills and skills in facilitating preventive and developmental education programs. College counseling and mental health centers have also been instrumental in developing many peer education programs and in training the participants. As previously discussed in some detail, providing training in counseling and in psychoeducational skills as well as supervision of this training requires careful planning and decisions about resources.

A number of suggestions for research in college counseling and student mental health were presented in Chapter Thirteen. There are viable research possibilities for even the smallest counseling and mental health centers, but little research will take place unless specific resources are allocated to it. In many instances, the counseling center can also contribute research expertise to student affairs or institutional research efforts.

Funding

The funding of counseling and mental health services has become increasingly complex. For many years these services were funded from the regular university budget or from a health fee. More recently, fee-for-service, mandatory fees, and outsourcing have been explored as funding alternatives. Bishop (1995) discussed the advantages and disadvantages of various revenue sources. He concluded that fee-for-service has limited possibilities for generating significant amounts of revenue, that mandatory student fees offer centers the advantage of not being dependent on general university revenues but these fees are dependent on enrollment, and that outsourcing or contracting with private firms to provide counseling may reduce initial expenditures somewhat but typically does not provide an adequate range of services.

Outsourcing is an issue on a number of campuses where private organizations have attempted to persuade college administrators that they can save money by contracting for counseling services. Phillips, Halstead, and Carpenter (1996) surveyed thirty-one colleges and universities and one state system that had considered privatization. The authors concluded that although some colleges had considered privatization, there was little evidence that this trend is widespread. Of the institutions they surveyed, nine had opted for some type of contracted service for counseling. All but one of these were small institutions, under three thousand students, and all had contracted for personal counseling only, not for career or academic counseling. Cost was the most significant factor, but another theme was dissatisfaction with present services. Three of these institutions had longstanding contracts for counseling services (ten to twenty years). Six institutions, ranging in size from 1,200 to 22,500 students, and the state system (twenty-one campuses) had considered privatization but had opted to stay with a college-operated counseling service. Thirteen more of the institutions had considered some degree of privatization but had not contracted out services. Three colleges had abandoned previously contracted services to return to a college-operated counseling service. Among a number of conclusions, the authors suggested that centers that are more clinically oriented are more vulnerable to competition from outside agencies.

The multicampus, systemwide decision about outsourcing and privatization is noteworthy. The board of trustees of the California State University System accepted the recommendations of a consulting firm, Stephen L. Becky and Associates, concerning health services for the state system. In response to the consultants' recommendations, the board passed a resolution that systemwide affiliation with HMOs and other health-care companies should not occur at this time (Welty, 1995).

The arguments against privatization are persuasive and can be summarized as follows:

- College counseling and mental health centers have a much broader scope than just one-on-one counseling. Outsourcing to private mental health companies would likely result in the loss of prevention, wellness, and developmental programs.
- Easy access to counselors for consultation by faculty and staff would be lost.
- On-campus crisis intervention services would likely be limited.
- Participation in campuswide task forces and committees (women's issues, advisement, athletic council, drug abuse education, and so on) would be lost.

- Easy access for students and a "nonclinical" approach to counseling would be lost.
- Outreach to minority students and other groups that do not access counseling easily would be lost, because counselors for private companies would lack the necessary on-campus contacts and credibility.
- Retention of students with a combination of academic and personal problems would decrease under privatization.
- Campus counseling helps provide a personal touch and counter the feeling of anonymity that so many students report as a negative campus experience.

The two most basic arguments against outsourcing seem to be the potential loss of many unique services that a general health-care HMO or managed-care group cannot offer, and the need for accessibility of and ease of entry into the counseling system. Private companies contend that they can bring the cost of counseling services down, but they typically are not able to offer the range of services needed, nor do they have the unique experience and expertise needed to work within an academic community.

The threat of competition posed by privatization brings into clear focus the need for centers to deliver high-quality services as efficiently as possible. It also requires college counselors to clearly communicate the extent and breadth of their services so that college and university administrators do not make poorly informed decisions about outsourcing. Funding and budgeting for counseling and mental health services in general require considerable communication skills, particularly on the part of the director.

Managed care and its implications for funding and organization will be discussed later, but it is important to note here that managed care and national and state health-insurance laws and policies are having and will continue to have profound effects on the funding of college counseling and mental health services.

Because of the unique situation on every campus, it is not possible or desirable to recommend particular funding patterns. It certainly behooves counseling and mental health centers to consider student-generated fees as well as direct support from the institutional budget. Inherent in these funding questions are the earlier questions raised about roles and functions as well as the ultimate decisions about the organizational model adopted on a particular campus.

Campus Organizational Structures

Schoenberg (1992) discussed campus organizational structures in his monograph on models for college and university counseling centers. He noted that campuses have different needs and therefore different structures. A perusal of his study of eleven different counseling centers supports the notion that differences in both internal and external organizational structures are common.

At least four different organizational units can provide the services outlined in the discussion of counseling roles and functions. The history of two of these, counseling centers and mental health units, and their relationship to each other were discussed in the Introduction. In addition to these common counseling units, many campuses have a separate career counseling/development unit as well as a learning-skills center. The two factors most responsible for the particular structure of these units on any campus are size and individual history. Small campuses, by necessity, have few separate units, so the counseling operation performs many different functions. Large campuses are likely to have specialized services, with separate counseling, mental health, career, and learning-skills operations.

As is the case with nearly all organizations, periodic changes occur in the organizational structure of counseling functions. A new vice president might decide to shift functions and units around. Or a faculty committee may call for certain changes. Or the loss of a director may lead to a merger. Almost all such changes are carried out in the name of increased efficiency or cost savings (or both). Federman and Emmerling (1996) studied thirty-seven campuses that had recently merged their counseling and mental health services. They concluded that there is no clear trend in the direction of organizational mergers and that no specific organizational configuration is more effective or desirable than any other.

On campuses with more than one counseling service—a counseling center and a mental health center, for example—issues of overlap and duplication of service must be addressed. Usually, because of limited resources, there is more than enough "business" for each service; however, the appearance of duplication of services can be problematical. If the services are truly different or have different priorities or emphases, it is helpful to make those clear to the campus community. For example, if one service has an eating disorders program and another a stress-management clinic, these unique features should be publicized. If possible, the two organizations should work cooperatively to ensure coverage and to provide a reasonably comprehensive program of services for the campus. Holding regular meetings and establishing communication channels can help different counseling services function together efficiently and can minimize confusion in the campus community concerning the location of various services. It is important not to assume, without examining individual cases, that two services are less efficient than one. In fact, two services may be more effective than one for a particular campus. Drum (1998) suggests that few mergers of counseling and health services in colleges and universities include an adequate consideration or a clear vision of how health care can be better provided on campus. Rather, they are usually a result of funding or cost considerations. He suggests that functional mergers, which involve a realignment of how the two services are coordinated and contractually listed, are generally more effective because they result in an overall administrator, encouraging a more integrated health-care system, and because they allow current units, such as counseling and mental health, to maintain campus identities.

Although a number of the factors influencing decisions about organizational change and mergers are unique to particular institutions and their organizational dynamics, some general implications of how counseling functions are structured may have considerable importance for the future development of counseling services. As Steenbarger (1994) pointed out, there may be a great advantage to a counseling service in closely linking itself to health services because it will then be positioned to become a managed-care provider for students and faculty. Because managed care requires a "seamless" provision of health-care services, lack of involvement with a comprehensive medical group virtually eliminates any possibility of participating as a provider. From another perspective, the loss of responsibility for career and academic counseling or the separation of a learning-skills center might jeopardize a counseling or mental health center's relationship to the central educational mission of the university. Questions about the placement of various units in the organizational structure are of particular interest on large campuses. On the one hand, if a comprehensive counseling center is an umbrella for all kinds of services and programs, is this an organizational advantage? On the other hand, the close linking of personal and emotional counseling with career, learning, and other specialized services allows counselors to work easily with the personal aspects of career choice, learning problems, and so on. Some would argue, in fact, that such links are a necessity if quality services are to be offered.

Implications of Managed Care

Although managed care is closely related to funding and to organizational structure, it deserves discussion as a separate topic because of the important implications for the future of college counseling and mental health. The previous discussion about privatization and outsourcing is clearly relevant here. The organizations seeking to provide "private" mental health care for campuses are in fact managed-care companies of one kind or another. As mentioned previously, Steenbarger (1995b) has argued that college counseling will become a part of integrated managed-care systems. "There is absolutely no doubt about it" (p. 3). He contends that it is "incumbent upon college counseling professionals to understand managed care trends and to learn to work within these" (p. 3). His view is essentially that college counseling and mental health services will, by necessity, have to become part of "seamless" health-care systems that provide a full range of medical services. He further states that the lack of medical coverage in most counseling centers raises quality and malpractice questions and that if counseling centers do not become part of a large health-care system, they will be seen as low-quality providers. Finally, he notes that most college counseling centers are underproductive in comparison with managed-care mental health services, where the average clinical caseload for providers is thirty to thirty-five hours of direct service (Steenbarger, 1995b).

Ironically, from a certain perspective college counseling and mental health services have been in the managed-care business for a long time. They typically provide a limited array of counseling and mental health services for a capitated group—that is, they receive per-head funding to provide these services to a college student community. Steenbarger's basic point is that this kind of small-scale managed care is no longer viable because it sets itself up in opposition to the medical model. "Opposing the developmental model to a medical model and advocating for single specialty staffing of services is suicidal" (p. 3).

The possibility of universal health care, which was unsuccessfully proposed during the early 1990s, is relevant here. If it were to be enacted at some point in the future and included extensive mental health benefits, the increase in the number of students with such benefits would certainly have an impact on college counseling and mental health services. Would a college or university be willing to fund mental health counseling, even if it were only short-term, if reimbursement were possible for all or most of the students? The most salient question for counseling and mental health services would be whether to become part of a large, comprehensive health-care network in order to share in the reimbursements available. And, if they did that, could they retain any of their previous identity as educators who are an essential part of the higher education enterprise?

College counseling and mental health services must consider the possibility that the costs of their service will be examined and perhaps compared with those in private managed-care systems. Although the many arguments in favor of in-house counseling that were presented previously are strong, it is important to look at financial concerns. Drum (1994) suggested that counseling and mental health centers must focus on four important factors: price, product, customer satisfaction, and quality. If, when compared with managed care, a college counseling or mental health center offers better and more comprehensive services at a competitive price and if the services are successful and highly valued by students, it is less likely that the college or university will see managed care as a cost-saving alternative. The key here is the quality of services and their relevance to the higher education enterprise. In addition to offering cost-efficient and high-quality counseling, college counselors must be able to describe the nonmedical preventive and developmental aspects of their services and articulate the value of these services to the college or university.

Drum's suggestions for counseling centers do not speak directly to Steenbarger's (1995b) contention that the centers must become part of managed health care. Steenbarger's contention is however supported by Cummings's (1995) prognostications about the health-care market. Cummings suggests that existing managed-care companies will eventually be taken over by a few large health-care conglomerates. Clearly, counseling and mental health centers need to grapple with the possibility that sometime in the not-too-distant future mental health services may be available for large numbers of students through some type of comprehensive health-care system. This is an extremely important consideration for college counseling services as they contemplate the future.

Models for Counseling Centers

A number of possible organizational models are described below, primarily as a stimulus for thinking about organizational issues. The models give a consistent representation that seldom exists in reality, and counseling and mental health services typically do not pick a particular model or type of operation. For the most part they inherit a service, structure, and funding pattern that has evolved over time. Given the widely varying sizes, locations, and philosophies of colleges and universities, it is risky to suggest any one model for college counseling and mental health centers. The authors, however, recommend the last model described, which includes comprehensive counseling and community development services, as the ideal organizational approach to accomplishing the programs and goals described in this book.

A Center Providing Educational Services

In this model all counseling-center services must be directly tied to the educational mission of the institution. Individual counseling is offered with an emphasis on career and educational issues. Students with moderate or severe personal and mental health problems are referred to private therapists. Workshops, groups, and other programs emphasize acquiring skills (study skills, career choice) and overcoming problems (speech anxiety, test anxiety) that are directly related to the educational mission. Personal development programs (on relationship issues, values clarification, human sexuality) may be offered in conjunction with other student affairs units if they are deemed part of the educational mission. It is important to note here that the educational mission of institutions varies considerably, at least in reality if not in terms of catalogue platitudes. For example, a small, church-affiliated liberal arts college may be much more interested in personal and character development than a large research multiversity. Thus, application of this model may look quite different for different schools.

Community-development and campus environmental work in this model focuses on the campus educational and intellectual environment. Prevention activities, such as drug-abuse prevention and sexual-violence prevention, are handled by another organization, probably a health education unit in the student health service.

Funding for centers using this model comes directly from the university budget or student fees, and no student health fees are utilized. Research and training are important. Staff may well be charged with carrying out major research on students for the institution, and training and teaching are major roles for the staff.

A Counseling Center for Students and Employees

This model is based on the assumption that emotional and mental health problems interfere with productivity for all members of the educational community. Consequently, brief and easily accessed counseling is made available to everyone. Counseling is limited to only a few sessions with referral to other mental health practitioners as needed. Funding may come from a variety of sources: the regular university academic budget, the personnel budget, faculty or student insurance.

Two concomitant major outreach efforts are important. The first is an ongoing effort to inform various campus groups about the service and how to refer people to it. The second effort consists of a variety of prevention programs targeting different campus groups. These prevention programs focus on mental health concerns (stress, depression, self-esteem) and problematic behaviors (alcohol abuse, relationship violence, eating disorders). An additional outreach effort aimed at modifying organizational cultures may be directed toward the larger campus community. In this model, center staff do not teach or do research, except perhaps as part of needs-assessment and evaluation activities. Staff are not likely to hold doctorates because the major counseling focus is on brief intervention and referral.

A Health-Service Counseling Center

Counseling under this paradigm is defined in medical terms. Students (patients) are diagnosed according to DSM-IV and receive therapy (treatment) or medication (or both) for their difficulties. Comprehensive medical mental health services are available, including inpatient psychiatric care if needed. The focus of counseling in this model tends to be remedial rather than developmental, although many college mental health counselors attempt to follow a growth-oriented model. Career, study-skills, and academic problems are handled only as they relate to personal and mental health problems. Staff in this model are usually housed in a general health facility and work closely with physicians and other medical staff. Outreach and consultation efforts typically emphasize health education and prevention of major public health problems on campus. Funding comes from student health fees or student health insurance or both rather than from the regular operating budget. This kind of service may also be part of an HMO, depending on the organization of the institution's health services. Staff therapists in this model tend not to be involved in the educational aspects of the college or university, mostly because they are funded entirely as health-care workers. Training programs in counseling, psychology, or medicine may place practicum students, residents, and interns in this setting for clinical training; however, their clinical work must support any expenditure of training time by the staff.

A Privately Contracted Counseling Service

In this model counseling and other related services are contracted out to a private group or corporation. Services to be provided are spelled out in a contract that is usually renewed on a yearly basis. The contractor agrees to provide services to a specific population (students, faculty, staff). Although the extent and range of such services may vary considerably, the typical contract is somewhat narrow in scope, usually covering only counseling and emergency services, primarily because colleges and universities opting for this model usually do so to cut costs, and less service means less expense. Counselors are not employed by the university and are not directly involved in campus activities. Space is usually provided on campus as part of the contract.

A Center Providing Consultation for Organizational and Community Development

A center operating under this model does not provide individual counseling. Staff focus on community and organizational development with the assumption that organizations and communities that are operating effectively greatly enhance student mental health and the educational process. Such a center can be funded through the regular university budget or through student fees. Faculty departments, student groups, employee groups and departments can all make use of the organizational consultation provided. Although it is unlikely that this center would be operated without some kind of related counseling service, a college or university might decide to rely on some other source for counseling services (private contract, local resources, mental health center). This kind of center could be charged with both proactive and reactive organizational consultation as well as with environmental assessment and intervention. For example, the center might work closely with student affairs offices in regard to the campus climate for students, with the personnel office in regard to the environment for faculty and staff, and with the institutional research office in regard to institutional goals.

A Center Providing Comprehensive Counseling Services and Community Development

Counseling services in this type of center include career, educational, and personal. Outreach and consultation services provide preventive and developmental programs and focus on campus subsystems and the general campus environment. The mission also includes research, teaching, and training of graduate and paraprofessional counselors. Some or all of the staff are faculty members affiliated with an academic department, and they teach at least one course per year. The staff includes counseling generalists and, if appropriate, specialists in career, learning, and other specialty areas. Priority is given to research conducted on students and on various aspects of the university environment. Psychiatric consultation and extended mental health care are available through referral to on- or off-campus hospitals and mental health facilities. Community-development work for the entire campus is a major focus with connections to many different campus offices, departments, and populations.

Funding Options

These different types of counseling centers can be funded in one of two ways. With the first option, the center is funded through a combination of the regular university or college budget, student health fees, and possibly third-party insurance reimbursements (some colleges and universities require all students to have health insurance). The regular budget allocation supports the functions related to the educational mission of the institution, while the health fee or insurance supports personal and mental health counseling.

With the second funding option, the center is designated as a managed-care provider in cooperation with a local HMO, managed-care group, or university health service. Funding for some of the counseling services offered then comes from student participation in an HMO or managed-care plan, while funding from the regular university budget is used to cover nonmedical counseling and services directly connected to the educational mission, such as career counseling, learning-skills workshops, teaching, research, and training programs. The continued viability of this option is not certain, but it is nonetheless recommended here as a possible alternative if it makes sense in a particular setting.

◆ ◆ ◆

It should be clear from the models described above that many different organizational structures are possible for different campuses and that each carries implications for the kinds of services offered. The descriptions of the models and the previous discussions of general issues are intended primarily to stimulate consideration of the implications and assumptions of the different approaches and to help counselors and administrators think through plans for future changes and reorganizations.

CHAPTER SEVENTEEN

PROVIDING LEADERSHIP FOR QUALITY IN CAMPUS COUNSELING

College counseling and mental health centers tend to be relatively flat organizations with few bureaucratic levels. They are similar in many respects to traditional academic departments, with a director, a number of professionals (psychologists, counselors, social workers, psychiatrists), and support staff. They usually operate on the same sort of collegial principles as academic departments, but their functions are more varied and involved. Because of the sensitivity and complexity of these functions, counseling and mental health centers require more managerial and administrative activity. Also, as previously discussed, national developments in managed care and general tightening of higher education funding make efficient management of resources increasingly imperative. Consequently, a focus on the management of counseling and mental health operations is vital. In this chapter a number of important internal-management topics will be addressed, including internal organizational models, management practices (including leadership), quality control, and staff development.

Internal Organizational Models

Size of the center and the range of services it provides are the most important factors in determining the internal organization of a counseling or mental health service. However, the interests and abilities of available personnel also often play a surprisingly significant role. Even in a one-person counseling or mental health service some kind of model or plan for how the various functions are to be accomplished is useful. Whatever basic organizational structure exists, it usually must include the traditional functional areas—counseling services, outreach, consultation, training, and research—as well as the administrative functions of personnel management, accountability and quality control, and marketing and campus leadership.

One particularly critical question concerns the degree to which staff members are involved in the management of various functions and of the agency. In medium to large centers, coordinators and sometimes assistant and associate directors help in management and administration, usually with a committee structure. For example, a coordinator of clinical services, together with a small committee, might be charged with overseeing that particular function. Often these coordinators and groups provide day-to-day management and also recommend policy changes to the director and to the staff as a whole. Modern management theory seems to favor the involvement of staff in the management and administration of organizations. According to Merryman (1994), in an article applying TQM (total quality management) principles to counseling centers, teamwork and employee involvement are important parts of both employee empowerment and a process/systems perspective, two of the guiding principles of the TQM approach.

The key issue for a "staff-involvement" organizational model is maintaining an appropriate balance between time spent on administrative work and committee meeting and time spent on provision of services and programs. Although there is clearly value in staff involvement and in allowing a number of staff members to participate in administration and management, there is also the possibility of using up too much staff time in discussing, evaluating, and continually changing procedures and methods. Continued analysis, evaluation, reorganization, and change for the purpose of improving quality and efficiency are noble goals, and they are supported by contemporary management theories such as TQM; but an overemphasis on process and on staff involvement can also lead to instability and inefficiency. The following suggestions can be helpful in developing and evaluating internal organizational models:

1. The size and scope of the agency should justify the complexity of the coordinator and committee structure. Sometimes coordinatorships and committees can be combined to save time and effort. The director and the staff should have a clear idea of how much time is spent on these functions and periodically evaluate and justify it.

2. The director should have sufficient contact (meetings, informal check-ins) with coordinators to provide guidance and to trouble-shoot problems.
3. Staff charged with coordination should be willing and able to provide leadership in a particular area. At the level of assistant or associate director, salary supplements should be provided.
4. The director should make it clear to coordinators and other staff what authority they have to change policy and make decisions.
5. Those designing the organizational structure should be aware that it plays an important role in determining priorities. If a center has a coordinator of clinical services with a related committee but has no special committee or coordinator for outreach and consultation services, then the clinical-service aspect of the agency is likely to be emphasized.
6. Line supervision arrangements should be unambiguous. For example, if the director of training is directly responsible for all trainees or if the coordinator of paraprofessional services is directly responsible for all paraprofessionals, those lines of authority should be clear.
7. On occasion, ad hoc, time-limited committees and coordinators can be appointed. They provide opportunities for creative contributions to the organization. For example, a center may want to spruce up the physical appearance of its facility, or it may want to address the issue of staff burnout. Either of these goals might be met by appointing a committee and perhaps a coordinator to develop and implement new ideas and procedures.

Internal organization is not as much of an issue for small counseling centers or mental health services as it is for large centers. Operations with only a few staff members do not need or have time for coordinators; however, it is still useful for these services to examine their functions and how they are handled. Even with only two or three staff members, there is room for a division of some responsibilities. In a sense, internal organization in small centers refers to how individuals divide their time and how they manage to accomplish a myriad of tasks. On one hand, the having the luxury of being a small, informal center with limited bureaucracy is highly advantageous. For example, in a two-person operation communication, planning, and all meeting agendas might be taken care of at an informal coffee time for a few minutes at the beginning of the day. On the other side, the danger of becoming too reactive to the pressures of the moment can make it difficult to maintain a well-balanced counseling program. The sole counselor in a center usually finds it hard not to respond to various requests that come from faculty and staff with whom the counselor has a fairly close relationship. Time for planning, reflecting on priorities, and allocating resources is difficult to come by.

Management Practices and Leadership

A number of management areas are of particular importance in the administration of college and university counseling and mental health services, including staff supervision, budget and priority setting, strategic planning, maintenance of group culture, policies and procedures, and leadership style.

Supervision of Staff

Staff supervision is certainly one of the most challenging tasks for directors. Counselors are typically professionals at either the doctoral or master's level, and they spend a good part of their time working independently in counseling or other professional activities. They are often licensed, have considerable experience, and do not usually see themselves as requiring close supervision. Yet directors are responsible for the overall operation of centers and for the quality of programs and services, so they must provide some level of supervision. This supervision can be divided into several components.

The director must work with counselors to communicate agency and institutional expectations. Typically, there is some kind of contract in which duties are laid out, often in terms of weekly time commitments as well as annual goals. Many agencies have guidelines specifying the number of hours to be spent in clinical service, training, outreach, and so forth. The details of this contract should reflect the center's needs as well as the staff member's professional goals and growth needs. For example, a staff member who wants to work on writing a research article might be allocated specific time during a particular term to work on that project. Time might also be given for professional development activities, such as workshops and coursework. In some centers a block of time is allocated weekly for professional development, reading, research, writing, planning. In other settings larger blocks of time are given for nonclinical activities during vacation periods. Whatever kind of contract is used, it should be made clear to staff members that they will be evaluated at the end of the term or year on the basis of how well they achieved the goals set forth in the contract. Periodic individual sessions with each staff member to discuss progress can be useful. The director can play an important role as a motivator and encourager in this regard. Moreover, this kind of process allows for supervision that helps both the agency and the staff member. Yearly evaluations can easily be tied to the contract.

In addition to this kind of ongoing, activities-related supervision, there are often occasions when more targeted feedback is desirable or required. For example, if the agency receives a complaint about a counselor, the director will typically discuss the complaint with the staff member. Or if the staff member's work habits or professional demeanor are problematical, some action needs to be taken. These kinds of situations can be difficult because often staff members have close relationships and they need to interact and work as a professional team. At times problems with one staff member may affect the entire staff to such an extent that the director must deal with the staff as a group. It is important for the director to set limits in this kind of situation and to structure a discussion with explicit boundaries. Consultation from outside the center can be useful. Members of professional organizations, such as national or regional associations of center directors, can be effective consultants.

Directors have considerable power as motivators and reinforcers, both in their individual contacts with staff and in the tone they set. A well-functioning counseling staff is like a family in many ways, and staff members look to each other for support. The director should never miss an opportunity to recognize achievements and contributions made by staff members. Although part of the rewards for performance may be financial, these rewards are rather limited in most counseling and mental health settings. Explicit and frequent praise and recognition by colleagues as well as by the director can make an enormous difference. The culture of the agency (to be discussed later) must include norms that support and reinforce staff members' achievements.

It is also important for the director to develop an explicit and fair system for distributing periodic salary increases. Many colleges and universities have regulations that govern how these monies are distributed. A process for faculty at most colleges and universities involves peer review of performance and recommendations for merit raises. However, student affairs divisions, within which most counseling operations reside, often do not have as organized a process. Although the director usually makes the final decision on allocation of raises, the method used should be discussed with staff members, and they should have a clear understanding of how these decisions are made.

Supervision of clerical and support staff is also crucial. These personnel are often poorly paid yet are called on to perform professional-like tasks. Receptionists, for example, frequently must deal with disturbed and upset students, often when a counselor is not immediately available. Frequently the skill and sensitivity required are not recognized by the college or university personnel system, so it is incumbent on the director and the professional staff to provide reinforcement and appreciation. It is not unusual for these staff members to feel left out and second-class because of their nonprofessional status. This problem can be especially vexing in a counseling or mental health center because of the additional expectations placed on support personnel and because of the often close relationships between professional and nonprofessional staff. Directors should not underestimate the importance of support staff, and they should allocate time for their supervision and development. Depending on the organizational structure, it may be desirable to include support staff in various meetings and staff-development sessions. In addition, it is helpful for the director or the direct supervisor of support staff to help them in their career development and progression.

Setting Budgets and Priorities

Three aspects of budgeting deserve attention: budget requests, control and accounting, and the fit with priorities. Without doubt, the most challenging part of budgeting is the annual request and accompanying justification. The way in which the director and the staff argue for and support their budget request is important to the agency and to the students served. This is a complex and often politically sensitive process that is directly connected to relationships with higher-level administrators and to the ongoing efforts to demonstrate the importance of counseling services to the college or university mission. Clearly, the director needs to have an understanding of institutional priorities and how the counseling and mental health service budget fits into those priorities, as well as an understanding of the budget process and how decisions are made. In reality, a counseling or mental health center often has little room to negotiate. The largest budget item by far is salaries (probably about 80 percent), and typically salaries and raises are determined within a fairly narrow range.

A counseling or mental health center should have an effective system for determining how much various programs and functions cost so that reasoned judgments can be made about where to put resources. For example, a center should know how much an individual and a group session cost, how much outreach and consultation programs cost, and how much training programs cost. If necessary, the director or other responsible person should get outside advice on developing an accounting system to determine these costs. Complexity usually correlates with size; however, regardless of size, it is absolutely crucial that all staff activities, programs, and services be included in this kind of cost accounting. If all activities are not taken into account, the costs of the more obvious functions, like counseling, will be greatly inflated.

The most effective budget process involves the entire staff on some level, both in an advisory capacity to the director and as partners in the ongoing process of providing accountability and proof of effectiveness. Priority setting, which has been discussed in several previous chapters, involves budgetary decisions.

Strategic Planning

Strategic planning is an extremely important function for any organization. The involvement of counseling-center and mental health service staff in planning activities leads to an effective organization whose members know their individual goals and those of the organization. Strategic planning should take place periodically in a setting that allows staff to free themselves from daily activities in order to focus on priorities and long-range issues. Retreats off-campus are ideal for this activity.

Program Example: Staff Retreats

The professional development program at the Center for Counseling and Student Development of the University of Delaware includes three annual retreats attended by all professional staff members and interns. All the retreats are scheduled for a day and a half and take place at off-campus locations that provide overnight accommodations and meals. The first retreat is usually scheduled during the week that precedes the return of students for the fall semester. This is usually the first opportunity that new staff members and interns have to spend a significant amount of time with the returning staff. This retreat focuses on the upcoming academic year, with particular emphasis on those activities and procedures that are new. In short, the retreat serves as an extended orientation for both new and returning staff members.

The second retreat is scheduled for the midway point in the academic year. It affords an opportunity for the staff to assess the particular services and activities it identified as priorities at the beginning of the year. Often a guest presenter provides some professional development for the staff as well.

The third retreat is designed as an end-of-the-year evaluation of the Center's programs, services, and priorities. Decisions are often made that will affect the Center's priorities in the following year. The summer months are then used to develop the plans that are adopted.

Overall, this program of regularly scheduled off-campus retreats helps not only in developing the direct-service and programming priorities of the Center but also in creating and maintaining a team spirit among staff members. All the expenses associated with these retreats are covered by the Center budget, so individual staff members incur no financial obligations.

Source: J. Bishop, assistant vice president, Center for Counseling and Student Development, University of Delaware, Newark, Delaware, personal communication, 1997.

With medium to large staffs it can be helpful for the director to appoint a small committee to develop a strategic planning process for the entire staff. The process should include setting short- and long-term goals as well as discussion of resources and means to achieve the goals. By necessity, this process almost always involves grappling with limits and priorities. Difficult though it is, a realistic strategic plan intentionally sets some goals at the expense of other needed activities. The challenge is to harness the excitement of commitment to the most important goals yet accept the limitation of other worthwhile activities. After a plan is developed, periodic review and evaluation of progress toward goals are necessary.

Building an Organizational Culture

Attending to the organizational culture of a counseling or mental health center can make the difference between having an exciting, enjoyable, and productive work environment and having one that is static and limited in its rewards and challenges. Organizational culture can be defined as the informal norms that govern the behavior of members of any group. An organizational culture often has historical roots in the traditions and stories that get passed down over the years. Effective work groups, staffs, and organizations typically have rich traditions and group norms that facilitate communication and reward effort and accomplishment. These traditions are often related to social activities, such as retreats, holiday parties, trips, and birthday celebrations, and they serve to remind staff members that they belong to an organization that is significant and important. Counselors and psychologists are often good at developing these kinds of traditions to emphasize the human part of work relationships. Older members of the organization often pass down stories, anecdotes, and humorous events that have taken place in the life of the organization. Some counseling and mental health centers and services even have written histories, and some of the larger centers have celebrated anniversaries (twenty-fifth, fiftieth) by inviting past staff and interns to a reunion conference. All these activities are important. It is easy for administrators to get caught up in the day-to-day crises and neglect the development and maintenance of organizational culture.

Following are examples of activities, most of them gleaned from the authors' experiences at various college and university counseling centers, that can contribute to an effective and positive organizational culture:

1. Annual retreats with some of the time devoted to recreation, nice meals, informal contact.
2. Recognition of birthdays and other significant events in special ways (cards, balloons, cakes, special lunches, singing).
3. Yearly parties to celebrate events such as the beginning or ending of the school year or the departure of interns or practicum students.

4. Oral or written histories commemorating significant and humorous events; having senior staff share memories and stories during informal staff times together.
5. Time in staff meetings for sharing accomplishments and for recognizing contributions to the organization.
6. Welfare or wellness committees charged with planning activities that enhance the work environment and make it fun. (See Archer and Probert, 1985, for a description of a counseling center's wellness breaks.)
7. Establishment and maintenance of norms encouraging caring and concern for each staff member's personal and career development, modeled and facilitated by the director.

None of these suggestions or the emphasis on a positive organizational culture is meant to imply that a staff member's personal life or privacy should be violated. Staff members do not have to socialize with each other (except for organizational events), and they do not necessarily have to be close friends. However, a professional relationship, particularly in a mental health setting, includes a certain degree of personal sharing and a willingness to engage with other members of a staff. Directors may have particular problems with this kind of professional-personal engagement because of their additional role as supervisor. However, the director's role as limit-setter and giver of negative feedback need not conflict with his or her role as facilitator of and participant in the development of a positive and supportive group culture.

Policies and Procedures

The establishment and the articulation of policies and procedures are perhaps not as interesting to directors of college counseling and mental health centers as the people-oriented management functions, such as supervision or the development of organizational culture, but setting policies and procedures is crucial for successful operation of a center, particularly one that is medium-size or large. Written and well-articulated policies are important for several reasons: organizational effectiveness, staff communication and coordination, liability protection, and goal direction and evaluation.

An organization cannot be effective unless all its members have a clear vision of its goals and functions and in general agree on how the goals will be pursued and the functions carried out. Clearly articulated policies, typically contained in a manual or other publication, provide guidelines and ready reference when questions come up. They also set expectations and help staff deal with the considerable ambiguity always present in counseling and human service work. These guidelines are particularly important for new staff, interns, and practicum students, who are trying to learn how the organization works. These materials also allow for reasonable discussion of various policies and procedures with the goal of customer satisfaction and program effectiveness. Communication can be stymied when there is not clear agreement on the parameters of the discussion. Of course, students and other users of the service also deserve a clear explanation of what they can expect. For example, if there are policies regarding access to counseling or consultation, each consumer of the service should get about the same response when making a request. Without clear guidelines, the services provided can be somewhat haphazard and an impression of inconsistency, disorganization, and even favoritism can be conveyed.

A balance is needed between detail and comprehensiveness. It is rather easy in any organization to get carried away with developing guidelines, regulations, and policies. Depending on personal characteristics, preferences, and personality type, some staff members will favor detailed descriptions of policies and procedures, while others will opt for sketchy guidelines or just want to operate on the basis of common sense. The director and staff should, indeed, be circumspect about establishing policies and procedures. The consequences of setting a definitive policy need to be examined closely. In some instances it may be desirable not to have a written policy in order to gain flexibility.

Following are some guidelines for setting policies and procedures:

1. A written copy of policies and procedures should be provided to each staff member.
2. This document should be updated periodically.
3. Each policy should be dated to indicate when it was updated.
4. Orientation of new staff and students should include discussion of the policies and procedures.
5. Staff should discuss changes and updates. Policies and procedures are likely to be followed if staff members are involved in creating them.
6. Staff should avoid getting bogged down in detail in discussions and in creating policies and procedures.
7. If possible policies and procedures should be well indexed so that they can be accessed easily. A table of contents or computer file with a search feature can be helpful. Staff and students will search for policies and procedures only if they can find them with reasonable effort.
8. If certain policies and procedures are problematical or are not being followed, they need to be identified and discussed with the individuals not following

them. If lack of compliance is widespread, reconsideration of the usefulness of the policy or procedure is indicated.

9. Policies and procedures that are out-of-date, that have been superseded, or that are ignored should be eliminated. Having a large manual of policies and procedures that are haphazardly followed or benignly ignored makes it difficult to maintain a reasonably efficient operation.

Leadership Style

Leadership by the director of a counseling or mental health center is required in a number of different arenas. Many of the internal arenas have been discussed under management practices. Although the directors of large centers may share leadership with associates and assistants, they are clearly the ones most responsible. There is no one style that necessarily works best for the leader of a counseling or mental health center. However, given the fact that the professional staff are counselors, a style in which there is recognition of the importance of collegial relationships and decision making is preferable. Staff leadership includes proficiency in the management areas outlined earlier, but it also includes communication of vision, purpose, and optimism. A director should have a mission and a clear view of how this mission can be accomplished. A director needs to be an optimist and persistent in the face of setbacks and slow progress.

Providing leadership involves working outside the counseling or mental health center as well as with professional and support staff. Counseling and outreach services are seen in most higher educational institutions as support or ancillary services, so the director must be able and willing to fight a constant and uphill battle to educate all of the publics within and even outside the college or university about the relevance and centrality of counseling to higher education. As spokesperson for counseling to the entire campus, the director should be able to give speeches, visit with faculty and student groups, and mix well with administrators. It is not a position for someone who cannot assume extroverted, energetic, and persuasive roles as required.

Quality Control

Quality control has always been an important issue for counseling and mental health centers. With the increased emphasis on accountability, cost containment, and effective resource utilization, which has been discussed throughout this book, effective quality control and the provision of high-quality, consumer-oriented services and programs have become necessities. As previously mentioned, Drum (1994) suggested a focus on four important quality-control factors: price, produce, customer satisfaction, and quality. Steenbarger and Smith (1996), in discussing developments in quality control for managed mental health care, reported that the National Committee for Quality Assurance is testing guidelines for mental health care and will begin accrediting organizations that provide managed mental health services. They believe that it is likely that the following standards will eventually apply to all campus-based mental health services:

1. *Quality improvement:* ongoing structure and process for assessing quality and improving services based on that assessment, and a formal, written quality-improvement plan and a designated committee to implement that plan.
2. *Access, availability, referral, and triage:* formal standards for telephone access, triage, risk assessment (using data-based standards) supervised by a board-certified psychiatrist.
3. *Standards for utilization management:* a written plan for managing utilization, published policies and procedures to review care, and procedures for denials reviewed by a psychiatrist or psychologist.
4. *Credentialing and recredentialing:* written policies and procedures for reviewing credentials of providers; providers must be licensed and must permit records review as part of site visits to assess quality.
5. *Patient rights and responsibilities:* patients must have access to written policies guaranteeing them information about benefits and decisions about care, with formal procedures for addressing complaints.
6. *Preventive services:* screening of population for mental health problems and accessible programs for prevention in areas like child abuse, depression, eating disorders, alcohol and drug use, sexually transmitted diseases, parent training, and stress management.
7. *Treatment services:* formal standards for clinical records documenting all aspects of patient care.

Although formulated in medical language, these standards are equivalent to many of those already in use in college counseling, which are included in IACS standards for accreditation of counseling centers and American Psychological Association standards for accreditation of psychology internship programs. The major differences appear to be in the level of explicitness required for policies and procedures and in the degree to which quality and consumer satisfaction must be documented.

In Chapter Thirteen, the importance of research in college counseling was emphasized from a variety of perspectives. One of these was quality control and accountability. A major task of any research program in a college counseling or mental health center must be evaluation and documentation of effectiveness and of patient progress (Howard and others, 1996). The most difficult challenge with this kind of quality control is the need to go beyond satisfaction measures and demonstrate effectiveness of treatments. Whatever model a college counseling or mental health center adopts, counselors will be called on to demonstrate the results of their efforts.

A task force of the AUCCCD is working on a model for quality control (Association of University and College Counseling Center Directors, 1996). The following competency checklist from the working document of the task force asks the relevant questions:

1. What do we do?
   - tracking system
   - data system
   - contracts and goals for staff
2. How well do we do it?
   - quality assurance
   - client satisfaction
   - outcome research
   - environmental assessment
3. Are we doing what we should be doing?
   - needs assessment
   - contextual mapping
   - benchmarking
4. Who knows what we are doing?
   - marketing to multiple customers
   - marketing to funding sources
   - understanding client needs and integrated marketing
5. How can we improve what we do?
   - continuous quality improvement
   - strategic plan
6. As the director, what do I need to know?
   - leadership qualities
   - staff management skills
   - quality management
   - resource management skills

This approach by AUCCCD demonstrates this organization's understanding of how important quality control and assurance are to the future of college counseling and mental health services.

Implementation of these kinds of quality-control goals, mechanisms, and processes can be especially challenging on a small campus. In most of these settings counseling and mental health services are one- or two-person operations. How can what seem like rather elaborate quality-assurance requirements be applied? Clearly, small campuses do not have the resources to set policies and procedures, to establish committees, and to conduct outcome research as called for in the different recommendations for quality control. One solution would be for a consortium of small-college counseling and mental health directors to establish a quality-control policy that makes sense for small colleges. Because small centers may have trouble evaluating client satisfaction and outcome, staff from different schools can be utilized as consultants or even as quality-assurance assistance teams. Often, small campuses do not have the benefit of the accreditation teams and visits that are so helpful in the quality-assurance process of medium-size and large centers. Standardized forms and methods of evaluation would also be helpful for small centers. For example, a standardized form and procedure to assess client satisfaction and to measure counseling outcomes would allow small centers to use these tools without having to develop them. Generic quality-assurance policies and procedures could easily be adopted or adapted without the need to reinvent the wheel at each college. Standardization would also allow for large, aggregate-data comparisons among small colleges similar to the college counseling Research Consortium Project.

Staff Development

Stone and Archer (1990) presented three basic challenges in facilitating staff development in college and university counseling centers. Staff must be provided with viable career paths, effective ways to counter stress and burnout, and training opportunities to keep up with current research and clinical practice. Another way of looking at staff development was provided in a study by May (1990), who identified four main reasons why psychologists left counseling centers: money and status, factors not related to the job, growth and autonomy, and job-related conflict issues. Bishop (1995) reiterated the importance of positive career development opportunities, citing the desirability of career ladders. Parham (1994) discussed the key career issues for counseling-center psychologists after seven to ten years of service. He noted the following three common developmental problems:

1. *Burnout:* Staff member feels used, overworked, unappreciated, and underpaid; feels that he or she is seeing more disturbed students in fewer sessions with

fewer resources; and perceives limited opportunities for advancement as well as institutional indifference.

2. *Difficulty finding time for other activities:* The first six years are characterized by involvement in various self-enhancement projects. Seven-to-ten-year staff member begins to see costs of overextension, experiences stress of involvement in diverse activities and often of trying to start private practice.

3. *Shift of age relative to students:* Staff member becomes noticeably older than traditional-age students, questions career choice, burnout, awareness of aging.

Clearly, the director and all the staff need to pay attention to career development needs. It is rather widely recognized that counseling and mental health work in colleges and universities is not particularly lucrative; therefore, working conditions, learning opportunities, and other factors play an important role in career satisfaction. Following are a number of suggestions for enhancing career development and satisfaction in college counseling and mental health settings:

1. Develop and maintain a supportive and positive agency culture that provides encouragement and stimulation for growth for staff members at all levels of career development.
2. Develop a nonadministrative career ladder that allows for advancement, including salary increases, for staff counselors and psychologists.
3. Provide opportunities for leadership and administrative skill development for staff interested in administration.
4. Provide regular continuing-education sessions for staff.
5. Develop a career development plan with each staff member and provide time and resources to assist that staff member in reaching goals. These resources might include sabbatical leave and weekly assignment to career development and career enhancement activities.
6. Provide a formal or informal mentor program for new staff members.
7. Allow for variation of duties and assignments, particularly for staff members who are in mid-career or late career.
8. Within resource and priority limits, encourage staff to develop new programs in their areas of interest.
9. Encourage staff to participate in professional organizations and if desired to pursue leadership positions within these organizations.
10. Encourage and support licensing and advanced certification (such as a diplomate).
11. If desired, encourage staff to conduct research and publish in professional journals and to present at professional conferences.

12. Attend to the differential needs of staff members at different phases in their careers. A regular discussion of career growth with each staff member as part of a goal-setting process will provide a focus on career development issues.
13. Confront career development problems and issues such as burnout, semi-retirement while getting paid for full-time work, lack of focus, and professional weaknesses directly but from a developmental perspective. The initial thrust should always be to help the staff member get back on a growth-oriented career path. Administrative actions may be necessary later.
14. Keep all staff members personally involved in the planning and operation of the agency.

Although career development is a crucial issue for staff during all phases of their careers, attending to their development in this area during the first year or two is of particular importance. Olson, Downing, Heppner, and Pinkney (1986, pp. 416–418) described six myths or irrational beliefs that new psychologists may hold:

- As soon as I unpack my bags, I will be settled.
- My new associates will welcome me enthusiastically and accept me as one of them.
- I will never be an apprentice again.
- I will easily master the varied demands of my job.
- I must perform perfectly, lest someone discover that I am a fraud.
- Because I worked so hard to get here, I will love my job.

An understanding of these common myths will help counseling and mental health staff respond in helpful ways to new professionals. One effective response is formally or informally assigning a mentor who can help the new professional work through irrational expectations and other transition issues.

Helping staff members cope with burnout deserves special mention because the emotional demands of counseling often exact a toll from counselors at all levels of career development. Corey (1996) offers a number of suggestions to counselors to prevent burnout:

1. Evaluate your goals, priorities, and expectations to see whether they are realistic and whether they are getting you what you want.
2. Find other interests besides work, especially if your work is not meeting your most important needs.
3. Think of ways to bring variety into your work.

4. Attend to health through adequate sleep, an exercise program, proper diet, and meditation or relaxation.
5. Find meaning through play, travel, or new experiences.
6. Learn your limits and learn to set limits with others.

Many counselors and psychologists working in college mental health are high achievers and strive for lofty goals. Individuals who set impossible or difficult goals for themselves are never totally satisfied. Goals and priorities, as previously mentioned, also change over the course of one's career. The director must stay in close touch with all staff counselors and help them set goals and priorities. This may be a tricky task because at times the goals and priorities of the agency may be different from the goals and priorities of the individual. Generally, a compromise is possible.

Although directors are obviously most concerned about work-related activities, they may find it useful and helpful to point out a staff member's over-reliance on work for life satisfaction. It is certainly not unusual to find a counselor who is too involved in work and who needs help and permission to seek satisfaction and balance in nonwork areas such as hobbies, sports, travel, or relationships with others. The director should be wary of any staff member who does not have time for a vacation or who will not leave campus for a sustained period of time.

Exercise, nutrition, and relaxation are the mainstays of most stress-management programs, and one would expect counselors to be aware of their value. This is not necessarily so, and directors sometimes need to help staff members find the time and energy to use these simple but important stress-management techniques. Group staff activities to promote wellness and to encourage relaxation are helpful. Humor is also a great ally in burnout prevention. There is nothing so deadly as a too-serious staff meeting.

Setting limits is another area where the director may have dual interests. Clearly, staff members who work sixty-hour weeks are helpful to the agency, but in the long run can they sustain that pace without burnout? Part of a director's responsibility is to point out the need for limits to staff counselors and if necessary to help them learn to set these limits for themselves.

It should be obvious from this chapter that the director's position in a college counseling or mental health center is complex. In small operations the director must provide a considerable amount of the clinical and other services and at the same time be responsible for management, leadership, quality control, and staff development. In large centers the job becomes mostly managerial, with the increased complexities of more staff and more formalized operating procedures. Not all professional counselors or psychologists are suited for this leadership position, and it is important for the staff and the vice president or other administrator in charge to spend considerable time in the recruitment and selection of the director.

Concluding Thoughts

As we move toward the beginning of a new century, higher education in the United States is facing unprecedented challenges that may radically change the way colleges and universities operate. Because of the rapid social and economic changes that are part of this transformation, college counseling and mental health services are more important to our students and to the educational enterprise than ever before. With the costs of educating students under close scrutiny, it is crucial for colleges and universities to examine the educational process and its efficiency. We can no longer afford to spend millions of dollars to set up state-of-the-art educational facilities and to pay high-quality faculty without making certain that students can effectively use these resources to their best advantage. This need to ensure that students have the personal resources and opportunities to function effectively as students makes counseling and related activities a must for colleges and universities. And, as we have outlined, a number of social and economic forces have contributed to increasing demands from students and their parents for help in dealing with a multitude of psychological and social issues.

Counseling and mental health services, however, cannot meet these profound challenges without new and creative approaches and methods of operation. They must develop ways to continue to meet the demand and need for counseling and at the same time help colleges and universities manage problems like racism, violence, gender discrimination, homophobia, and excessive stress. New approaches, models, and technology are called for but will have to be developed within a general higher education community that is scrutinizing its resources and demanding accountability and demonstrated effectiveness.

In this book we have attempted to review the most recent writing and research in the general area of college counseling, and we have made a number of recommendations and suggestions, some that require new and perhaps risky changes and some that incorporate much of the excellent work that has already been done by counseling and mental health services across the country. We echo the caution regarding prediction provided by Stone and Archer (1990) in their monograph on counseling centers in the 1990s. It remains extremely difficult to predict the future and equally difficult to generalize across colleges and universities with different missions, sizes, and contexts.

With this caveat in mind, the following summary of general recommendations is offered. College and university counseling and mental health centers should do the following:

1. Adopt and further refine models of brief therapy with an emphasis on process, assessment, and treatment strategies rather than on specific session limits.
2. Use groups as the treatment of choice for many typical problems of college students.
3. Foster the development and support the use of faculty, students, and others to function in "helper" roles on campus.
4. Increase the use of adjuncts and alternatives to counseling. This can be accomplished through the use of current and emerging self-help technology (such as the Internet, computer-assisted counseling, and emerging campus information systems) as well as more traditional self-help books and pamphlets, through increased use of support groups, and through access to and appropriate use of psychotropic treatments, particularly as new medications and new applications are developed.
5. Continue to develop treatment programs and approaches for serious and life-threatening problems such as depression and suicide, eating disorders, sexual abuse and violence, and alcohol and substance abuse, while at the same time maintaining counseling resources that focus on more common and less serious but nevertheless important developmental issues and problems.
6. Increase staff skills and knowledge in order to counsel and assist students who are members of special populations, such as minorities, women, GLB students, and students with disabilities.
7. Adopt an initiator-catalyst approach to outreach and consultation that encourages community development and systems change.
8. Serve as an initiator-catalyst for faculty development and student development programs that are embedded in the fabric of the institution.
9. Take an activist, initiator-catalyst approach to prevention programs that target serious campus health problems.
10. Take an activist, initiator-catalyst approach to address campus diversity issues and to move the campus toward a culture that celebrates diversity.
11. Increase applied-research and evaluation activities, particularly those that tie into the overall accountability and outcome measures of the college or university mission.
12. Continually confront and wrestle with contemporary ethical and legal dilemmas with a focus on constant self-evaluation of counseling-center policies and professional behavior.
13. Whenever feasible provide training opportunities and programs for paraprofessional counselors and peer educators, practicum students, and interns with an understanding that these programs are vital educationally and also for staff growth and development.
14. As an organization, take an active and political role on campus with a reasoned but decisive approach to campus needs and issues.

15. Maintain a healthy and creative organizational culture with internal norms and management practices that sustain and motivate staff. This requires a collaborative yet strong leadership style by a director who has vision and flexibility and is willing to listen and lead.

◆ ◆ ◆

The future offers exciting possibilities for college counselors. We have attempted to review the challenges that we see and some of the changes and developments in college student counseling and mental health that we feel will be required to continue the vitality and creativity that college counselors have demonstrated in the past.

REFERENCES

Abraham, S., & Llewellyn-Jones, D. (1989). *Eating disorders: The facts.* New York: Oxford University Press.

Adams, M. (1992). *Promoting diversity in college classrooms: Innovative responses for the curriculum, faculty, and institutions.* San Francisco: Jossey-Bass.

Aizenman, M., & Kelly, G. (1988). The incidence of violence and acquaintance rape in dating relationships among college men and women. *Journal of College Student Development, 29,* 305–311.

Albertson, M., & Kagan, M. (1988). Dispositional stress, family environment, and class climate among college teachers. *Journal of Research and Development in Education, 21,* 54–61.

Alexander, D. K., & Baron, A. (1995, Oct.). Nature and severity of college students' counseling concerns: A preliminary analysis comparing the 1991 clinical sample and the 1994–95 non-clinical sample. Paper presented at the annual convention of the Association of University and College Counseling Center Directors. Newport, R.I.

Allan, R., & Sipich, V. F. (1997). Developing a self-help brochure series: Costs and benefits. *Journal of Counseling and Development, 65,* 257–258.

Altrocchi, J. (1972). Mental health consultation. In S. E. Golann & C. Eisdorfer (eds.), *Handbook of community mental health.* Englewood Cliffs, N.J.: Appleton-Century-Crofts.

Amada, G. A. (1993). The role of the mental health consultant in dealing with disruptive college students. *Journal of College Student Mental Health, 8*(1), 121–137.

American Psychological Association. (1982). *Ethical principles in the conduct of research with human participants.* Washington, D.C.: American Psychological Association.

American Psychological Association. (1993). Guidelines for providers of psychological services to ethnic, linguistic, and culturally diverse populations. *American Psychologist, 48*(1), 45–48.

American Psychological Association. (1994). *Answers to your questions about sexual orientation and homosexuality.* Washington, D.C.: American Psychological Association.

American Psychological Association. (1995a). *Ethical principles of psychologists and code of conduct.* Washington, D.C.: American Psychological Association.

American Psychological Association. (1995b). *Suggestions for affirmative psychotherapy with lesbians and gay men.* Washington, D.C.: American Psychological Association.

Andrews, H. B. (1995). *Group design and leadership: Strategies for creating successful common theme groups.* Needham Heights, Mass.: Allyn & Bacon.

Andrews, K. (1994). ED-media. Paper presented at the 1994 World Conference on Educational Media and Hypermedia, Vancouver, Canada. (ED 388 316)

Aplin, J. C. (1985). Business realities and organizational consultation. *Counseling Psychologist, 13,* 396–402.

Archer, J., Jr. (1991). *Counseling college students: A practical guide for teachers, parents, and counselors.* New York: Continuum.

Archer, J., Jr. (1992). Campus in crisis: Coping with fear and panic related to serial murders. *Journal of Counseling and Development, 71,* 96–100.

Archer, J., Jr., Bishop, J., Gallagher, B., & Morgan, J. (1994). Combining counseling center needs assessment data: A multi-university study. Unpublished paper, Counseling Center, University of Florida.

Archer, J., Jr., & Kagan, N. (1973). Teaching interpersonal relationships on campus: A pyramid approach. *Journal of Counseling Psychology, 20,* 535–540.

Archer, J., Jr., & Probert, B. S. (1985). Wellness breaks. *Journal of College Student Personnel, 26*(6), 558–559.

Ascher, C. A. (1994). Changing student health needs and college and university health services. *Higher Education Extension Service Review, 5*(1), 1–7.

Association of University and College Counseling Center Directors. (1996, June). Elements of excellence competency checklist. *AUCCCD Newsletter, 7.*

Astin, A. (1993a). Diversity and multiculturalism on campus: How are students affected? *Change, 25*(2), 44–49.

Astin, A. (1993b). *What matters in college: Four critical years revisited.* San Francisco: Jossey-Bass.

Atkinson, D. R., Jennings, G. R., & Liongson, L. (1990). Minority students' reasons for not seeking counseling and suggestions for improving services. *Journal of College Student Development, 31,* 342–350.

Atkinson, D. R., Morten, G., & Sue, D. W. (eds.). (1993). *Counseling American minorities: A cross cultural perspective.* (4th ed.) Madison, Wis.: Brown & Benchmark.

Aulepp, L. A., & Delworth, U. (1978). A team approach to environmental assessment. In J. Banning (ed.), *Campus ecology: A perspective for student affairs.* Cincinnati, Ohio: National Association for Student Personnel Administration.

Baker, E. (1988). *Use of journal writing for psychologists.* Sarasota, Fla.: Professional Resource Exchange.

Bandura, A. (1994). Social cognitive theory and control over HIV. In R. J. DiClemente & J. L. Peterson (eds.), *Preventing AIDS: Theories and methods.* New York: Plenum.

Barba, W. C. (ed.). (1995). *Higher education in crisis: New York in national perspective.* Garland Studies in Higher Education 3. (ED 387 038)

Baron, A., Jr. (1992). Valuing ethnic diversity. A day long workshop for university personnel. *Journal of College Student Development, 33*(2), 178–181.

Baron, A., Jr. (1993). *Report of the Research Consortium of Counseling and Psychological Services in Higher Education.* Austin: University of Texas Counseling Center.

Barrow, J. C., Harsilano, L., & Bumbalough, P. (1987). Adapting the ecosystem model for environmental assessment and redesign. *Journal of College Student Personnel, 28*(4), 378–379.

Beck, A. T., Rush, J., Shaw, B., & Emery, G. (1979). *Cognitive therapy of depression.* New York: Guilford Press.

Beck, A. T., & Weishaar, M. E. (1989). Cognitive therapy. In R. Corsini & D. Wedding (eds.), *Current psychotherapies.* (4th ed.) Itasca, Ill.: Peacock.

Beck, K. H., & Lund, A. K. (1981). The effects of health threat seriousness and personal efficacy upon intentions and behavior. *Journal of Applied Social Psychology, 11,* 401–415.

Berg-Cross, L., Starr, B. J., & Sloan, L. R. (1993). Race relations and polycultural sensitivity training on college campuses. *Journal of College Student Psychotherapy, 8*(1), 151–175.

Bergan, J. R. (1977). *Behavioral consultation.* Columbus, Ohio: Merrill.

Berkowitz, A. (1992). College men as perpetrators of acquaintance rape and sexual assault: A review of recent research. *Journal of American College Health, 40,* 175–181.

Berkowitz, A. (1993). *Hobart College acquaintance rape prevention workshop for men.* Geneva, N.Y.: Counseling Center, Hobart College.

Berne, L. A. (1992). Homosexuality: Exposing your feelings. *Journal of Health Education, 23*(5), 307–309.

Bertocci, D., Hirsh, E., Sommer, W., & Williams, A. (1992). Student mental health needs: Survey results and implications for service. *Journal of American College Health, 41,* 3–10.

Betz, N. E., & Fitzgerald, L. F. (1987). *The career psychology of women.* Orlando, Fla.: Academic Press.

Bishop, J. B. (1995). Emerging strategies for college and university counseling centers. *Journal of Counseling and Development, 74,* 33–38.

Bishop, J. B., Bauer, K. W., & Becker, E. T. (1998). A survey of counseling needs of male and female college students. *Journal of College Student Development, 39*(2), 205–210.

Bishop, J. B., & Richards, T. F. (1987). Counselor intake judgments about white and black clients in a university counseling center. *Journal of Counseling Psychology, 34*(1), 96–98.

Bishop, J. B., & Trembley, E. L. (1987). Counseling centers and accountability: Immovable objects, irresistible forces. *Journal of Counseling and Development, 65,* 491–494.

Blazina, C., & Watkins, C. E., Jr. (1996). Masculine gender role conflict: Effects on college men's psychological well-being, chemical substance usage, and attitudes toward help seeking. *Journal of Counseling Psychology, 43*(4), 461–465.

Bloom, B. L. (1992). *Planned short-term psychotherapy: A clinical handbook.* Needham Heights, Mass.: Allyn & Bacon.

Bodensteiner, I. E., & Levinson, R. B. (1997). *State and local governments' civil rights liability.* Vol. 1. Dearfield, Ill.: Clark, Boardman, & Callahan.

Boesch, R., & Cimbolic, P. (1994). Black students' use of college and university counseling centers. *Journal of College Student Development, 35,* 212–216.

Botvin, G. J., & Dusenbury, L. (1992). Substance abuse prevention: Implications for reducing risk of HIV infection. *Psychology of Addictive Behaviors, 6,* 70–80.

Boyd, V. S., Roberts, R., & Cook, D. (1994). Assessing the college students: Use of data by counseling centers. *AUCCCD Proceedings,* 89–91.

Boylan, J. C., Malley, P. C., & Scott, J. (1995). *Practicum and internship: Textbook for counseling and psychotherapy.* (2nd ed.) Muncie, Ind.: Accelerated Development.

Brouwers, M. (1994). Bulimia and the relationship with food: A letters-to-food technique. *Journal of Counseling and Development, 73,* 220–222.

Browning, C., Reynolds, A. L., & Dworkin, S. H. (1991). Affirmative psychotherapy for lesbian women. *Counseling Psychologist, 19*(2), 177–196.

Bruch, M. A. (1997). Positive thoughts or cognitive balance as a mediator of the negative life events-dysphoria relationship: A reexamination. *Cognitive Therapy and Research, 21*(1), 25–38.

Bucknam, R. B. (1992). *The other side of the coin.* Washington, D.C.: Fund to Improve Postsecondary Education, U. S. Department of Education.

Buelow, G. (1995). Comparing students from substance abusing and dysfunctional families: Implications for counseling. *Journal of Counseling and Development, 73,* 327–330.

Burgess, A. W., & Holmstrom, L. L. (1979). *Rape: Crisis and recovery.* Bone, Md.: R. J. Bradley.

Burke, R. R. (1995, Apr.). *Critical issues in the lives of gay and lesbian students: Implications for counseling.* Report no. CG026466. Springfield, Va.: Resources in Education. (ED 386 646)

Burkhart, B. R., & Fromuth, M. E. (1991). Individual psychological and social psychological understandings of sexual coercion. In E. Grauerholz & M. A. Koralewski (eds.), *Sexual coercion: A sourcebook on its nature, causes, and prevention.* Lexington, Mass.: Heath.

Burnette, E. (1997, Mar). APA divisions give minorities a voice. *APA Monitor, 20*(3), 20.

Burns, D. (1993a.) *Ten days to self-esteem.* New York: Morrow.

Burns, D. (1993b.) *Ten days to self-esteem: The leader's manual.* New York: Morrow.

Caplan, G. (1970). *Theory and practice of mental health consultation.* New York: Basic Books.

Carden, A. D. (1994). Wife abuse and the wife abuser: Review and recommendations. *Counseling Psychologist, 22*(4), 539–582.

Carney, C. S. (1996). Dynamics of campus environments. In S. R. Komives, D. B. Woodard, Jr., & Associates, *Student services: A handbook for the profession.* (3rd ed.) San Francisco: Jossey-Bass.

Carter, K., Feldbaum, K., & Puzycki, V. (1996, Mar.). Talk is cheap: Responding to GLB issues in our communities. Paper presented at the annual convention of the American College Personnel Association, Baltimore, Md.

Carter, S. D. (1997). Security on campus, inc. [http://www.soconline.doc].

Cass, J. C. (1979). Homosexual identity formation: A theoretical model. *Journal of Homosexuality, 4,* 219–235.

Chartrand, J. M. (1992). An empirical test of a model of nontraditional students' adjustment. *Journal of Counseling Psychology, 39*(2), 193–202.

Cheatham, H. E., Ivey, A. E., Ivey, M. B., & Simek-Morgan, L. (1993). Multicultural counseling and therapy: Changing the foundations of the field. In A. E. Ivey, M. B. Ivey, & L. Simek-Morgan (eds.), *Counseling and psychotherapy: A multicultural perspective.* (3rd ed.) Needham Heights, Mass.: Allyn & Bacon.

Chickering, A. W. (1969). *Education and identity.* San Francisco: Jossey-Bass.

Chickering, A. W., & Reisser, L. (1993). *Education and identity.* (2nd ed.) San Francisco: Jossey-Bass.

Chojnacki, J. T., & Gelberg, S. (1995). The facilitation of a gay/lesbian/bisexual support-therapy group by heterosexual counselors. *Journal of Counseling and Development, 73,* 352–354.

Clack, J. (1995). *Counseling center referral database.* Presentation at the annual meeting of the American College Personnel Association, Boston.

Clark, C. A. (1993). Life skills enhancement groups as an alternative for waiting-list clients. *Journal of College Student Development, 34,* 382.

Cole, J. (1992). *Facing our future: From denial to environmental action.* Novato, Calif.: Growing Images.

Constantinople, A., Cornelius, R., & Gray, J. (1988). The chilly climate: Fact or artifact? *Journal of Higher Education, 59,* 527–550.

Conyne, R. K. (1987). *Primary prevention counseling: Empowering people and systems.* Muncie, Ind.: Accelerated Development.

Conyne, R. K., & Clack, R. J. (1981). *Environmental assessment and design.* New York: Praeger.

Conyne, R. K., & others. (1994). Applying primary prevention precepts to campus substance abuse programs. *Journal of Counseling and Development, 72,* 603–607.

Cooper, S. E. (1984). A spiral-ecological approach to supervision. *Clinical Supervisor, 2,* 79–80.

Cooper, S. E. (1989). Chemical dependency and eating disorders: Are they really so different? *Journal of Counseling and Development, 68,* 102–105.

Cooper, S. E. (1990). Stress management techniques. Unpublished manuscript, Valparaiso University.

Cooper, S. E. (1994). Prevention and interventions of drug abuse among college students. In P. Venturelli (ed.), *Drug use in America: Social, cultural, and political perspectives.* Boston: Jones & Bartlett.

Cooper, S. E., & Passafume, J. A. (1996). The gender climate revisited. Unpublished manuscript, Valparaiso University.

Cooper, S. E., Passafume, J. A., Satkamp, S. D., & Gaebel-Morgan, B. (1996). *Counseling services policies and procedures manual.* Valparaiso, Ind.: Student Counseling and Development Center, Valparaiso University.

Cooper, S. E., & Robinson, D. A. (1989). Childhood play activities of females and males entering engineering and science careers. *School Counselor, 36,* 338–342.

Corazzini, J. G. (1994). Staff beliefs which hinder the use of group treatment. In C. Sieber (ed.), [Theme issue: Group work in counseling centers], *Commission VII Counseling and Psychological Services Newsletter, 21,* 3.

Corey, G. (1996). *Theory and practice of counseling and psychotherapy.* (5th ed.) Pacific Grove, Calif.: Brooks/Cole.

Corey, G., & Corey, M. S. (1997). *I never knew I had a choice.* (6th ed.) Pacific Grove, Calif.: Brooks/Cole.

Corey, G., Corey, M. S., & Callanan, P. (1997). *Issues and ethics in the helping professions.* (5th ed.) Pacific Grove, Calif.: Brooks/Cole.

Crawford, M., & MacLeod, M. (1990). Gender in the college classroom: An assessment of the "chilly climate" of women. *Sex Roles, 23,* 101–122.

Crego, C. A. (1990). Challenges and limits in search of a model. *Counseling Psychologist, 18,* 608–613.

Crego, C. A. (1995). The medicalization of counseling psychology: Managed care vs. developmental models in university and college counseling centers. *Commission VII Counseling and Psychological Services Newsletter, 21*(3), 9.

Crites, J. O. (1981). *Career counseling: Models, methods, and materials.* New York: McGraw-Hill.

Cummings, N. (1990). Brief intermittent psychotherapy throughout the life cycle. In J. K. Zeig & S. G. Gilligan (eds.), *Brief therapy: Myths, models, and metaphors.* New York: Brunner/Mazel.

Cummings, N. (1995). Impact of managed care on employment and training: A primer for survival. *Professional Psychology, 26,* 10–15.

D'Andrea, V. J. (1987). Peer counseling in colleges and universities: A developmental viewpoint. *Journal of College Student Psychotherapy, 1*(3), 39–55.

Das, A. K. (1995). Rethinking multicultural counseling: Implications for counselor education. *Journal of Counseling and Development, 74,* 45–52.

D'Augelli, A. R., & Rose, M. L. (1990). Homophobia in a university community: Attitudes and experiences of heterosexual freshmen. *Journal of College Student Development, 31*(6), 484–491.

Daugherty, A. M. (1995). *Consultation: Practice and perspectives in school and community settings.* (2nd ed.) Pacific Grove, Calif.: Brooks/Cole.

Daugherty, R., & O'Brien, T. (1995). *On campus talk about alcohol.* Lexington, Ky.: Prevention Research Institute.

Delworth, U., & Moore, M. (1974). Helper plus trainer: A two-phase program for the counselor. *Personnel and Guidance Journal, 52*(6), 423–433.

Deressa, B., & Beavers, I. (1988). Needs assessment of international students in a college of home economics. *Educational Research Quarterly, 12,* 51–56.

Desiderato, L. L., & Crawford, H. J. (1995). Risky sexual behavior in college students: Relationships between number of sexual partners, disclosure of previous risky behavior, and alcohol use. *Journal of Youth and Adolescence, 24*(1), 55–68.

DeStefano, T. J. (1995). Critical incidents stress debriefing: A summary. *Commission VII Counseling and Psychological Services Newsletter, 22*(2), 1–4.

Dinklage, K. T. (1991). Counseling the learning disabled student. *Journal of College Student Psychotherapy, 5*(3), 3–27.

Dixon, W. A., Rumford, K. G., Heppner, P. P., & Lips, B. J. (1992). Use of different sources of stress to predict hopelessness and suicide ideation in a college population. *Journal of Counseling Psychology, 39,* 342–349.

Drucker, P. F. (1994). The age of social transformation. *Atlantic Monthly, 274*(5), 53–80.

Drum, D. J. (1994). Keynote address presented at the annual meeting of the Association of University and College Counseling Center Directors, Memphis, Tenn.

Drum, D. J. (1998). Merging healthcare on college campuses. *Commission VII Counseling and Psychological Services Newsletter, 24*(3), 2–3.

Drum, D. J., & Baron, A., Jr. (1996). Prepared protocol—Research Consortium. Unpublished manuscript, AUCCCD Research Consortium, Austin, Tex.

Drum, D. J., & Knott, J. E. (1977). *Structured groups for facilitating development: Acquiring life skills, resolving life themes, and making life transitions.* New York: Human Sciences Press.

Drum, K., & Lawler, A. (1988). *Developmental interventions: Theories, principles, and practice.* Columbus, Ohio: Merrill.

Dworkin, D. S., & Lyddon, W. J. (1991). Managing demands on counseling services: The Colorado State University experience. *Journal of Counseling and Development, 69,* 402–408.

Dworkin, S. H., & Guiterrez, F. (eds.). (1989). Gay, lesbian, and bisexual issues in counseling [special issue]. *Journal of Counseling and Development, 68,* 6–96.

Dworkin, S. H., & Pincu, L. (1993). Counseling in the era of AIDS. *Journal of Counseling and Development, 71,* 275–281.

Dye, A., & Borders, D. (1990). Counseling supervisors: Standards for preparation and practice. *Journal of Counseling and Development, 69,* 27–29.

Ehrlich, H. V. (1995). Prejudice and ethnoviolence on campus. *Higher Education Extensions Service Review, 6*(2), 1–15.

Eigen, L. D., & Quinlan, J. W. (1991). OSAP college drinking campaign: "Put on the brakes: Take a look at college drinking." *Alcohol Health & Research World, 15*(1), 87–89.

Ellis, A. (1989). Rational-emotive therapy. In R. Corsini & D. Wedding (eds.), *Current psychotherapies*. (4th ed.) Itasca, Ill.: Peacock.

Ellis, A. (1993). The advantages and disadvantages of self-help therapy materials. *Professional Psychology, 24,* 335–339.

Elwood, J. A. (1992). The pyramid model: A useful tool in career counseling with university students. *Counseling Development Quarterly, 41,* 51–54.

Enns, C. Z. (1994). Archetypes and gender: Goddesses, warriors, and psychological health. *Journal of Counseling and Development, 73*(2), 127–133.

Essandoh, P. K. (1996). Multicultural counseling or the "fourth force": A call to arms. *Counseling Psychologist, 24*(1), 126–137.

Farber, E. W. (1994). Psychotherapy with HIV and AIDS patients: The phenomenon of helplessness in therapists. *Psychotherapy, 31*(4), 715–724.

Farberow, N. L., & Frederick, C. J. (1990). *Training manual for human service disaster workers in major disasters.* Rockville, Md.: National Institute of Mental Health.

Fassinger, R. E. (1991). The hidden minority: Issues and challenges in working with lesbian women and gay men. *Counseling Psychologist, 19*(2), 151–176.

Feagin, J. R., & Sikes, M. P. (1995). How black students cope with racism on white campuses. *Journal of Blacks in Higher Education, 8,* 91–97.

Federman, R., & Emmerling, D. (1996). An outcome of mergers between university student counseling centers and student health, mental health services. Unpublished manuscript, Counseling Center, East Carolina University, Greenville, N.C.

Firestone, P. W., & Serden, R. H. (1990). Psychodynamics in adolescent student suicide. *Journal of College Student Psychotherapy, 4,* 101–123.

Fitzgerald, L. F., Fassinger, R. E., & Betz, N. E. (1995). Handbook of vocational psychology: Theory, research, and practice. In W. B. Walsh & S. H. Osipaw (eds.), *Career counseling: Contemporary topics in vocational psychology.* (2nd ed.) Hillsdale, N.J.: Erlbaum.

Fitzgerald, L. F., & Nutt, R. (1986). The Division 17 principles concerning the counseling/psychotherapy of women: Rationale and implementation. *Counseling Psychologist, 14*(1), 180–216.

Flam, F. (1991). Still a chilly climate for women? *Science, 252,* 1604–1606.

Flynn, C. A., Vanderpool, N. M., & Brown, W. E. (1989). Reentry women's workshop: Program and evaluation. *Journal of College Student Development, 30*(4), 377.

Foreman, M. E. (1990). The counselor's assessment and intervention with the suicidal student. *Journal of College Student Psychotherapy, 4*(3–4), 125–140.

France, M. H., Cadieax, J., & Allen, E. (1995). Letter therapy: A model for enhancing counseling. *Journal of Counseling and Development, 73,* 317–318.

Frazier, P. A., & Cohen, B. B. (1992). Research on the sexual victimization of women: In preparation for counselor training. *Counseling Psychologist, 20,* 141–158.

Frazier, P. A., Valtinson, G., & Candell, S. (1994). Evaluations of coeducational interactive rape prevention program. *Journal of Counseling and Development, 73,* 153–158.

Friedlander, J. (1978). Student ratings of co-curricular services and their intent to use them. *Journal of College Student Personnel, 19,* 195–201.

Fulero, S. M. (1988). Tarasoff: 10 years later. *Professional Psychology, 19*(2), 184–190.

Funderburk, J. R., & Archer, J., Jr. (1989). This campus cares: A suicide prevention project. *Journal of College Student Development, 30,* 277–279.

Gallagher, R. P. (1993). *National survey of counseling center directors.* Alexandria, Va.: International Association of Counseling Services.

Gallagher, R. P., & Bruner, L. A. (1994). *National survey of counseling center directors.* Alexandria, Va.: International Association of Counseling Services.

Gallagher, R. P., & Bruner, L. A. (1995). *National survey of counseling center directors.* Alexandria, Va.: International Association of Counseling Services.

Gallagher, R. P., Golin, A., & Kelleher, K. (1992). The personal, career, and learning skills needs of college students. *Journal of College Student Development, 33,* 301–309.

Gelso, C. J. (1992). Realities and emerging myths about brief therapy. *Counseling Psychologist, 20,* 464–471.

Gelso, C. J., & Fretz, B. R. (1992). *Counseling psychology.* Orlando, Fla.: Harcourt Brace.

Gelso, C. J., & Johnson, H. D. (1983). *Explorations in time-limited counseling and psychotherapy.* New York: Teachers College Press.

Gibbs, A., & Campbell, U. M. (1984). Mandatory psychological evaluations: A balance between conflicting interests. *Journal of College Student Personnel, 25,* 115–121.

Gilbert, B. J., Heesacker, M., & Gannon, L. U. (1991). Changing the sexual-aggression-supportive attitudes of men: A psychoeducational intervention. *Journal of Counseling Psychology, 38,* 197–203.

Gilbert, L. A., & Rachlin, V. (1987). Mental health and psychological functioning of dual-career families. *Counseling Psychologist, 15,* 7–49.

Gilbert, S. P. (1992). Ethical issues in the treatment of severe psychopathology in university and college counseling centers. *Journal of Counseling and Development, 70,* 695–699.

Gilbert, S. P., & Sheiman, J. A. (1995). Mandatory counseling of university students: An oxymoron? *Journal of College Student Psychotherapy, 9,* 3–21.

Gilchrist, L. D., & Schinke, S. P. (1983). Coping with contraception: Cognitive and behavioral methods with adolescents. *Cognitive Therapy and Research, 7,* 379–388.

Gilles-Thomas, D. L. (1996). *Student counseling centers on the Internet: A directory for counseling center professionals.* Buffalo: Counseling Center, State University of New York.

Gilles-Thomas, D. L. (1997). Counseling Center self-help home page. [http://ub-counseling.buffalo.edu].

Gilligan, C. (1982). *In a different voice.* Cambridge, Mass.: Harvard University Press.

Gilligan, C., Rogers, A. G., & Tolman, D. L. (eds.). (1991). *Women, girls, and psychotherapy: Reframing resistance.* New York: Haworth Press.

Glick, I., Clarkin, J., & Kessler, D. (1987). *Marital and family therapy.* (3rd ed.) Philadelphia: Grune & Stratton.

Gluhoski, V. L. (1996). Cognitive therapy for clients newly diagnosed as HIV-positive. *Psychotherapy, 33*(3), 441–448.

Goebel, B. A., & Hall, J. C. (eds.). (1995). *Teaching a "new canon"? Students, teachers, and texts in the college literature classroom.* Urbana, Ill.: National Council of Teachers of English. (ED 384 912)

Goelyan, C. (1991). Women's psychological development: Implementations for psychoanalysis. In C. Gilligan, A. G. Rogers, & D. L. Tolman (eds.), *Women, girls, and psychotherapy: Reframing resistance.* New York: Haworth Press.

Golden, B. R., Corazzini, J. G., & Grady, P. (1993). Current practice of group therapy at university counseling centers: A national survey. *Professional Psychology, 24*(2), 228–230.

Gonsiorek, J. C. (1988). Mental health issues of gay and lesbian adolescents. *Journal of Adolescent Health Care, 9,* 114–122.

Gonzales, G. M., & Broughton, E. A. (1994). Changes in college student drug and alcohol knowledge: A decade of progress. *Journal of Alcohol and Drug Education, 39*(3), 56–62.

Good, G. E., & Wood, P. K. (1995). Male gender role conflict, depression, and help seeking: Do college men face double jeopardy? *Journal of Counseling and Development, 74*(1), 70–75.

Gooler, D. D. (1991). *Professorial vitality: A critical issue in higher education.* DeKalb, Ill.: LEPS Press.

Gottfriedson, L. S. (1981). Circumscription and compromise: A developmental theory of occupational aspirations. *Journal of Counseling Psychology, 28,* 545–579.

Gould, R. L. (1990). The therapeutic learning program (TLP): Computer-assisted short term therapy. In G. Gumbert & S. L. Fish (eds.), *Talking to strangers.* Norwood, N.J.: Ablex.

Grater, H. A. (1985). Stages in psychotherapy supervision: From therapy skills to skilled therapist. *Professional Psychology, 16*(5), 605–606.

Gray, M. D., Lesser D., Quinn, E., & Bounds, C. (1990). The effectiveness of personalizing acquaintance rape prevention: Programs on perceptions of vulnerability and reducing risk-taking behavior. *Journal of College Student Development, 31,* 217–220.

Grayson, P. A. (1986). Mental health confidentiality on the small campus. *Journal of American College Health, 34*(4), 187–191.

Grayson, P. A., & Cauley, K. (1989). *College psychotherapy.* New York: Guilford Press.

Gropper, R. E. (1991). Student support services: A needs identification process for the black college student athlete. Doctoral dissertation, Florida International University. *Dissertation Abstracts International, 52*(5), P1666A.

Gyorky, Z. K., Royalty, G. M., & Johnson, D. H. (1994). Time-limited therapy in university counseling centers: Do time-limited and time-unlimited centers differ? *Professional Psychology, 25*(1), 50–54.

Hackney, H. L., & Cormier, L. S. (1996). *The professional counselor: A process guide to helping.* (3rd ed.) Needham Heights, Mass.: Allyn & Bacon.

Hall, R. M., & Sandler, B. R. (1982). The classroom climate: A chilly one for women? In *Project on the Status and Education of Women.* Washington, D.C.: Association of American Colleges.

Hall, R. M., & Sandler, B. R. (1984). Out of the classroom: A chilly campus climate for women? In *Project on the Status and Education of Women.* Washington, D.C.: Association of American Colleges.

Harding, A. K., Gray, L. A., & Neal, M. (1993). Confidentiality limits with clients who have HIV: A review of ethical and legal guidelines and professional policies. *Journal of Counseling and Development, 71*(3), 297–305.

Harris, H. J., and Anntonen, R. G. (1986). Assessing needs of male and female college freshmen. *Journal of College Student Personnel, 27,* 277.

Hayes, S. C., Follette, V. M., Dawes, R. M., & Grady, K. E. (1995). *Scientific standards of psychological practice: Issues and recommendations.* Reno, Nev.: Context Press.

Heesacker, M., & Prichard, S. (1992). In a different voice, revisited: Men, women and emotion. [Special issue: Mental health counseling for men.] *Journal of Mental Health Counseling, 14*(3), 274–290.

Heinze, C. (1987). Gaining insight through journaling. *Academic Therapy, 22,* 489–495.

Helms, J. (1990). *Black and white racial identity: Theory, research, and practice.* Westport, Conn.: Greenwood Press.

Heppner, M. J., Humphrey, C. F., Hillenbrand-Gunn, T. L., & DeBord, K. A. (1995). The differential effects of rape prevention programming on attitudes, behavior, and knowledge. *Journal of Counseling Psychology, 42*(4).

Heppner, P. P., & Johnston, J. A. (1994). New horizons in counseling: Faculty development. *Journal of Counseling and Development, 72,* 451–453.

Heppner, P. P., & Neal, G. W. (1983). Holding up the mirror: Research on the roles and functions of counseling centers in families' education. *Counseling Psychologist, 11,* 81–98.

Herer, E., & Holzapfel, S. (1993). The medical causes of infertility and their effects on sexuality. *Canadian Journal of Human Sexuality, 2*(3).

Hill, C. E., Nutt-Williams, E., Heaton, K. J., Thompson, B. J., and Rhodes, R. H. (1996). Therapist retrospective recall of impasses in long-term psychotherapy: A qualitative analysis. *Journal of Counseling Psychology, 43*(2), 207–217.

Hills, H. I., & Strozier, A. L. (1992). Multicultural training in APA-approved counseling, psychology programs: A survey. *Professional Psychology, 23,* 43–51.

Hoffman, M. A. (1991). Counseling the HIV-infected client: A psychosocial model of assessment and intervention. *Counseling Psychologist, 19*(4), 467–542.

Hoffmann, F. L., & Mastrianni, X. (1989). The mentally ill student on campus: Theory and practice. *Journal of College Health, 38,* 15–20.

Holahan, W., & Gibson, S. A. (1994). Heterosexual therapists leading lesbian and gay therapy groups: Therapeutic and political realities. *Journal of Counseling and Development, 72,* 591–594.

Holloway, E. L. (1995). *Clinical supervision: A systems approach.* Thousand Oaks, Calif.: Sage.

House, R. M., Eicken, S., & Gray, L. A. (1995). A national survey of AIDS training in counselor education programs. *Journal of Counseling and Development, 74,* 5–11.

House, R. M., & Walker, C. M. (1993). Preventing AIDS via education. *Journal of Counseling and Development, 71,* 202–289.

Howard, K. I., Lueger, R., Maling, M., & Martinovich, Z. (1993). A phase model of psychotherapy: Causal mediation of outcome. *Journal of Consulting and Clinical Psychology, 61,* 678–685.

Howard, K. I., & others. (1996). Evaluation of psychotherapy: Efficacy, effectiveness, and patient progress. *American Psychologist, 51*(10), 1059–1064.

Huebner, L. A. (ed.). (1979). *Redesigning campus environments.* New Directions for Student Services, no. 8. San Francisco: Jossey-Bass.

Hurwitz, T., & Kersting, S. (1993). Some practical considerations for providing access to the postsecondary environment. *Journal of American Deafness and Rehabilitation, 26,* 29–36.

Ibraham, F. A. (1991). Contribution of cultural worldview to generic counseling and development. *Journal of Counseling and Development, 70,* 13–19.

Ivey, A. E., Ivey, M. B., & Simek-Morgan, L. (1993). *Counseling and psychotherapy: A multicultural perspective.* (3rd ed.) Needham Heights, Mass.: Allyn & Bacon.

Janz, N. K., & Becker, M. H. (1984). The health belief model: A decade later. *Health Education Quarterly, 11,* 1–47.

Javorsky, J., & Gussin, B. (1994). College students with attention deficit hyperactivity disorder: An overview and description of services. *Journal of College Student Development, 35,* 170–177.

Jobes, D. A., Jacoby, A. M., Cimbolic, P., & Hustead, L. A. (1997). Assessment and treatment of suicidal clients in a university counseling center. *Journal of Counseling Psychology, 44*(4), 368–377.

Joffe, P. (1995). *Psychological emergency service: Guidelines and instructions.* Urbana: University of Illinois.

Johnson, C. E., & Petrie, T. A. (1996). Relationship of gender discrepancy to psychological correlates of disordered eating in female undergraduates. *Journal of Counseling Psychology, 43*(4), 473–479.

Johnson, R. W., Ellison, R. A., & Heikkinen, C. A. (1989). Psychological symptoms of counseling center clients. *Journal of Counseling Psychology, 36,* 110–114.

Johnston, M. W. (1989). AIDS issues and answers for university counseling center staff. Unpublished manuscript, California State University at Long Beach.

June, L. N. (1990). Challenges and limits: A provocative but limited view. *Counseling Psychologist, 18,* 623–627.

Juntunen, C. (1996). Relationship between a feminist approach to career counseling and career self-efficacy beliefs. *Journal of Employment Counseling, 33*(3), 130–143.

Kain, C. D. (1988). To breach or not to breach: Is that the question? A response to Gray and Harding. *Journal of Counseling and Development, 66,* 224–225.

Kashubeck, S., & Mintz, L. (1996). Eating disorder symptomatology and substance use in college females. *Journal of College Student Development, 37*(4), 396–404.

Katz, M. R. (1975). *SIGI: A computer-based system of interactive guidance and information.* Princeton, N.J.: Educational Testing Service.

Katz, M. R. (1993). *Computer-assisted career decision making: The guide in the machine.* Hillsdale, N.J.: Erlbaum.

Kazdin, A. E. (1993). *Behavior modification in applied settings.* (5th ed.) Pacific Grove, Calif.: Brooks/Cole.

Keeling, R. P. (ed.). (1989). *AIDS on the college campus.* Rockville, Md.: American College Health Association.

Keeling, R. P. (1991). Time to move forward: An agenda for campus sexual health promotion in the next decade. *Journal of American College Health, 40,* 51–53.

Kelly, K. (1987). AIDS and ethics: An overview. *General Hospital Psychiatry, 9,* 331–340.

Kerns, J. G., & Fine, M. A. (1994). The relation between gender and negative attitudes toward gay men and lesbians: Do gender role attitudes mediate this relation? *Sex Roles, 31*(5–6), 297–307.

Kiracofe, N., & others (1994). IACS accreditation standards for university and college counseling centers. *Journal of Counseling and Development, 73,* 38–44.

Kitchener, K. S. (1986). The reflective judgement model: Characteristics, evidence, and measurement. In R. A. Mines & K. S. Kitchener (eds.), *Cognitive development in young adults.* New York: Praeger.

Kite, M. E. (1994). When perceptions meet reality: Individual differences in reactions to lesbians and gay men. In B. Green & G. M. Herek (eds.), *Lesbian and gay psychology: Theory, research, and clinical applications.* Vol. 1. Thousand Oaks, Calif.: Sage.

Kivlighan, D. M., Johnston, J. A., Hogan, R. S., & Mauer, E. (1994). Who benefits from computerized career counseling? *Journal of Counseling and Development, 72*(3), 289—292.

Klerman, G., Weissman, M., Rounsavile, B., & Chevron, E. (1984). *Interpersonal psychotherapy of depression.* New York: Wiley.

Knefelkamp, L. L., & Slepitza, R. (1976). A cognitive developmental model of career development—An adaptation of the Perry scheme. *Counseling Psychologist, 6*(3), 53–58.

Kolata, G. (1984). Equal time for women. *Discover, 5,* 24–27.

Koplik, E. K., & DeVito, A. J. (1986). Problems of freshmen: Comparison of classes of 1976 and 1986. *Journal of College Student Personnel, 27,* 124–130.

Koss, M. P., Gidyez, C. A., & Wisneiwski, J. (1987). The scope of rape: Incidence and prevalence of sexual aggression and victimization in a national sample of higher education students. *Journal of Consulting and Clinical Psychology, 55,* 162–170.

Kramer, P. D. (1993). *Listening to Prozac.* New York: Viking Penguin.

Kuh, G. D. (1982). Purposes and principles of needs assessment in student affairs. *Journal of College Student Personnel, 23*(2), 202–209.

Kuh, G. D. (1996). Guiding principles for creating seamless learning environments for under-graduates. *Journal of College Student Development, 37*(2), 135–148.

Kunkel, C. A. (1994). Women's needs on campus: How universities meet them. *Initiatives, 56*(2), 15–28.

Kurth, C. L., Krahn, D. D., Nairn, K., & Drewnoswski, A. (1995). The severity of dieting and bingeing behaviors in college women: Interview validation of survey data. *Journal of Psychiatric Research, 29,* 211–225.

Lamb-Porterfield, P., Jones, C. H., & McDaniel, M. L. (1987). A needs assessment survey of re-entry women at Arkansas State University - 1985. *College Student Journal, 21,* 222–227, 243–247.

LaPerriere, A., & others. (1991). Psychoimmunology and stress management in HIV-1 infec-tion. In J. M. Gorman & R. M. Kertzner (eds.), *Psychoimmunology update.* Washington, D.C.: American Psychiatric Press.

Latham, P., & Latham, P. (1995, Apr.). ADD and the law. Paper presented at the annual ADD conference. Merriville, Ind.

Leong, F. T. (1992). Guidelines for minimizing premature termination among Asian American clients in group counseling. [Special issue: Group counseling with multicultural populations.] *Journal for Specialists in Group Work, 17*(4), 218–228.

Leong, F. T. (1996). Toward an integrative model for cross-cultural counseling and psy-chotherapy. *Applied and Preventive Psychology, 5*(4), 188–208.

Levant, R. F. (1996). The new psychology of men. *Professional Psychology, 27*(3), 259–265.

Levenson, J. L. (1986). Position paper on acquired immunodeficiency syndrome. *Annals of Internal Medicine, 105*(3), 466–467.

Lewis, J. A., Dana, R. Q., & Blevins, G. A. (1994). *Substance abuse counseling: An individualized approach.* (2nd ed.) Pacific Grove, Calif.: Brooks/Cole.

London, H. B. (1996). How college affects first-generation students. *About Campus, 1*(5), 9–13, 23.

Lonnquist, M. P., & Reesor, L. M. (1987). The Margaret Sloss Women's Center at Iowa State University: A model. *NASPA Journal, 25*(2), 137–140.

Lucas, M. (1997). Identity development, career development, and psychological separation from parents: Similarities and differences between men and women. *Journal of Counseling Psychology, 44* (2), 123–132.

Luzzo, D. A. (1995). Gender differences in college students' career maturity and perceived barriers in career development. *Journal of Counseling and Development, 73,* 319–322.

Lynch, S. K. (1993). AIDS: Balancing confidentiality and the duty to protect. *Journal of College Student Development, 34,* 148–153.

MacKenzie, R. (1993). Time-limited group theory and technique. In A. Alonso & H. I. Swiller (eds.), *Group therapy in clinical practice.* Washington, D.C.: American Psychiatric Press.

MacKenzie, R. (1995). *Effective use of group therapy in managed care.* Washington, D.C.: American Psychiatric Press.

Magoon, T. (1992). *Data bank: College and university counseling centers.* College Park: University of Maryland Counseling Center.

Magoon, T. (1993). *Data bank: College and university counseling centers.* College Park: University of Maryland Counseling Center.

Maher, C. A. (1981). Intervention with school social systems: A behavioral-systems approach. *School Psychology Review, 10*(4), 499–510.

Malley, P., Gallagher, R., & Brown, S. M. (1992). Ethical problems in university and college counseling centers: A Delphi study. *Journal of College Student Development, 33,* 238–244.

Maloney, M. L. (1995). Preventing relationship violence: What you can do on your campus. *Catalyst, 1*(3), 3–5.

Mann, J. M. (1973). *Time limited psychotherapy.* Cambridge, Mass.: Harvard University Press.

Manuel, C., & others (1990). The ethical approach to AIDS: A bibliographical review. *Journal of Medical Ethics, 16,* 14–27.

Mark, D. M., and others. (1988). Assessment of a computer-assisted counseling program. Unpublished manuscript, University Counseling Services, University of Minnesota, Minneapolis, Minnesota.

Marlatt, G. A., & Gordon, J. R. (1985). *Relapse prevention: Maintenance strategies in the treatment of addictive behaviors.* New York: Guilford Press.

Marshall, D. L. (1993). Violence and the male gender role. *Journal of College Student Psychotherapy, 8,* 203–218.

May, R. (1992). Severe psychopathology in counseling centers: Reaction to Gilbert. *Journal of Counseling and Development, 70,* 702–703.

May, T. M. (1990). Psychologists who leave counseling centers: Job satisfaction and career options. *Journal of College Student Development, 31*(3), 270–275.

McBurney, D. H. (1994). *Research methods.* (3rd ed.) Pacific Grove, Calif.: Brooks/Cole.

McCann, I. L., Sailheim, D. K., & Abrahamson, D. J. (1988). Trauma and victimization: A model of psychological adaptation. *Counseling Psychologist, 16,* 531–594.

McClary, C., Pyeritz, E., Bruce, W., & Henshaw, E. (1992). A liberal arts health promotion course. *Journal of American College Health, 41,* 71–72.

McCollum, S., & Devore, H. (1988). Safe sex and AIDS: A successful education program. *AUCCCD Proceedings* (Snowbird, Utah), p. 72.

McFarland, B. (1995). *Brief therapy and eating disorders.* San Francisco: Jossey-Bass.

McHenry, S. S., & Johnson, J. W. (1993). Homophobia in the therapist and gay or lesbian client: Conscious and unconscious collusions in self-hate. *Psychotherapy, 30*(1), 141–151.

McKee, M. B., Hayes, S. F., & Axiotis, I. R. (1994). Challenging heterosexism in college health service delivery. *Journal of American College Health, 42,* 211–216.

McKusick, L., & others (1990). Longitudinal predictors of reductions in unprotected anal intercourse among gay men in San Francisco: The AIDS behavioral research project. *American Journal of Public Health, 80,* 978–998.

McLean, D. A. (1994). A model for HIV risk reduction and prevention among African American college students. *Journal of American College Health, 42,* 220–223.

McMurray, D. (1993). *Facing our future together. A trainer's guide.* Novato, Calif.: Growing Images.

Meara, N. M., Schmidt, L. D., & Day, J. D. (1996). A foundation for ethical decisions, policies, and character. *Counseling Psychologist, 24,* 4–77.

Mehlman, E. (1994). Enhancing self-discovery of the African American college student in therapy with the Caucasian therapist. *Journal of College Student Psychotherapy, 9*(1), 3–20.

Meichenbaum, D. (1985). *Stress inoculation training.* New York: Pergamon Press.

Meilman, P. W. (1992). Alcohol education and treatment: On the use of leverage in the college setting. *Viewpoint, 41,* 79–81.

Mendoza, D. W. (1993). A review of Gerald Caplan's *Theory and practice of mental health consultation. Journal of Counseling and Development, 71*(6), 529–535.

Merryman, H. M. (1994). TQM: A primer. *Commission VII Counseling and Psychological Services Newsletter, 20*(3), 3–5.

Miller, I. J. (1996). Time-limited therapy has gone too far: The result is invisible rationing. *Professional Psychology, 27*(6), 567–576.

Miller, T. K., Thomas, W. L., Looney, S. C., & Yerain, J. (1988). *Council for the Advancement of Standards for Student Services/Development Programs.* Iowa City, Iowa: American College Testing Program.

Miller, W. R. (1985, Aug.). Perspectives on treatment. Paper presented at the 34th International Congress on Alcoholism and Drug Dependence, Calgary, Canada.

Minatoya, L. Y., & King, B. (1984). A systematic approach to assessment and intervention for minority undergraduates. *Journal of College Student Personnel, 25,* 272–274.

Mitchell, J. T., & Everly, G. S. (1993). *Critical incident stress debriefing (CISD): An operations manual for the prevention of traumatic stress among emergency services and disaster workers.* Elliott City, Md.: Chevron Corporation.

Mooney, C. J. (1989, Apr. 12). Stanford University reports strained campus race relationships; University of Michigan faculty rejects required course on racism. *Chronicle of Higher Education,* p. A15.

Morgan, K. S., & Nerison, R. M. (1993). Homosexuality and psychopolitics: An historical overview. *Psychotherapy, 30*(1), 133–140.

Morrill, W. H., & Hurst, J. C. (1990). Factors in a productive environment: Colorado State University, 1964–1976. *Journal of Counseling and Development, 68,* 247–281.

Morrill, W. H., Oetting, E. R., & Hurst, J. C. (1974). Dimensions of counselor functioning. *Personnel and Guidance Journal, 52,* 354–359.

Murray, B. (1996). University "stress lab" helps students unwind. *APA Monitor, 27,* A43.

Nagel, J. E. (1995). Chemical Awareness Responsibility Education (CARE) substance abuse education class. Unpublished manuscript, Valparaiso University.

National Clearinghouse on Postsecondary Education for Individuals with Disabilities. (1992). Percent of college freshmen with disabilities increases. *Information from HEATH, 11*(2–3), 1.

National Occupational Information Coordinating Committee, U.S. Department of Labor. (1992). *The national career development guidelines project.* Washington, D.C.: U.S. Department of Labor.

Newton, F. (1993). Counseling service intakes and brief treatment: From assessment to outcome. Paper presented at the annual meeting of the American Psychological Association, Toronto.

Newton, F., Brack, C. J., & Brack, G. (1992). Autonomy training: A structured group experience. *Journal of College Student Development, 33,* 371–372.

Newton, F., & Krause, R. S. (1991). Student affairs administrators react. In R. I. Witchel (ed.), *Dealing with students from dysfunctional families.* New Directions for Student Services, no. 54. San Francisco: Jossey-Bass.

Olson, S., Downing, N. E., Heppner, P. P., & Pinkney, J. (1986). Is there life after graduate school? Coping with the transition to postdoctoral employment. *Professional Psychology, 17*(5), 415–419.

O'Neil, J. M. (1990). Assessing men's gender role conflict. In D. Moore & F. Leafgren (eds.), *Problem solving strategies and interventions for men in conflict.* Alexandria, Va.: American Counseling Association.

Orlinsky, D. E., & Howard, K. I. (1986). Process and outcome in psychotherapy. In A. E. Bergin & S. L. Garfield (eds.), *Handbook of psychotherapy and behavior change.* (3rd ed.) New York: Wiley.

Ostrow, D. G. (1989). AIDS prevention through effective education. *Daedalus, 118,* 229–253.

Pace, D., Stamler, V. L., & Yarris, E. (1992). A challenge to the challenges: Counseling centers of the 1990s. *Counseling Psychologist, 20,* 183–188.

Pace, D., Stamler, V. L., Yarris, E., & June, L. (1996). Rounding out the cube: Evolution to a global model for counseling centers. *Journal of Counseling and Development, 74,* 321–325.

Parham, T. A., & Helms, V. E. (1985). Attitudes of racial identity and self-esteem of black students: An exploratory investigation. *Journal of College Student Personnel, 26*(2), 143–147.

Parham, W. D. (1994). Personal and professional issues for counseling center psychologists: 7–10 years postdoctorate. *Counseling Psychologist, 20,* 32–38.

Parsons, R. D., & Meyers, J. (1984). *Developing consultation skills: A guide to training, development, and assessment for human services professionals.* San Francisco: Jossey-Bass.

Pascarella, E. T., & Terenzini, P. T. (1991). *How college affects students: Findings and insights from twenty years of research.* San Francisco: Jossey-Bass.

Patterson, A. M., Sedlacek, W. E., & Perry, F. W. (1984). Perceptions of blacks and Hispanics in two campus environments. *Journal of College Student Personnel, 25*(6), 513–518.

Pavela, G. (1985). *The dismissal of students with mental disorders.* Asheville, N.C.: College Administration Publications.

Payne, K. E. (1991, Apr. 3–7). The power game: Sexual harassment on the college campus. Paper presented at the annual meeting of the Southern States Communication Association, Tampa, Fla.

Pearson, C. S., Shavlik, D. L., & Touchton, J. G. (eds.). (1989). *Educating the majority: Women challenge tradition in higher education.* New York: American Council on Education.

Pederson, P. (1994). *A handbook for developing multicultural awareness.* (2nd ed.) Alexandria, Va.: American Counseling Association.

Perkins, W. P. (1995). Scope of the problem: Misperceptions of alcohol and drugs. *Catalyst, 1*(3), 1–2.

Perry, W. G. (1968). *Forms of intellectual and ethical development in the college years.* Austin, Tex.: Holt, Rinehart and Winston.

Pettigrew, T. F. (1994). Prejudice and discrimination on the college campus. *Higher Education Extension Service Review, 6*(1), 1–8.

Phillips, E. L., Gershenson, J., & Lyons, G. (1977). On time-limited writing therapy. *Psychological Reports, 41,* 707–712.

Phillips, L., Halstead, R., & Carpenter, W. (1996). The privatization of college counseling services: A preliminary investigation. *Journal of College Student Development, 37*(1), 52–59.

Pinkerton, R. S. (1996). The interaction between brief and very brief psychotherapy: Allowing for flexible time limits on individual counseling services. *Professional Psychology, 27,* 315.

Pinkerton, R. S., & Rockwell, W. J. (1994). Brief psychotherapy with college students. *Journal of American College Health, 42,* 156–162.

Pinkerton, R. S., & others. (1990). Psychotherapy and career counseling: Toward an integration for use with college students. *Journal of American College Health, 39,* 129–131.

Pollard, J. W., & Whitaker, L. C. (1993). Cures for campus violence, if we want them. *Journal of College Student Psychotherapy, 8*(3), 285–295.

Pope, M. (1995). The "salad bowl" is big enough for us all: An argument for inclusion of lesbians and gay men in any definition of multiculturalism. *Journal of Counseling and Development, 73*(3), 301–304.

Presley, C. A., & Meilman, P. W. (1992). *Alcohol and drugs on American college campuses: A report to college presidents.* Washington, D.C.: Fund for the Improvement of Postsecondary Education, U.S. Department of Education.

Presley, C. A., Meilman, P. W., & Lyerla, R. (1994). Development of the Core Alcohol and Drug Survey: Initial findings and future directions. *Journal of American College Health, 42*(6), 248–255.

Price, B. K., & McNeill, B. W. (1992). Cultural commitment and attitudes toward seeking counseling services in American Indian college students. *Professional Psychology, 23,* 376–381.

Price, L. A., Johnson, J. M., & Evelo, S. (1994). When academic assistance is not enough: Addressing the mental health issues of adolescents and adults with learning disabilities. *Journal of Learning Disabilities, 27*(2), 82–90.

Prochaska, J. O., & DiClemente, C. C. (1992). The transtheoretical approach. In J. C. Norcross (ed.), *Handbook of eclectic psychotherapy.* New York: Brunner/Mazel.

Prochaska, J. O., & Norcross, J. C. (1994). *Systems of psychotherapy: A transtheoretical analysis.* (3rd ed.) Pacific Grove, Calif.: Brooks/Cole.

Pruett, H. L., & Brown, V. B. (eds.) (1990). *Crisis intervention and prevention.* New Directions for Student Services, no. 49. San Francisco: Jossey-Bass.

Pryzwansky, W. B. (1977). Collaboration or consultation: Is there a difference? *Journal of Special Education, 11,* 179–182.

Puig, A. (1984). Predomestic strife: A growing college counseling concern. *Journal of College Student Personnel, 25*(3), 268–269.

Range, L. M., & Antonelli, K. B. (1990). A factor analysis of six commonly used instruments associated with suicide among college students. *Journal of Personality Assessment, 55*(3–4), 804–811.

Reifler, C. B. (1990). Clements Fry, if you could see us now: The Robert L. Arnstein Retirement Lecture. *Journal of College Student Psychotherapy, 5*(1), 3–18.

Richmond, R. (1992). Discriminating variables among psychotherapy dropouts from a psychological training clinic. *Professional Psychology, 23*(2), 123–130.

Ridley, C. R., Mendoza, D. W., & Kanitz, B. E. (1994). Multi-cultural training: Re-examination, operationalization, and integration. *Counseling Psychologist, 22*(2), 227–289.

Riggs, R. O. (1993). Sexual harassment in higher education: From conflict to community. ASHE-ERIC Higher Education Report 2. (ED 364 133)

Rivinus, T. M. (1993). Violence, alcohol, other drugs, and the college student. *Journal of College Student Psychotherapy, 8*(1), 71–119.

Roark, M. L. (1993). Conceptualizing campus violence: Definitions, underlying factors, and effects. *Journal of College Student Psychotherapy, 8*(1), 1–27.

Robertson, J. M., & Fitzgerald, L. F. (1992). Overcoming the masculine mystique: Preferences for alternative forms of assistance among men who avoid counseling. *Journal of Counseling Psychology, 39*(2), 240–246.

Robinson, D. A., & Gaw, K. F. (1995). Faculty advisor training and development, innovations in college counseling. Paper presented at the annual meeting of the American College Personnel Association, Boston.

Rockett, G. M. (1989). Confidentiality on the small campus: A counseling center perspective. *Journal of American College Health, 38*(3), 148–150.

Rosenstock, I. M., Strecher, V. J., & Marshall, H. B. (1994). The health belief model and HIV risk behavior change. In R. J. DiClemente & J. L. Peterson (eds.), *Preventing AIDS.* New York: Plenum.

Rosser, C. L. (1995, Mar.). Avoiding net-wreckage in cyberspace: A counseling service goes on-line. *Visions: ACCA, 3,* 4–5.

Rubin, D. C., & Feeney, C. (1986). A multicomponent stress management program for college students. *Journal of Counseling and Development, 64*(8), 531.

Ruffin, V. E. (1990). Retention of minority students: The counseling services role. *AUCCCD Proceedings,* 13.

Salovey, P., & D'Andrea, V. J. (1984). A survey of campus peer education activities. *Journal of American College Health, 32,* 262–265.

Sampson, J. P., & Krumboltz, J. D. (1991). Computer-assisted instruction: A missing link in counseling. *Journal of Counseling and Development, 69,* 395–397.

Sanchez, A. R., & King, M. (1986). Mexican Americans' use of counseling services: Cultural and institutional factors. *Journal of College Student Personnel, 27*(4), 344–349.

Sandler, B., & Hall, R. (1986). The campus climate revisited: Chilly for women faculty, administrators, and graduate students. Washington, D.C.: Project on the Status and Education of Women, Association of American Colleges.

Santrock, J. W., Minnett, A. M., & Campbell, B. D.(1994). *The authoritative guide to self-help books.* New York: Guilford Press.

Scarano, G. M., & Kalodner-Martin, C. R. (1994). A description of the continuum of eating disorders: Implications for intervention and research. *Journal of Counseling and Development, 72,* 356–361.

Schaef, A. (1992). *Beyond therapy, beyond science: A new model for healing the whole person.* San Francisco: Harper San Francisco.

Schaefers, K. G., Epperson, D. L., & Nauta, M. N. (1997). Women's career development: Can theoretically derived variables predict persistence in engineering majors? *Journal of Counseling Psychology, 44*(2), 173–183.

Schauble, P., Murphy, M., Cover-Paterson, C., & Archer, J., Jr. (1989). Cost effectiveness of internship training programs: Clinical service delivery through training. *Professional Psychology, 20,* 17–22.

Schein, E. H. (1978). The role of the consultant: Content expert or process facilitator? *Personnel and Guidance Journal, 56,* 339–343.

Schepp, K. F., & Snodgrass, G. (1995, Oct.). Psychological disability: A dialogue on counseling center involvement. Paper presented at the annual convention of the Association of College Counseling Center Directors, Newport, R.I.

Schlossberg, N. K., Waters, E. B., & Goodman, J. (1995). *Counseling Adults in Transition.* (2nd ed.) New York: Springer.

Schneider, D., & others (1994). Evaluating HIV/AIDS education in the university setting. *Journal of American College Health, 43,* 11–14.

Schoenberg, M. (1992). *Conceptualizations: Counseling center models.* Alexandria, Va.: International Association of Counseling Services.

Schreier, B. A. (1995). Moving beyond tolerance: A new paradigm for programming about homophobia/biphobia and heterosexism. *Journal of College Student Development, 36*(1), 19–26.

Schroeder, C. (1996). Focus on student learning: An imperative for student affairs. *Journal of College Student Development, 37,* 115–122.

Schulberg, C., & Rush, J. A. (1995). Clinical practice guidelines for managing major depression in primary care settings: Implications for psychologists. *American Psychologist, 49,* 34–41.

Schwitzer, A. M., Grogan, K., Kaddoura, K., & Ochoa, L. (1993). Effects of brief mandatory counseling on help-seeking and academic success among at-risk college students. *Journal of College Student Development, 34,* 401–403.

Seligman, L., & Moore, B. M. (1995). Diagnosis of mood disorders. *Journal of Counseling and Development, 74*(1), 65–69.

Seligman, M.E.P. (1995). The effectiveness of psychotherapy: The Consumer Reports study. *American Psychologist, 50*(12), 965–974.

Sesan, R. (1989). Peer educators: A creative resource for the eating disordered college student. *Journal of College Student Psychotherapy* [special issue], *3*, 221–240.

Sexual Orientation Diversity Allies Committee. (1995). *ALLY: A faculty and staff network affirming lesbian, gay, and bisexual people on campus.* Urbana: University of Illinois.

Shannon, J. W., & Woods, W. J. (1991). Affirmative psychotherapy for gay men. *Counseling Psychologist, 19*(2), 197–215.

Sharkin, B. S. (1997). Increased severity of presenting problems in college counseling centers: A closer look. *Journal of Counseling and Development, 75*(4), 275–281.

Sherry, P., Teschendorf, R., Anderson, S., & Guzman, F. (1991). Ethical beliefs and behaviors of college counseling center professionals. *Journal of College Student Development, 32*, 350–358.

Silverman, M. M. (1993). Campus student suicide rates: Fact or artifact? *Suicide and Life-Threatening Behavior, 23*, 329–342.

Simon, T. (1993). Complex issues for sexual assault peer education programs. *Journal of American College Health, 41*, 289–291.

Simpson, E. L. (1990). *Faculty renewal in higher education.* Malabar, Fla.: Krieger.

Skibbe, A. (1986). Assessing campus needs with nominal groups. *Journal of Counseling & Development, 64*(8), 532–533.

Slater, B. R. (1993). Violence against lesbian and gay male college students. *Journal of College Student Psychotherapy, 8*(1), 71–119.

Slimp, P. A., & Burian, B. (1994). Multiple role relationships during internship: Consequences and recommendations. *Professional Psychology, 25*, 39–45.

Smart, D. W., & Smart, J. F. (1997). DSM-IV and culturally sensitive diagnosis: Some observations for counselors. *Journal of Counseling and Development, 75*(5), 392–398.

Smith, J. C. (1993). *Understanding stress and coping.* New York: Macmillan.

Sobell, M. B., Maisto, S. A., Sobell, L. C., Cooper, A. M., Cooper, T., & Sanders, B. (1980). Developing a prototype for evaluating alcohol treatment effectiveness. In L. C. Sobell, M. B. Sobell, & E. Ward (eds.), *Evaluating alcohol and drug abuse treatment effectiveness: Recent advances.* New York: Pergamon Press.

Sorcinelli, M. D. (1994). Effective approaches to new faculty development. *Journal of Counseling and Development, 72*(5), 474–479.

Stachowiak, T. (1994). One-session counseling: A semester's end, waiting list alternative. *Journal of College Student Development, 35*, 144.

Steenbarger, B. N. (1992). Toward science-practice integration in brief counseling therapy. *Counseling Psychologist, 20*(3), 403–450.

Steenbarger, B. N. (1993). A multicontextual model of counseling: Bridging brevity and diversity. *Journal of Counseling and Development, 72*, 8–15.

Steenbarger, B. N. (1994). Duration and outcome in psychotherapy: An integrative review. *Professional Psychology, 25*, 111–119.

Steenbarger, B. N. (1995a). Changes in health care: Implications for college counseling and mental health: Part II. *Visions, 2*(3), 9–10.

Steenbarger, B. N. (1995b). Managed care and the future of university counseling centers. *Commission VII Counseling and Psychological Services Newsletter, 21*, 2–4.

Steenbarger, B. N., & Manchester, R. A. (1990). Research in college health I: An introduction to the research process. *Journal of American College Health, 39*, 119–124.

Steenbarger, B. N., & Manchester, R. A. (1993a). Research in college health II: Designing the study. *Journal of American College Health, 42*, 15–19.

Steenbarger, B. N., & Manchester, R. A. (1993b). Research in college health III: Representative designs and their challenges. *Journal of American College Health, 42,* 55–60.

Steenbarger, B. N., Schwartz, A. J., & Manchester, R. A. (1993). Research in college health IV: Analyzing and communicating results. *Journal of American College Health, 42,* 99–104.

Steenbarger, B. N., & Smith, H. B. (1996). Assessing the quality of counseling services: Developing accountable helping systems. *Journal of Counseling and Development, 75*(2), 145–150.

Stoltenberg, C. D., & Delworth, U. (1987). *Supervising counselors and therapists: A developmental approach.* San Francisco: Jossey-Bass.

Stoltenberg, C. D., McNeill, B. W., & Delworth, U. (1997). *IDM supervision.* San Francisco: Jossey-Bass.

Stone, G. L. (1993). Psychological challenges and responses to a campus tragedy: The Iowa experience. *Journal of College Student Psychotherapy, 8,* 259–271.

Stone, G. L., & Archer, J., Jr. (1990). College and university counseling centers in the 1990s: Challenges and limits. *Counseling Psychologist, 18*(4), 539–607.

Stone, G. L., & Lucas, J. (1990). Knowledge and beliefs about confidentiality on a university campus. *Journal of College Student Development, 31,* 437–444.

Stone, G. L., & Lucas, J. (1991). Research and counseling center: Assumptions and facts. *Journal of Counseling and Development, 32,* 497–501.

Stone, G. L., & Lucas, J. (1994). Disciplinary counseling in higher education: A neglected challenge. *Journal of College Development, 72,* 234–238.

Stone, G. L., & McMichael, J. (1993). Limits and entitlements in clinical procedures. Paper presented at the annual meeting of the American Association of Counseling Center Directors, Breckenridge, Colo.

Stone, G. L., & McMichael, J. (1996). Thinking about mental health policy in university and college counseling centers. *Journal of College Student Psychotherapy, 10*(3), 3–28.

Strange, C. (1994). Student development: The evolution and status of an essential idea. *Journal of College Student Development, 35,* 399–412.

Strupp, H. H., & Binder, J. L. (1984). *Psychotherapy in a new key: A guide to time-limited dynamic psychotherapy.* New York: Basic Books.

Sue, D. W. (1993). Multicultural counseling: The multiple roles of the helping professional. *AUCCCD Proceedings,* 19–20.

Sue, D. W., Arrendondo, P., & McDavis, R. J. (1992). Multicultural counseling competencies and standards: A call to the profession. *Journal of Counseling and Development, 70*(4), 477–486.

Sue, D. W., & Sue, D. (1990). *Counseling the culturally different: Theory and practice.* (2nd ed.) New York: Wiley.

Super, D. E. (1990). A life-span, life-space approach to career development. In D. Brown, L. Brooks, & Associates, *Career choice and development: Applying contemporary theories to practice.* (2nd ed.) San Francisco: Jossey-Bass.

Talley, J. E., & Rockwell, W. J. (1985). *Counseling and psychotherapy services for university students.* Springfield, Ill.: Thomas.

Talmon, M. (1990). *Single-session therapy.* San Francisco: Jossey-Bass.

Taylor, C. A. (1986). Black students on predominantly white college campuses in the 1980s. *Journal of College Student Personnel, 27*(3), 196–202.

Terenzini, P., Pascarella, E. T., & Blimling, G. S. (1996). Students' out-of-class experiences and their influence on learning and cognitive development: A literature review. *Journal of College Student Development, 37,* 149–162.

Tillitski, C. J. (1990). A meta-analysis of estimated effect size for group vs. individual vs. control treatments. *International Journal of Group Psychotherapy, 40,* 215–224.

Tomlinson, S. M., & Cope, N. R. (1988). Characteristics of black students seeking help at a university counseling center. *Journal of College Student Development, 29*(1), 65–69.

Toseland, R. W., & Siporin, M. (1986). When to recommend group treatment: A review of the clinical and research literature. *International Journal of Group Psychotherapy, 36,* 171–201.

Touchton, J. G., & Davis, L. (eds.). (1991). *Fact book on women in higher education.* Old Tappan, N.J.: Macmillan.

Trevino, J. G. (1996). Worldview and change in cross-cultural counseling. *Counseling Psychologist, 24*(2), 198–215.

Trimble, R. W. (1990). Campus suicide prevention: Issues for the counseling center director. *Journal of College Student Psychotherapy, 4*(3–4), 165–178.

Trippi, J., & Cheatham, H. E. (1989). Effects of special counseling programs for black freshmen on a predominantly white campus. *Journal of College Student Development, 30*(1), 35–40.

Trippi, J., & Cheatham, H. E. (1991). Counseling effects on African American college students' graduation. *Journal of College Student Development, 32*(4), 342–349.

Vannicelli, M. (1992). *Removing the roadblocks: Group psychotherapy with substance abusers and family members.* New York: Guilford Press.

Vollmer, B. M. (1996, Mar.). Counseling outcome research: Innovations in college counseling. Paper presented at the annual meeting of the American College Personnel Association, Baltimore, Md.

Walsh, W. B., & Osipaw, S. H. (1990). *Career counseling: Contemporary topics in vocational psychology.* Hillsdale, N.J.: Erlbaum.

Walter, J. L., & Pelletier, J. E. (1992). *Becoming solution-focused in brief therapy.* New York: Brunner/Mazel.

Warnath, C. F. (1973). *New directions for college counselors.* San Francisco: Jossey-Bass.

Watson, D. L., & Tharp, R. G. (1992). *Self-directed behavior: Self-modification for personal adjustment.* Pacific Grove, Calif.: Brooks/Cole.

Webb, R. E., & Widseth, J. C. (1991). Students we don't refer: "Holding" the unheld. *Journal of College Student Psychotherapy, 5*(2), 19–42.

Wechsler, H. (1995). *Binge drinking on American college campuses: A new look at an old problem.* Boston: Harvard School of Public Health.

Weidner, G., Kohlmann, C. W., Dotzauer, E., & Burns, L. R. (1996). The effects of academic stress on health behaviors in young adults. *Anxiety, Stress, and Coping, 9*(2), 123–133.

Weinrach, S. G., & Thomas, K. R. (1996). The counseling profession's commitment to diversity-sensitive counseling: A critical reassessment. *Journal of Counseling and Development, 74,* 472–477.

Weinstein, G., & Obear, K. (1992). Bias issues in the classroom: Encounters with the teaching self. In M. Adams (ed.), *Promoting diversity in college classrooms: Innovative responses for the curriculum, faculty, and institutions.* San Francisco: Jossey-Bass.

Weiss, C. R., & Orysh, L. K. (1994). Group counseling for eating disorders: A two phase treatment program. *Journal of College Student Development, 35*(6), 487–488.

Welch, B. (1990, Jan.). *An American Psychological Association statement on homosexuality.* Washington, D.C.: American Psychological Association.

Wells, J. T. (1995, Oct.). Safe zone awareness training for faculty, staff, and police. *AUCCCD Proceedings,* 209–212.

Welty, J. D. (1995). *Memo to CSU Task Force on Student Health Services.* Fresno: Office of the President, California State University.

Westefeld, J. S., & Furr, S. R. (1987). Suicide and depression among college students. *Professional Psychology, 18,* 119–123.

Westefeld, J. S., Whitchard, K. A., & Range, L. M. (1990). College and university student suicide: Trends and implications. *Counseling Psychologist, 18*(3), 464–476.

Whitaker, L. C. (1993). Violence is golden: Commercially motivated training in impulsive cognitive style and mindless violence. *Journal of College Student Psychotherapy, 8*(1), 45–69.

Whiteley, J. M. (1982). *Character development in college students.* Schenectady, N.Y.: Character Research Press.

Williamson, E. G. (1936). *How to counsel students.* New York: McGraw-Hill.

Williamson, E. G. (1961). *Student personnel services in colleges and universities.* New York: McGraw-Hill.

Wilson, S. B., Mason, T. W., & Ewing, M.J.M. (1997). Evaluating the impact of receiving university-based counseling services on student retention. *Journal of Counseling Psychology, 44*(3), 316–320.

Winston, R. B., Jr., Bonney, W. C., Miller, T. K., & Dagley, J. C. (1988). *Promoting student development through intentionally structured groups: Principles, techniques, and applications.* San Francisco: Jossey-Bass.

Witchel, R. I. (1991). The impact of dysfunctional families on college students' development. In R. I. Witchel (ed.), *Dealing with students from dysfunctional families.* New Directions for Student Services, no. 54. San Francisco: Jossey-Bass.

Wood, G. J., Marks, R., & Dilley, J. W. (1990). *AIDS law for mental health professionals: A handbook for judicious practice.* San Francisco: AIDS Health Project.

Woody, R. H. (1991). *Quality care in mental health.* San Francisco: Jossey-Bass.

Yapko, M. (1988). *When living hurts.* New York: Brunner/Mazel.

Zeig, J. K., & Gilligan, S. G. (eds.). (1990). *Brief therapy: Myths, models, and metaphors.* New York: Brunner/Mazel.

Zraly, K., & Swift, D. (1990). *Anorexia, bulimia, and compulsive overeating: A practical guide for counselors and families.* New York: Continuum.

Zunker, V. G. (1994). *Career counseling: Applied concepts of life planning.* Pacific Grove, Calif.: Brooks/Cole.

NAME INDEX

A

Abraham, S., 80, 81
Abrahamson, D. J., 83
Adams, M., 177
Aizenman, M., 17
Albertson, M., 178
Alexander, D. K., 207
Allan, R., 61
Allen, E., 67
Altrocchi, J., 122
Amada, G. A., 110
Anderson, S., 210, 218
Andrews, H. B., 44
Andrews, K., 3
Angell, J., 7
Anntonen, R. G., 139
Antonelli, K. B., 74
Aplin, J. C., 122
Archer, J., Jr., 4, 6, 7–8, 14–15, 19, 23–24, 25, 51, 56, 88, 90, 121, 128, 131, 141, 173n, 194, 225, 259, 264, 268
Arnstein, R., 7
Arrendondo, P., 94, 230
Ascher, C. A., 84
Astin, A., 183

Atkinson, D. R., 21, 94, 95, 176, 182
Aulepp, L. A., 126
Axiotis, I. R., 105

B

Baker, E., 67
Baker, T. 52n
Balistrieri, T., 154n
Bandura, A., 161
Barba, W. C., 2
Baron, A., Jr., 2, 183n, 207
Barrow, J. C., 126–127
Bauer, K. W., 204n
Beard, W., 233
Beavers, I., 139
Beck, A. T., 28, 75
Beck, K. H., 161
Becker, E. T., 204n
Becker, M. H., 161
Bergan, J. R., 122
Berg-Cross, L., 176
Berkowitz, A., 17, 163–164
Berne, L. A., 185
Bertocci, D., 14, 139
Betz, N. E., 90, 99

Binder, J. L., 28
Bishop, J. B., 14–15, 25, 94, 204n, 237, 240, 257n, 264
Blazina, C., 102
Blevins, G. A., 78
Blimling, G. S., 100, 150, 151
Bloom, B. L., 26, 28, 30, 32
Bodensteiner, I. E., 109
Boesch, R., 21, 94
Bonney, W. C., 43
Borders, D., 227
Botvin, G. J., 161
Bounds, C., 163
Boyd, V. S., 194, 195–196
Boylan, J. C., 227
Brack, C. J., 45n
Brack, G., 45n
Broughton, E. A., 15
Brouwers, M., 81
Brown, S. M., 209–210, 218
Brown, V. B., 88
Brown, W. E., 114n
Browning, C., 104
Bruce, W., 172n
Bruch, M. A., 170
Bruner, L. A., 6, 14, 17, 19, 24, 74, 162, 210, 214

Gilbert, B. J., 163
Gilbert, L. A., 99
Gilbert, S. P., 111, 215, 216
Gilchrist, L. D., 161
Gilles-Thomas, D. L., 64, 134–135
Gilligan, C., 22, 100, 125
Gilligan, S. G., 28
Glick, I., 4
Gluhoski, V. L., 85
Goebel, B. A., 4
Goelyan, C., 99
Golden, B. R., 38
Golin, A., 139
Gonsiorek, J. C., 103
Gonzales, G. M., 15
Gonzales, T., 107n
Good, G. E., 102
Goodman, J., 125, 126
Gooler, D. D., 146
Gordon, J. R., 78, 161
Gottfriedson, L. S., 178
Gould, R. L., 68
Grady, K. E., 25
Grady, P., 38
Grater, H. A., 227–228
Gray, J., 178
Gray, L. A., 168, 214
Gray, M. D., 163
Grayson, P. A., 92, 211
Grogan, K., 112
Gropper, R. E., 139
Gussin, B., 71
Gutierrez, F., 104
Guzman, F., 210, 218
Gyorky, Z. K., 33

H

Hackney, H. L., 185
Hall, J. C., 4
Hall, R. M., 100, 178–179
Halstead, R., 241
Harding, A. K., 214
Harris, H. J., 139
Harsilano, L., 126–127
Hayes, S. C., 25
Hayes, S. F., 105
Heath, D. H., 127
Heesacker, M., 102, 163
Heikkinen, C. A., 14
Heinze, C., 67
Helms, J., 21, 182

Helms, V. E., 94
Henshaw, E., 172n
Heppner, M. J., 161–162, 206n
Heppner, P. P., 7, 146, 154, 213, 266
Herer, E., 168
Hill, C. E., 201
Hillenbrand-Gunn, T. L., 161–162, 206n
Hills, H. I., 94
Hirsh, E., 14, 139
Hitchcock, E., 7
Hoffman, M. A., 85
Hoffmann, F. L., 109
Hogan, R. S., 205n
Holahan, W., 105
Holloway, E. L., 227
Holmstrom, L. L., 82–83
Holzapfel, S., 168
Hotelling, K., 82n
House, R. M., 84, 168–169
Howard, K. I., 39, 199, 204, 263
Huebner, L. A., 126
Humphrey, C. F., 161–162, 206n
Hurst, J. C., 8, 43, 127, 128, 132
Hurwitz, T., 139
Hustead, L. A., 75

I

Ibraham, F. A., 94
Ivey, A. E., 94
Ivey, M. B., 94

J

Jacoby, A. M., 75
Janz, N. K., 161
Javorsky, J., 71
Jenkins, B., 184n
Jennings, G. R., 21, 94
Jobes, D. A., 75
Joffe, P., 77n
Johnson, C. E., 100
Johnson, D. H., 33
Johnson, J. M., 189n
Johnson, J. W., 105
Johnson, R. W., 14
Johnston, J. A., 146, 154, 205n
Johnston, M. W., 85
Johnston, P., 113n
Jones, C. H., 139

June, L. N., 128, 132, 141n
Jung, C. G., 102
Juntunen, C., 100

K

Kaddoura, K., 112
Kagan, M., 178
Kagan, N., 51, 131
Kain, C. D., 86
Kalodner-Martin, C. R., 80
Kanitz, B. E., 96
Kashubeck, S., 100
Katz, M. R., 90, 205
Kaye, S., 41n
Kazdin, A. E., 201
Keeling, R. P., 84, 85
Kelleher, K., 139
Kelly, G., 17
Kelly, K., 86
Kerns, J. G., 185
Kersting, S., 139
Kessler, D., 4
King, B., 139
King, M., 94
Kiracofe, N., 193, 232, 237
Kitchener, K. S., 150
Kite, M. E., 105
Kivlighan, D. M., 205n
Klerman, G., 75
Knefelkamp, L. L., 89
Knott, J. E., 43, 44
Kohlberg, L., 127
Kohlmann, C. W., 170
Kolata, G., 178
Koplik, E. K., 14
Koss, M. P., 17
Krahn, D. D., 5
Kramer, P. D., 221
Krause, R. S., 18
Krumboltz, J. D., 68
Kuh, G. D., 138, 146
Kunkel, C. A., 179
Kurth, C. L., 5

L

Lamb-Porterfield, P., 139
LaPerriere, A., 86
Latham, P., 187
Latham, P., 187
Lawler, A., 123

SUBJECT INDEX

A

Academic success, and student development, 147–149

Accreditation: of centers and programs, 232–234; and quality, 262; and roles and functions, 237

Accreditation Association for Ambulatory Health Care, 232

Acquaintance rape, 162–164

Action markers, for brief therapy, 34–35

Adult learners: approaches and program example for, 114; and developmental theories, 125–126; and multiculturalism, 189–190

African American students: and need for services, 21; peer mentors for, 184. *See also* Minority students

AIDS: approaches for, 84–86; challenge of, 5; and duty to warn, 214; and need for services, 17–18; and prevention interventions, 133, 135; and public health, 167–170

Alcohol abuse. *See* Substance abuse

Alcoholics Anonymous (AA), 16, 60, 69, 70, 78

American Association of Marriage and Family Therapy, 94

American College Health Association, 204, 234

American College Personnel Association, 204; Tomorrow's Higher Education project of, 127

American Council on Education, 189

American Counseling Association, 94, 204, 222

American Psychological Association: and accreditation, 232, 233, 262; Committee for the Advancement of Professional Practice of, 204; ethical code of, 218, 222; Psychotherapy Task Force of, 103; and research, 202, 203, 204; and special populations, 94, 101, 102

Americans with Disabilities Act (ADA) of 1990: and brief therapy, 27; and practice limits, 215, 238; and students, 4, 106–107, 108, 109, 111

Amherst College, services at, 7

Anxiety, approaches for, 86–88

Appalachian State University, Uncle Sigmund at, 66

Assessment: for brief therapy, 29–30, 32–36; and data use, 140–141; of environment, 126–127; of learning disabilities, 107–108; mandatory, 113, 216–217; of needs, 14–15, 138–141, 179–180

Association of University and College Counseling Center Directors (AUCCCD): and accreditation, 234; Clearinghouse of, 45; and disciplinary counseling, 111; Elements of Excellence Task Group of, 2; and psychological disabilities, 108; and quality, 263; Research Consortium of, 207